EXPERIMENTS IN A JAZZ AESTHETIC

Louann Atkins Temple Women & Culture Series

EXPERIMENTS IN A JAZZ AESTHETIC

Art, Activism, Academia, and the Austin Project

Edited by
OMI OSUN JONI L. JONES, LISA L. MOORE,
AND SHARON BRIDGFORTH

University of Texas Press ᐊᐅᐅ Austin

The Louann Atkins Temple Women & Culture Series is supported by Allison, Doug, Taylor, and Andy Bacon; Margaret, Lawrence, Will, John, and Annie Temple; Larry Temple; the Temple-Inland Foundation; and the National Endowment for the Humanities.

Requests for permission to reproduce material from this work should be sent to:
  Permissions
  University of Texas Press
  P.O. Box 7819
  Austin, TX 78713-7819
  www.utexas.edu/utpress/about/bpermission.html

♾ The paper used in this book meets the minimum requirements of ANSI/NISO Z39.48-1992 (R1997) (Permanence of Paper).

Library of Congress Cataloging-in-Publication Data

Experiments in a jazz aesthetic : art, activism, academia, and the Austin Project / edited by Omi Osun Joni L. Jones, Lisa L. Moore, and Sharon Bridgforth. — 1st ed.
      p.   cm. — (Louann Atkins Temple women & culture series)
   This book is both an anthology of writing by participants of the Austin Project and a sourcebook for those who would like to use creative writing and performance to energize their artistic, scholarly, and activist practices.
   Includes bibliographical references and index.
   ISBN 978-0-292-72204-0 (cloth : alk. paper) — ISBN 978-0-292-72287-3 (pbk. : alk. paper)
   1. Performance poetry—Authorship—Handbooks, manuals, etc.   2. Creative writing—Handbooks, manuals, etc.   3. Performance art—Texts.   4. Performance poetry.   5. American poetry—Women authors.   6. Music and literature—United States.   7. African American aesthetics.   8. Performance art—Social aspects—United States.   9. Art and social action—United States.   10. Austin Project.   I. Jones, Omi Osun Joni L., 1955–   II. Moore, Lisa L. (Lisa Lynne)   III. Bridgforth, Sharon.
   PN4151.E97   2010
   808.5'4—DC22

                                                          •   2010001031

CONTENTS

HOW TO USE THIS BOOK

In Austin, Texas, in 2002, a group of artists, activists, and academics formed the Austin Project (tAP), which provides a space for women of color and their allies to write and perform in a jazz aesthetic as a strategy for social change. This volume assembles the work of many of these individuals. In addition to the pleasure and inspiration we hope you will find in the writing collected here, we offer tools you can use to create similar projects in your own communities. We invite and challenge you to take the personal, political, and artistic risks made possible by these prompts and ideas, and to seek the private and communal joy that this work can yield.

The book is organized in three parts. Part I, titled "Framing the Work," sets up the context from which the writing and dialogue collected in this book emerged. An introductory chapter by Omi Osun Joni L. Jones discusses the Austin Project with regard to other community-based art and activism projects and the history of the performance tradition of the jazz aesthetic. The next chapter is a guide to the Finding Voice method written by the method's originator, Sharon Bridgforth. With these two chapters, Part I shows you how and why this work emerged as it did, and invites you to make it your own.

Part II is an anthology of writing produced in the Austin Project's workshops and by Guest Artists during the first five years (2002–2006). Chapter Three collects pieces by (almost) every one of the nearly fifty women who participated in the workshops and performances throughout this period. Chapter Four offers full-length original scripts by Guest Artists Laurie Carlos, Daniel Alexander Jones, Carl Hancock Rux, Maiana Minahal, and Robbie McCauley, who shared excerpts or earlier versions of this material with participants and the public during their residencies with the Austin Project. Chapter Five gathers writing by other Austin artists working in the jazz aesthetic. These community artists performed these "pre-show" pieces in 2002 and 2003 as opening acts for the Austin Project performances with the goal of linking local and national artists through the work of the Austin Project. Finally, these individual voices build to an orchestra: the script documenting the 2005 performance by the Austin Project constitutes Chapter Six. That year, we worked with Laurie Carlos in a two-week residency, combining our individual pieces of writing into a full-length performance. The script published here did not exist in 2005; this version was painstakingly amassed by Anastasia Coon from our scribbled notes and from grainy, nearly inaudible videos of the performance. Aside from being a work of literature in itself, Chapter Six is a methodological model for documenting the ever-vanishing present moment of performance in the jazz aesthetic.

Part III documents the widening circles of influence of the Austin Project. In Chapter Seven, four participants talk about their respective academic, artistic, and activist works, reflecting on how the Austin Project experience transformed their practices and offering models for others who may also be looking to counter burnout or refresh their commitments to these arduous paths. Chapter Eight transcribes a remarkable conversation that Austin Project women had with poet and spiritual elder raúlrsalinas in 2006. This open-ended discussion demonstrates the power of the jazz aesthetic to transform the spiritual practice and understanding of its participants as well as their artistic, activist, and academic work. Chapter Nine constitutes a kind of appendix: it's a narrative history of the first five years of the project that we hope can provide a starting point for leaders in other places who want to know the nuts and bolts of the communities and practices described here. In other words, the book ends with a pebble thrown into the lake in which the reader is standing. Where will the ripples take you?

We think there is something for everyone in this book. Specifically:

Community organizers and activists

Read Chapter One for a discussion of the mission and structure of the Austin Project. This chapter offers a useful guide for developing similar work across class, sexual, and racial boundaries. Women of color are central to the Austin Project. This chapter offers ways of thinking about the roles of women of color as leaders and white women as allies that model the most progressive, Black feminist approach to community work. Also, read Chapter Nine for a narrative chronological account of community building and performance in the jazz aesthetic.

Teachers and scholars in performance studies, creative writing, and related fields

Chapters Three, Four, and Six are excellent introductions to the jazz aesthetic for your students. Some discussion questions might include: How do the women of the Austin Project shape language to express their identities? Do the works of nationally known theater artists Laurie Carlos, Robbie

McCauley, Carl Hancock Rux, Maiana Minahal, and Daniel Alexander Jones share formal or thematic concerns? Does the Austin Project script in Chapter Six have similar or different concerns? What other traditions and genres (artistic, activist, spiritual, cultural) does this work reference?

Workshop leaders

Start with Chapter Two, a handbook on the Finding Voice method of facilitation. Try some of the exercises with your classes or workshops. They are appropriate for workshops seeking to deepen participants' work in terms of writing, performance, spirituality, identity exploration, personal history, and community building. They are excellent team-building exercises for people working together on many kinds of projects.

Writers

Read Chapters Three, Four, Five, and Six to find examples of writing that move you. Read Chapter Two and use some of the writing prompts to get started on some free writing of your own.

Theater artists

Mount a production based on the script in Chapter Six. Alternatively, use the process described in Chapter Two to work collaboratively with a group of artists and develop your own script. Try mixing experienced artists with emerging artists, or mix artists with activists and academics that share similar interests. Should you need replenishing, read Chapter Eight to be reminded of the spiritual authority invested in your creative work.

Omi Osun Joni L. Jones

I thank the joyous healing power of the river for sustaining me, for opening me to the idea of the Austin Project.

N'o máà sìn ọ.	*Always worship you, I will!*
Eni tí o fìmọ̀ jọ ọ kìí tẹ.	*Anyone with knowledge similar to yours is never humiliated.*
Ọṣun Yeye Onímọ̀.	*Osun, Mother of Wisdom!*
Ọ̀rẹ́ Yeye O!	*Oh, my Maternal Friend!*

I thank Leigh Gaymon-Jones for choosing me as her mother! Her patience, love, and wisdom have kept me buoyed, have taught me how to be courageous in the world.

I thank Sharon for being my dear and abiding friend, for providing steadfast support and kindness, for agreeing to be Anchor Artist to the Austin Project and steering so masterfully, for simply being fearless in her embrace of spirit.

I thank Lisa for sitting me down in her office and nudging me to narrate what a book about the Austin Project might be while she typed my thoughts into her computer, for seeing within those notes an actual book proposal, for being willing to be wrong and to be right, for being a wizard who declares it and thereby makes it so!

I thank each woman of the Austin Project for believing in the idea, for giving their vulnerability and strength to build it, for standing strong in reimagining themselves.

I thank the Guest Artists for lending so much rigor and love to our process.

I thank the Austin-based artists for their willingness to join the jazz journey.

I thank Anastasia Coon and Shawn Sides for the exceptional job they did transcribing tapes, editing text, envisioning orchestration, herding cats, and feeling so empathetically with each breath on the page.

I thank Darwin Smith for the preliminary work he did to transform Chapter Eight into a readable conversation.

I thank Layne "Eleventh Hour" Craig, Celeste Henery, and Beliza Torres Narvaez for dotting each "i" and crossing each "t."

I thank all those audience members who said yes.

I thank the John L. Warfield Center for African and African American Studies at the University of Texas at Austin for being the Hush Harbor, for nurturing my impulses.

I thank Theresa May for believing in this project and expertly guiding it to completion.

Lisa Moore

I'd like to acknowledge, first and foremost, my collaborators, Sharon Bridgforth and Omi Osun Joni L. Jones, who generously included me in this transformative project. Omi, as my colleague, has been a model of institutional change and academic activism. Sharon, my teacher, helped me find my voice as a poet again after many years. Their friendship and our working relationship are precious to me. The women who participated in the Austin Project from 2002–2006 are patient, inspiring, brilliant, and beautiful, and I thank them for their insistence on my growth as a writer and ally.

We have been fortunate to work with two brilliant artists as editorial assistants on this project. Anastasia Coon, with astonishing creativity and painstaking rigor, developed a language for documenting the 2005 performance and put that script together. I'm forever in her debt. Shawn Sides's exquisitely sensitive and intelligent editing of the manuscript is the only thing that made it possible to deliver it to UT Press in readable shape. I thank Shawn for herding the cats, as we so often said, so effectively and diplomatically.

Layne Craig put the icing on the cake of many years of admiration by pushing us gently but firmly through the last stages of copy editing. My thanks and appreciation to her.

I thank Madge Darlington for all the childcare, artistic support, inspiration, and loving attention through this process and always, and especially for the excellent idea of putting together a script of the 2005 performance. I thank Max and Milo Darlington for continuous inspiration and for writing some of my best lines.

Sharon Bridgforth

Always/I thank and appreciate my daughter and our family for their Love and support.

I would like to thank Omi for all of the years of friendship and Work/ walking with/Joy and adventure—for being bold enough to imagine the

Austin Project/for asking me all those years ago in the garden at Cafe Mundi to be the Anchor Artist. I thank JLW/CAAAS for supporting this project/my Work/and so much more.

I'd like to thank Lisa L. Moore for bringing me into her classroom all those years ago/for teaching my books and for giving me courage and the gift of being seen and heard.

Omi and Lisa, you rock! Editing this book with you two has been a wonderful Journey. We have a perfect mix and flow of temperaments, energy, abilities, and humor.

Shawn/Layne/Anastasia/I don't know how you guys did it but you pulled all the magic that this book is into a manifested form. University of Texas Press/you have been amazing! Thank you.

Each one of our Guest Artists is my hero/she'ro. You Inspire me. I Love you all!

To each of the Austin Project participants, thank you! You are my teachers. Your trust and your courage/your talents and kindness/helped me give voice to my facilitation method. Because of you I have been able to grow into myself more fully. It's on and poppin' y'all.

EXPERIMENTS IN A JAZZ AESTHETIC

PART I

Framing the Work

Chapter One

MAKING SPACE

Producing the Austin Project

OMI OSUN JONI L. JONES

In this chapter, Austin Project founder and producer Omi Osun Joni L. Jones describes the theoretical and historical context out of which her vision emerged. Jones identifies several ways in which the Austin Project is distinctive. The Austin Project works from the premise that all women—all people—are inherently creative, are artists in their own right, and that claiming this identity can be transformative for individuals and communities. Rather than training teachers, the Austin Project offers rigorous discipline in writing and performance that participants take back to their own work—as artists, activists, academics, or in other roles—and enrich their own practice. Finally, this introduction identifies the foundational precepts of the jazz aesthetic, the philosophical and artistic basis for the methods of the Austin Project.

WHEN I FIRST CONCEIVED THE IDEA OF THE AUSTIN PROJECT IN THE fall of 2002, I didn't know that I was trying to save my life. Perhaps each attempt at art or scholarship or activism is a way to ward off the annihilation of the self. Even as the idea began to acquire clear contours, I just thought it would be a good thing to do—bring together artists, activists, and scholars to collaborate on artwork and thereby share their individual techniques for bringing about social change. Now, eight years later, I know that I started the Austin Project (tAP) to invent the community I most wanted to live in—a place where there were no divisions between the passions in one's life, where writing one line of prose through the ache of truth telling was as necessary and transformative as community organizing, where research into the details of human lives was a compelling form of scholarship, where talk of spirit was the norm because it was understood that all things are spiritual.

And the Austin Project did save my life. I can't be certain of its full impact on the other women, but for me it was the place where I couldn't hide and ultimately did not want to: there I was required to be free. The Austin Project pushed me to unearth the moldy, dank places of fear, and to fully be.

I realize now that these places of fear were born of the rejection I had come to think of as the expected response to my very existence. I do not exactly know how this expectation crystallized into my worldview but it was surely some mix of childhood loneliness, institutional racism, unconscious and pervasive sexism, implicit homophobia, and the U.S. class structure that leaves the middle class and underclass longing for material possessions as evidence of worth. By 2002 these forces had left me empty, almost broken, and in need of a way to live with the joy, wisdom, and peace that I believe enable us to be personally and communally fulfilled.

The Austin Project (tAP) is a collaborative venture of female artists, scholars, and activists of color from diverse races, ages, sexualities, and backgrounds, and our white women allies, who come together to create art—mostly writing—while learning new strategies for social change. Under the guidance of an Anchor Artist and a Producer, the women meet once a week for eleven consecutive weeks. Anchor Artist is a title I created to signify the way this person must hold the ship steady through the eleven weeks of each tAP term. The Anchor Artist facilitates the weekly workshops and courageously pushes the women to examine the choices that impede their development as present and responsive human beings. Since tAP's inception, Sharon Bridgforth has served as Anchor Artist; her work has given a distinctive force to tAP's presence in the world. I have been the Producer, shaping the weekly meetings, securing resources, providing managerial services, and, over time, creating physical exercises for tAP. Guest Artists provide additional workshops and offer public performances of their works in progress. The women are encouraged to use the techniques from tAP for their own projects, and to acknowledge tAP on their résumés, bios, curriculum vitae, and other such public documents.

During approximately the same time that I began tAP, other similar initiatives were already underway in the United States. In 1997, Anna Deavere Smith initiated the Institute on the Arts and Civic Dialogue at Harvard University with several goals: "to support the creation of artistic works that address the issues of our time and enhance discourse by citizens in our democracy; to explore how those works can attract and engage audiences whose members cross boundaries created by economics, social class, and cultural differences; to create opportunities for the arts to offer themselves as new modes of public discourse; and to use the arts as a middle ground in debates that are frequently divided along strict lines."[1]

Over the course of three summers, Smith set in motion an impressive series of collaborations among artists and scholars who then shared their work with audiences primed for dialogue about the ideas, issues, and images that the collaborations evoked. According to press materials and website narratives, a primary goal of the Institute was to stimulate discourse. Smith created what she called a "think and do tank" where activists, scholars, and audiences would encourage artists to move outside of studios to "deal with the world in a more provocative way." Like tAP, the Institute wanted to shift the ways in which people experience art so that more deep engagement and transformation might occur. Unlike tAP, the Institute worked primarily, often exclusively, with nationally recognized artists and scholars and with local participants as witnesses and discussants. tAP is a training ground and a method rather than a space specifically designed to raise questions and to showcase art. Indeed, tAP encourages all the women—artists, scholars, and activists—to imagine their everyday choices as the choices of creators, of those who make things manifest, of artists.

The Animating Democracy Initiative (ADI) began in 1999 "based on the premise that democracy is animated when an informed public engages in issues affecting people's daily lives."[2] Through the Animating Democracy Lab, ADI supported thirty-two artistic and cultural projects around the United States including work by Urban Bush Women, the Lower East Side Tenement Museum, the Out North Contemporary Art House of Anchorage, the San Francisco Opera, Junebug Productions of New Orleans, and the Esperanza Peace and Justice Center of San Antonio. Like Smith's Institute, much of the focus of ADI was in stimulating meaningful dialogue between audiences and art makers. While tAP, like ADI, seeks to create art and generate dialogue, tAP also seeks to provide new tools for making everyday choices.

I didn't realize it in 2002, when tAP began, but June Jordan's famed Poetry for the People had aims similar to those of the Austin Project. Jordan began Poetry for the People in 1991 as a writing seminar at the University of California at Berkeley. This seminar evolved into what Jordan called "something faithful and literate and individual and collective and technical and creative and systematic and unexpected and unpredictable," something that understood poetry as "a political action."[3] While both tAP and Poetry for the People believe that art is a major strategy for social change, Poetry for the People is invested in training student-teacher poets to teach writing as social action, and tAP is committed to giving people the rigorous artistic tools to transform their individual lives. Had I known of Poetry for the People, and the subsequent documentation of that artistic and academic rebellion housed in *June Jordan's Poetry for the People: A Revolutionary Blueprint*, I might have spared myself some of the missteps I took with tAP.

But I was not to fully discover Poetry for the People until after tAP was born and some of its graduates began to work with us.[4]

Just as I wasn't sure of what the Austin Project might be when it was first formed, I was unsure about the methods that would shape the group. I now know that we were all creating new ways of living inside of a jazz aesthetic[5]—the very form that the Anchor Artist and so many of the invited artists had already worked in for years.

What I know now is that the Austin Project is an ongoing experiment in the structures of jazz as applied to writing, theatrical performance, and daily life. As tAP developed, I discovered that my own jazz practice rested on a few foundational precepts.

Be present. To do this work, a woman has to show up, to bring her full self, to feel exactly what she is feeling right now. This single task is the most difficult.

Breathe. Take life fully into the body. Contribute the rhythm of one's breathing to the communal song. Breathing and being present go hand in hand.

Listen. Deep listening necessitates a simultaneous connection to one's own breath and to the sensory stimuli in the external environment.

Improvise. Spontaneous creation requires courage and dexterity. The skills of listening and being present are essential.

Simultaneous truths. Jazz aesthetics rely on the ability to imagine more than one event, sound, or idea at a time. Sometimes this will feel like competition, other times it will be synthesis, and other times it could be chaos. The work valorizes multiplicity rather than singularity. The work encourages layering of images, ideas, sound, experience. Polyphony and multivocality are mandatory.

Collaboration. Working with others insists on individual clarity and humility. It rests on the belief that individuals learn themselves more fully in interaction with others, and that there is virtue in collective power. Choral work enhances vibrancy.

Virtuosity. It is an individual's responsibility to bring forth her specific and idiosyncratic self into the world. The vocalizations, the gestures, the thinking, and the beauty are honed through repeated experiences that support solo gifts and the development of a personal voice.

Body-centered. Jazz aesthetics recognize the body as a site of knowledge. Cellular learning is linked to emotional and intellectual learning. Memory and daily living are lodged in the muscles, and must be restructured to ensure the radical reality of joy and health. Shifting these visceral knowledge systems generates social change. Experience is passed on, person to person.

Metamorphosis. Repeated practice of these principles changes spirit and thinking and behavior and knowledge. This is the basis for the formation of a just, humane community.

These precepts evolved into a manifesto for the Austin Project.

THE JAZZ AESTHETIC MANIFESTO

The jazz aesthetic as used in the Austin Project is a way to forestall the erosion of human connection by bringing to voice women of color and those white women who are able to learn the role of allies. Using the governing dictum of the Combahee River Collective Statement as a model, jazz aesthetic practitioners believe when women of color are free, everyone is free.[6] The body-to-body presentness, the immersion in individual artistry through a strong community ethos, the necessity for and valorizing of multiplicity, the activism inherent in moments of choice and empowerment, the reclamation of what Katherine McKittrick calls "geographies of domination,"[7] and the use of safer geographic and psychic spaces all work to create the method for social reconstruction known as the jazz aesthetic.

The Audience Collaborators

Bringing people together who would not otherwise meet shifts the chemistry without even trying. This is not only true of the participants but of the audience members as well. Jill Dolan speaks of utopian theatre, and some of that conception relies on a diverse audience.[8] I have often talked to Jill about how monolithic the audiences are in the theatre that we sometimes attend together; that is not my utopia. I sometimes get uncomfortable in predominantly white audiences, fearful that this is *it*, that life won't get any better than this—one Black woman in a sea of white people who believe themselves liberal and therefore above self-interrogation.

I wanted the work of the Austin Project to reach as wide a range of audience members as possible. For this reason, I attempted to have the women's work performed in both a university venue and a local venue each year. The University of Texas has a difficult history with many people of color in Austin. It might not be possible to get these potential audience members to attend a performance across I-35, the highway that separates the university from a predominantly Black and Latino/a part of town. If the work remained only on the campus of the University of Texas, it would only be associated with that institution and would not speak beyond its usual constituents.

The Pedagogical Strategy

The Austin Project uses the apprenticeship structure of jazz and life training as its pedagogical strategy. We learn by doing and creating, and we model strength, courage, and innovation for each other. It is a system that honors the wisdom of elders—those teachers who have learned something about the roads we are traveling, and who may or may not be our chronological seniors. Eldership was most easily expressed through the Guest Artists who conducted workshops for tAP and gave public performances of their work, often testing new material in the relative security of small, generally supportive audiences. This structure was more challenging when Sharon and I facilitated the weekly workshops. We are elders to most of the women by age and experience, but some of the women were more comfortable having peer relationships with us. The hierarchy implied during apprenticeships contradicts feminist models of leadership that encourage peer relationships. In addition, I have practiced Theatre of the Oppressed techniques for facilitation in which there is surely one "leader" (or Joker, as named in that tradition), but a goal of Theatre of the Oppressed is for those present to feel empowered to create their own fate rather than bend to the expertise of a presumed elder.[9]

As a facilitator, leader, and producer with tAP, I have had to create coping strategies for the painful internal work associated with leadership. The facilitators are given little space to stumble, but when we do, we must be prepared to offer the group adequate forms of redress. As much as I would like to do otherwise at times, I know that I must follow the guidelines the group establishes. I created Letters of Agreement (not to be confused with Sharon's Agreements for Safety, discussed in the next chapter) that the women signed, giving me permission to use their video images and recorded words for educational purposes, and I signed a similar form which pledged my commitment to fulfill my role as producer as thoroughly and respectfully as possible. I want their trust, and I can gain it by being accountable to them as a responsive producer.

The Cultivation of Allies

In my original conception of the Austin Project, I thought the group would include men and women of many backgrounds and races. After the initial meeting with Sharon to discuss her role as Anchor Artist, she made it clear that she was interested in working with women of color. She had learned over years of facilitation that this visible yet marginalized group had precious few spaces for reflection and declaration, and she wanted most to speak with them. My own feelings of isolation in academic institutions reinforced her point, and I agreed. However, we decided to invite one or two white women to join the group each year.[10]

Ideally, the white women learn that "the circle,"[11] *this circle* in particular, is not guaranteed to them as so many other circles are. They learn to earn the right to be there, they learn that being there in that circle with women of color is a privilege. They have to trade their unconscious privilege for a conscious privilege that they must work every day until they have acquired new muscles for it.

Ultimately, the white women were in the Austin Project to give all of us present another way to grow. How can the women of color speak to the white privilege in the room so that everyone can walk away with dignity? Could white women truly be allies against racism, and what would that look like? My feeling was that the presence of whiteness would stimulate a series of internal and external conversations that are a part of our mutual empowerment.

The Habit of Freedom

Activism has too narrowly been associated with overt political acts—sit-ins, marches, petitions, casting ballots. Such definitions render invisible the daily acts of activism that people perform. An aim of the jazz aesthetic is for the courageous choices of the artist to evolve into everyday habitual acts of freedom. Ntozake Shange references Frantz Fanon's use of the term "combat breath" as a way to acknowledge the breath of life itself as an activist tool[12]—it is a ready pose to push back external definitions and conformity to the ideas and images that collapse our humanity into unrecognizable distortions. More precisely, the jazz aesthetic trusts the process of "embeddedness" in which the women of tAP take their discoveries of clarity and authority and insinuate them into their homes, workplaces, and gardens.[13] The transformations they experience in tAP inevitably make their way to the larger world as the women practice, at every turn, the power they have learned. In a similar vein, Joanna Brooks notes the revolution inherent in the act of feeling when she tells us:

> It is not around virtuoso individual performances that newness comes into the world, but in open-ended, imperfectly realized, sublegible, occasionally disorienting pursuits of the transformative possibilities of feeling. That is the work we are doing when we organize ourselves, as scholars, as feminists, in our work. . . . In a time of shifting empires, a time of organized abandonment and dehumanization, we are claiming

and renovating spaces for feeling. . . . We are calling poets like Phillis Wheatley and Audre Lorde into this room, and we are saying, help us remember what it feels like to be fully human.[14]

What Brooks calls a "conscientious regard for feelings" is central to tAP's process, and restructures how the women conceive of themselves and their relations with others. tAP believes in this deep personal renovation as a prerequisite to radical social change. In describing how African American artists in the academy use jazz aesthetics across art forms as a distinctive pedagogy, Theresa Jenoure speaks of the personal work as a continuous practice when she writes, "[personal discovery] necessitates our moving in closer to the center of ourselves and coming to terms with deep-rooted impulses. Embarking on an introspective path, but ultimately working toward the full, healthy function of the group, we need to evaluate our own strengths and weaknesses on an ongoing basis, using everything we produce as a barometer for growth."[15] The ongoing work that Jenoure describes makes practitioners anew; this newness is unleashed into the world, generating change through gesture, eye contact, stance, and word, as well as sit-ins, marches, petitions, and ballots. In other words, new people create new worlds.

To get at the deepest of unconscious, and therefore insidiously entrenched habits, there must be focused attention on the body, the repository of all experience. tAP insists that the women examine the narratives lodged in their bodies that impede their full freedom. M. Jacqui Alexander discusses the necessity of muscular freedom when she tells us, "So much of how we remember is embodied: the scent of home; of fresh baked bread . . . or running from the rain the same way that our mothers and grandmothers did. But violence can also be embodied, that violation of sex and spirit, which is why body work is healing work is justice work."[16] In tAP, the women are encouraged to write the truths their bodies have been terrorized into keeping silent.

A World of One's Own

Women must seize space and time as radical acts of self-making and social transformation: a space to do their work and time that is controlled only by their own needs and desires. Seventy years after Virginia Woolf insisted that women needed a room of their own to truly create art,[17] commandeering such space still remains vital. With the Austin Project, this space is not only necessary for the creation of art but the creation of a truly authentic life. In this way, it is important that the spaces where this creation occurs are not only private spaces—a room of one's own as Woolf suggested—but also include public spaces where the everyday and mundane and commonplace and political and social and commercial realities become remade through the alchemical freedom the tAP women bring to those spaces. As I look toward the next cycle of the Austin Project, I have learned lessons that will guide me, and I am excited by the possibilities ahead. tAP is a way to stave off the decimation of the soul as we women push ourselves beyond fear and loneliness and despair. I know now that I need the courageous community that tAP has created, and my own soul survival rests on keeping that community strong.

FINDING VOICE

Anchoring the Austin Project's Artistic Process

The Facilitation Method Used during the Austin Project

SHARON BRIDGFORTH

In this chapter, Sharon Bridgforth, the Austin Project's inaugural Anchor Artist, describes the genesis and technique of her Finding Voice method of workshop facilitation. She offers a handbook for those who wish to use this approach in their own teaching and facilitation, and includes a series of sample exercises and handouts.

NEW DRAMATISTS MEMBER SHARON BRIDGFORTH IS A TWO-TIME Alpert Award nominee in theater and the recipient of the 2008 Alpert/ Hedgebrook Residency Prize. She received a National Performance Network Creation Fund Award for *delta dandi*, which was commissioned by Women & Their Work and the NPN. Bridgforth is the author of the Lambda Award–winning *the bull-jean stories* and the performance novel *love conjure/blues*, both published by Redbone Press. Bridgforth is the fall 2009 Artist-in-Residence at Northwestern University in the Department of Performance Studies. For more, go to www.sharonbridgforth.com.

> Because I have written *White Chocolate*, I can now speak about other things that are not autobiographical, and that are also not in my child's voice, which I had been unable to do for a while. . . . I have given voice to my matriarchal lineage. It is for those women who couldn't speak, for those women who were speaking for themselves but were never heard.
>
> Laurie Carlos, Moon Marked and Touched by Sun:
Plays by African-American Women

memphis
the home house
biscuits and bacon
my grandmother's laughter

backyard parties bid whist and beer.
neckbones greens and cobbler/sweet tea
Little Stevie Wonder the Staples Singers Jerry Butler Cannonball Adderley
great aunts great uncles cousins/dancing.
just beyond the railroad tracks
there is blood.

los angeles
my mother remembering
reaching forward.
cars buses exhaust sirens screaming billboards and concrete.
porkchops potato salad orange crush sweet potato pie
Otis Redding Martha Reeves and the Vandellas B. B. King Aretha
the radio. up up and away/my mother's laughter
the Ocean the Waves dancing my mother dancing her friends dancing
us children dancing/dancing new stories to Life.

i am from the blues.
hard times remembered recounted like mantras/lest we forget. chants about
survival and daddies taken in the night. moans in the subtext of dreams.
with chicken frying music loud finger popping and laughter
i learned how to tell stories from my family.
see Jazz is a blood memory. something deep in the bones.
a charge. a responsibility. a gift/experienced

like those stories
long before the books the mentors the theatre the words formed
there was my mother's laughter and her mother's and hers . . .

> *i am an urban born southern Spirited/Black/lesbian*
> *working-class-raised/activist/mother/two-Spirited/artist.*
> *i learned a long time ago that the process*
> *of writing/working/and living is as important as*
> *the outcome   a well written story/a great performance.*
> *i have seen artists—i have been an artist/bitter & burned out—living in lack*
> *indulging in addictive behavior*
> *rather than daring*
> *to Dream to receive to embody self-Love.*
> *it has been critical to my sanity/Healing and development*
> *that i consider each moment of the day/part of my writing process/*
> *part of the measure of my success.*

i do mothering/sistering/wo'mn loving
i am daughter/i mentor/do correspondence/my administrative work/travel/
read/make theatre/teach/write/eat real good/dance/drink strong coffee
this is what my life as an artist is like
it is me Living fully in
joy gratitude health and Abundance
Being the Dream.
this is how i Pray.
the Art is my Spiritual Practice
it is how i serve.

back in the day/before i had language for any of this
back when i was three years sober and
unpracticed in the Art of living in Abundance
i was on the phone with Laurie Carlos one day/complaining really
stressing/whining about my life. after awhile Laurie said
"you need to mentor somebody. help someone. and
ask for Divine opportunity to come to you with Grace
and in a perfect way."
uh okay
was all i could think to say in response.
shortly after that conversation i received a grant from the theatre
communications group/national endowment for the arts to be in residence
at frontera@hyde park theatre (Vicky Boone was artistic director at the time
and had encouraged me to apply). this grant gave me enough resources to be
able to write without having two/three/four jobs
for the first time in my life. remembering Laurie's advice i designed a
residency that included opportunities for me to facilitate and curate a
workshop and poetry/performance series for emerging local artists. i ended
up working with Florinda Bryant, Da'Shade Moonbeam (Jeff Johnson),
Zell Miller III, Virginia Grise, K. Bradford, Piper Anderson, Marian
Thambynayaga, Andre Landcaster, Firesong, Elisa Durrette, Vincent
Woodard, and many others in an intense and ongoing manner. the groups
included rappers/spoken word & slam artists/poets and performance artists/
straight lesbian bi-sexual gay/men women transgendered/folk from many
races and ethnic groups/community-based and from universities/from all over
the world/with varied religious beliefs/and economic realities. Yo/this was
my Tribe!

i put everything i hoped, believed, and had learned over the years into
the pot/including some dismantling-oppression facilitation techniques

that i learned from Luz Guerra and Hugh Vasquez (during a training
session about unlearning oppression and building multicultural alliance
given by TODOS: Sherover Simms Alliance Building Institute) the
work happened in my living room/at poetry spots/at frontera@hyde
park theatre/at resistencia bookstore/stonehaven ranch/on the phone/
online/in the car/at coffee shops/during retreats and workshops
inside and outside institutions and organizational support/continuing
long after my formal residency ended.
during this time of teaching/mentoring/curating
i stumbled
fell down/fell out
learned a lot
and grew.
these artists taught me about freestyling/traditional hip-hop/the slam scene/
poetry and theatre.
they challenged me to examine and articulate what i believed art and life
to be/inspired me to teach by example/are part of the reason i have made a
lasting commitment to my personal growth and development as an artist.
they via Laurie's wisdom
began my journey with finding voice.
with these experiences under my hat i facilitated a series of ongoing creative
writing circles for allgo, a statewide queer people of color organization. those
circles included Rajasvini Bhansali, Lorenzo Herrera y Lozano, Ramki
Ramakrishnan, Jackie Cuevas, Jen Margules, Maria Limon, Martha
Duffer, and many others.
so
by the time Omi approached me to be the anchor artist for the austin project
i had been flipped dipped and seasoned.
i knew a few things and
i knew that i didn't know a few things.

Omi's vision for the Austin Project is artists, scholars, activists, and community members coming together for a creative process. The Austin Project
organically grew to become a group for women. As it turned out, working
intensely with a women's group led to discovering that my facilitation method
works best with women. In fact, what I now know is that Finding Voice
circles work best when they are composed of women that identify as writers,
when there is a predominant number of women of color in the circle, and
when some of the women identify as queer (variations and combinations
of the above work well also). This is because Finding Voice is based in a
(theatrical) jazz aesthetic. The jazz aesthetic is an African American art-

creation. It necessitates the fact that when the individual works from a place of deep truth, works hard to achieve an advanced level of craftspersonship, and unmasks, unleashes, and reveals spirit, the individual is able to hear more deeply and therefore is better able to create in concert with others.

The jazz aesthetic is female in its creative energy and lives in the idea that art:

—is about revolution/the revolution of spirit.

—is at its best used for the purpose of building, nurturing, extending, and celebrating the humanity, liberation, and dignity of all people globally.

—asserts that the *process* of creating art is as important as the outcome.

Some of the ingredients in the gumbo of jazz are: virtuosity, improvisation, being present, listening, witnessing, expansion and exploration of time, polyrhythms, non-linear forms, breath, synchronicity, and transcendence.

The Finding Voice method is not about crafting writing; it is about the *process* of writing. It is about walking with people as they journey into a deep place in themselves for the sake of artistic expression. The reason I say this work is female in its creative energy is that the magic the group creates comes as a direct result of their willingness to be open, nurturing, and supportive of others while practicing being present during a process that demands rigorous revealing, unpeeling, unmasking, and truth telling. It is generative. In my experience, this aesthetic fits in the world that women of color, queer women, and white women that have done rigorous work on dismantling their racism are most likely to inhabit naturally. Writers do the work of opening themselves, of going in deep, articulating, and returning. The writer's job is to *feel*. Though writers need help, support, and nurturing in this process, they are usually used to "going there" without causing permanent harm. Some of the Austin Project women identify as writers, some do not. I ask each member of the Austin Project to agree to call themselves a writer during our time together.

One thing that I know is that with this method the facilitator's body is the instrument through which group transformation is possible. This means that the work starts with you. Though I would not suggest trying this facilitation method without formal training, I am very interested in opening, revealing, articulating, and sharing my experience as the Austin Project Anchor Artist within the context of my work as a Finding Voice facilitator.

The Finding Voice facilitator's job is to:

—be a witness for the miracle of transformation.

—be an advocate for the inner voice of each person in the circle.

Framing the Work

—keep the circle safe.

—encourage writers to break form, to mix languages, to use the page as a canvas for their personal style, rhythm, and voice.

—create exercises that encourage writers to unpeel, unearth, unmask, reveal, and speak their truths.

—offer writers the opportunity to use the personal—identity, culture, memory, family history, personal experiences, and aspirations—as a base for writing.

—to help writers form support networks that will last beyond the workshop structure.

Since writing is the vehicle for work done in the circle, Finding Voice is best facilitated by individuals that are living as writers.

Now, I am no angel. I practice mindfulness and I work on personal elevation and progress daily, but, being human, I am not always my best self. I have, at times, been rude, impatient, and unclear in circles. When I, as a facilitator, don't rest, don't have my coffee, have too much coffee, or haven't eaten right, it sometimes bleeds over. During my work with the Austin Project over the years, I have come into the circle with a broken heart, exhausted, cross, with spiritual conflicts, and with serious physical illness (more on that later). When I find that I have been in a state of bad nerves, bad mind, poor spirit, or bad behavior, I try to not beat myself up, but instead to be honest, to let my integrity guide me, to find courage as quickly as possible, to say I'm sorry when it's due, and to learn whatever my lesson in the moment is.

Answering the questions below is necessary before a facilitator even thinks about creating a Finding Voice circle. The questions are broken up to encourage the idea of dealing with each questionnaire as a separate experience.

Facilitator Questionnaire 1

A) How do you define art?

B) Is there a difference between the artist that makes art by cooking for her family and the artist whose work is her professional life?

C) What, in your opinion, makes art "good" and "important"?

D) What is your artistic aesthetic?

E) What are your beliefs or politics about the place of artists in communities?

F) Do you think artists function as activists? If so, how? If not, why?

G) How is the work of an artist different in times of war?

H) How do you think artists should make a living?

I) What are your short-, mid-, and long-term artistic goals?

J) What is your plan for achieving these goals?

Facilitator Questionnaire 2

A) What is your life work?

B) What place does the facilitation of creative process have in your life work?

C) In what tradition is your facilitation of creative process based?

D) Write your facilitation mission statement.

E) How does your life work inform and support your facilitation mission?

F) Why do you want to use the Finding Voice method as a base for facilitation? How will this method support your facilitation mission?

Facilitator Questionnaire 3

A) What do you know that you know but tell yourself that you don't know? What is that about, and how might it affect your work as a facilitator?

B) What does internalized oppression look like in your life, and how might that affect your work as a facilitator?

C) Do you have a spiritual belief system? If so, what is it? If not, why not?

D) What ghosts might you walk with during facilitation? What might they say? Whose voices are they? Why do they get to walk with you?

E) What control issues do you have? How might they affect you as a facilitator?

F) What are your triggers?

G) What do you know about jazz?

H) What work have you done to dismantle oppression in your personal life?

I am a big believer in questions. I can ask questions all day long. In fact, half the work in facilitating the Finding Voice method is being present enough to hear the questions that need to be asked of individuals in the circle in order to help them move through and process feelings, their work, and difficult moments. The keys to the kingdom in this context are the following questions: *What am I feeling? What is that (the feeling) about? How does this (whatever the feeling is about) affect how I live as a writer?*

These questions are the road map. They keep the writer grounded in the work of opening up. They lead individuals to places of unblocking and discovery. They offer witnessing as a community system of support, nurturing, and growth.

The facilitator's job is to see, believe, and nurture the humanity of each individual in each circle. However, to ensure that the circle works, one must make sure that the right people are in the circle. I was blessed because, though she ultimately chose the Austin Project participants, Omi and I had a long wonderful work history and a shared vision long before we started working on the Austin Project.

A few years into working with tAP we fell in love. A few years after that we broke up. Then we got back together, but that's a whole nutha story/yeah. Anyway, Omi respected my method and process. I trusted her completely and she always conferred with me before making final decisions about new members.

Well, to put it lightly, Omi and I deeply regretted the times we weren't vigilant in sticking to what we knew to be true about creating a good circle. A couple of times we got too thrilled with ourselves or got caught up in the hype of the Austin Project's success and invited people that we shouldn't have, made some circles impossibly big, etc. Unfortunately, over the years we've had to uninvite a couple of people, which, in essence, means that we invited people that were more committed to fear than grace. Omi eventually instituted a very successful process that involves alumni members in selecting new members. Still, there may be folk whose backbiting behavior (i.e., fear) will attempt to undermine the entire project. The following questions can be helpful to consider in an attempt to avoid such a mess, and they will help you in checking yourself.

A) Why am I creating this circle?
B) Whom will this circle serve?
C) How will I create a call that will clearly, honestly, and lovingly reflect the invitation?
D) What will the member-selection process be?
E) How will the organization that sponsors the circle affect, inform, and support the process?
F) Is each person that I am considering ready and able to embody grace, courage, and generosity?
G) How often will the circle meet? How long will meetings be?

H) What is the minimum and maximum number of people appropriate for the circle?

I) Write your circle invitation.

Very often in our desire to be open and democratic it becomes hard to say no to people or to not invite people. For the purposes of creating these circles you must be clear and selective. Otherwise you are operating from your own fears, which you will need to examine carefully, quickly, and honestly.

I recommend that the number of meetings be high and the length of each meeting be as long as possible. The more time you have with a Finding Voice circle, the more effective your work will be. Omi asked me in our initial meeting what I thought would be good. She then factored in her own producer considerations. As a result, we ended up instituting the Austin Project as meeting, on average, four hours a week for eleven weeks annually, culminating with two performances, one community-based and one on the University of Texas campus. Below are other things to consider as you move forward in creating circles.

—People should not be in an immediately unstable mental, emotional, or spiritual state.

—The circle should not function as therapy, though the process may propel participants to therapy.

—Facilitators will need to watch for triggering; work in the circle should not force people to go places they cannot come back from.

—It is ideal to work with a co-facilitator. Omi and I began co-facilitating in 2005. Prior to that, we worked as a producer-facilitator team. It is important to have a peer in the process to check in with, to debrief, and to plan with.

—It is best that you don't facilitate when you are seriously ill or mentally, emotionally, or spiritually unstable. (I learned this the hard way.)

Omi is a masterful host, and the John L. Warfield Center for African and African American Studies (JLW/CAAAS) is fully committed to the Austin Project with a fierceness, so the Austin Project participants are cared for in every way, down to snacks and space. I really believe that good snacks, coffee, and water help keep loving energy moving in the circle. The space that houses the circle should be comfortable, private, and quiet. If at all possible, try to always meet in the same space. The space should function like a touchstone, an environment that holds and comforts the circle. If you can't afford to feed the people, suggest that everyone bring something. We did a sign up sheet and asked women that were able to sign up to bring snacks for different meetings. We always eat really well.

One important aspect of holding the circle sacred is establishing Agreements for Safety. I was first exposed to this concept as a trainee in a TODOS workshop back in the early '90s. Agreements for Safety serve as the group norms that guide how the group creates and builds community. Through trial, error, and participant recommendations, I have come up with my own standard list of agreements (below) and I have learned the following with regard to being a facilitator.

—The facilitator's commitment to lovingly, firmly enforcing rules of safety allows people in the circle the opportunity to respect and trust you and to fully give themselves to the process.

—It's important to be flexible—have a plan but be open to honoring the moment and shifting your plans. Don't be afraid to throw your great workshop outline out the window.

—Remember, this is jazz. Being present is the tool that improvisation comes out of. Trust and employ your virtuosity, your humanity, and all your senses in the art of spontaneously honoring the magic of the moment.

—Maintain a sense of humor. If you take yourself too seriously you will find that you are full of yourself.

—Remember, it's not about you. Talk about yourself and your experiences infrequently but intentionally, i.e., sometimes it is good to answer a question that you pose to the circle first as an illustration and/or to build the group's trust in you through sharing.

—Don't take resistance personally.

—Encourage the circle to meet, to talk, and to go to events outside of group meetings as a way of nurturing independence and a sense of community that will continue once the circle formally ends.

—Focus on the fact that you are facilitating a writing group. Focus on the work. This is not therapy.

—Fixing or controlling people is not and should not be part of the process.

—Allow space for people in the circle to cry, to feel their feelings, but keep the energy in the group moving so that people don't get stuck.

—It is often good to ask the group what they need (a break, time to talk, etc.).

—Live what you teach.

—Stay present, keep breathing, be gentle with yourself and others.

—Work on your personal issues outside of the circle.

—Expect miracles.

Below is a sample of the standard Agreements for Safety that I use. I always ask each group for additional suggestions for agreement they'd like to add to the list.

Sample Agreements for Safety

—Respect yourself and others.
—Maintain confidentiality: what is said in workshop stays in workshop.
—Try on the process.
—Ask permission before speaking to someone else's experience.
—Be open.
—Make a personal commitment to honesty.
—Be present.
—Be vulnerable.
—Be open to transformation.
—Be available to walk with and witness one another's process.
—Breathe.
—Be an active listener.
—Be gentle with yourself and others.
—If you must talk about what's going on inside the group to someone outside the group, frame your remarks so that you are not breaking confidentiality.
—Use "I" statements.
—Focus on yourself (your feelings, your experience, your needs). The facilitator is the only "digger."

The following questionnaire is useful when considering agreements and safety:

Facilitator Questionnaire 4

A) What rules for safety will you ask the circle to agree to?
B) What will you do to make sure the rules for safety are honored?
C) What is one thing that you fear may happen while you are facilitating?
D) What are your weaknesses as a facilitator?
E) What are your strengths as a facilitator?
F) Which personal issue is likely to come up for you as you facilitate?
G) What support systems are available for you as a facilitator?
H) What support systems are available for people in the circle?

Create a list with contact information for AA meetings, writing groups, therapists, etc.

In terms of workshop structure, each meeting should include exercises that encourage each person in the circle to achieve the tasks in the following list. The more time you spend on each item below the better. For example, I have facilitated entire weekend retreats focusing on unpeeling. It is important to end each session with resurfacing and closure exercises.

—Break assumptions (about each other).
—Identify (race, ethnicity, class status, gender identity, sexuality, body challenges or abilities, year born, place of birth, birth language(s), current language(s), etc.).
—Unpeel/witness (tell something personal).
—Unmask/witness (tell a personal truth).
—Reveal/witness (tell personal truths in a way that uncovers something that you usually don't share with people).
—Be in the body (be present).
—Resurface (speak a healing, affirming, present-moment truth).
—Achieve closure (final words, rituals, send-offs).

Depending on how much time you have per workshop session, and depending on how the session goes and how present you are in allowing the process to unfold (as opposed to controlling it), you may find that you need to alter the structure.

Creating several exercises for each category below will give you options that will allow you to move confidently and quickly as you make decisions about what to do inside the circle. I said this earlier but I am going to repeat it because it is really important: remember, this is jazz. Being present is the tool that improvisation comes out of. Trust and employ your virtuosity, your humanity, and all your senses in the art of spontaneously honoring the magic of the moment. Again, don't be afraid to throw your great workshop outline out the window. Or better yet, walk in without a plan, and sit openly and honestly in the *what is* of the day.

Sample Workshop Outline

The first workshop (in a series of meetings) should begin with the group's Agreements for Safety being stated, written, and posted. A good time to do this is after introductions are made but before any workshop activities begin.

Exercises should move participants deeper and deeper in reflection, truth telling, and personal examination as the day's work session goes forward. Exercises must later transition energy up, moving participants from their emotional depths, so that they may safely reenter the world out of the circle. Be intentional in inviting and structuring ways for people in the circle to witness each other's truths with no cross talk or judgments. Workshops should combine writing, talking, witnessing, and movement.

Keeping these points in mind, create exercises for each category below. Each should last between ten and forty-five minutes.

breaking assumptions
identity
grandmother/mother/daughter
grandfather/father/son
unpeeling
unmasking
revealing
being in the body
being present
resurfacing
being gentle
closure

my Work with the Austin Project has been an unbelievable journey
a privilege/a personal Blessing.
over the years these wy'mn have become my family/celebrating all manner of
things with me. supporting me unfailingly.
in 2005 i was diagnosed with cervical cancer. during my recovery/they were
on point—giving me rides feeding me taking my at-home nursing crew (my
mom and my daughter) to the mall and to community events so they could
have breaks (i had a radical hysterectomy/am cancer free). there simply isn't
enough space to go into the number of ways that they continue to inspire
and support me/have supported each other/and other communities of artists
around the globe.

in the Austin Project i have become a better me.
the determination courage fiercenesses
commitment to sisterhood
to writing/to truth/to self examination
to moving powerfully forward that the Austin Project wy'mn embody
has helped me to work harder

to walk with more dignity and integrity
than i could have mustered on my own
of course during the process
i have stumbled
fallen down/fallen out
at times have been ungraceful
and of course
i have learned a lot
and i have grown.

all because of Omi's remarkable vision.

because of the resources that JLW/CAAAS put into the Austin Project.
because of the work/the Lives/the example/
the sisterhood of these wonderful wy'mn
i have fully realized my method of facilitation
and was able to create my own facilitation manual.
the gumbo is ready y'all.
ummhumm, sho nuff/indeed . . .

PART II
Working the Work
An Anthology of Austin Project Writings

POLYPHONY

Writings by Ensemble Members

At the heart of the Austin Project is the personal work—whether it be creative, political, or spiritual—of each participant. This chapter includes writing produced in the workshop by most of the women who participated in the first five years of the Austin Project (2002–2006). An anthology of poetry, prose, memoir, playwriting, and spiritual reflection, this chapter is a snapshot, in panoramic view, of what the Austin Project feels like and what it produced.

Shannon Baley

SHANNON'S MAIN CLAIM TO FAME IS HAVING MOVED THIRTY-FIVE TIMES by the time she was twenty-one years old. She is currently a recovering graduate student, a teacher, a poet, a performer, and a mama. She lives with her husband, Stephan, her daughter, Fiona, a baby-to-be, and three rambunctious cats in Austin, Texas. Her work has previously appeared in *Farelu Literary Magazine, Texas Borderlands Poetry Review,* and *di-vêrse'-city: The Austin International Poetry Festival Anthology.*

six days of christmas

I

season of joy and giving, we stake out
parking spots, credit card bills and barbed wire
around long distance phone calls.

my childhood has been annexed
because my mother had none herself
and every morning in november
i awake from dreams of kittens
and road trips and sinks full of dirty dishes.
infected, my shoes fill up with water.

II

that year i walked into the office,
you screaming at me to get out
to shut the door. frightened to the roots
of my hair, i hid under the bunk beds
until you fetched me out
to interrogate what i had seen.
i remembered nothing except shame,
until i saw the homemade dolls
under the tree at 5 a.m.

santa became a woman, mouth full of pins and
needles, spitting mad at the surprise
ruined.

III

when was it that the joy left you?
did your children grow up too fast or too slowly?
was it sucked out like milk, or gradually dispersed
like flour sprinkled on the counter once weekly
and pounded into smooth loaves,
while your small daughters sat on stools
aproned and chattering away?

or was it gone before we even arrived,
stolen by endless christmases of
free-for-all ripping and tearing
and too much to drink around the
family turkey?

did you think of leaving, of putting up
a gate around the christmas tree,
locking up the gifts,
tiptoeing off late one night
with only your thoughts
and an overnight bag?

did you dream of escaping to yourself?
do you still?

IV

sister sets up holidays
like matchsticks
temporary and
flammable

V

what was the hardest, though, were the thousand
little rituals they demanded, tradition building upon
tradition each year until december was a march of musts
and everything in its place. children love consistency

and somewhere along the line consistency becomes nostalgia,
a longing for what *was* even if it never existed in the first place,

no matter how carefully they placed the animals in the crèche
or advent calendars on the walls of the thousand
little houses in the thousand new cities
until they too were adults, rigid with memories.

VI

mama,
these are the gifts I would give you:

things, a mountain of them, all shiny
and glittery with remarkable usefulness,
easily returned, recycled.

yards and yards of supple young men,
well toothed and well read.

firewood for the bonfire of your childhood
(i would light the match
and
BURN
baby
burn).

rest. free from care, to smooth out
worry lines and restless mind,
gnawing at itself
at 2 a.m.

truth and the courage to tell it.

beauty and the courage to know it.

love and the courage to take it.

Rajasvini Bhansali

RAJASVINI BHANSALI IS A POET, DANCER, AND SOCIAL ENTREPRENEUR.
She co-founded Sukuma for Opportunities, an international NGO that
works for secure livelihoods in Kenya, and serves as a board member for
CUSO-VSO, an international development organization that serves in
the global south. A Kathak dancer since age three, Rajasvini trained to
use poetry, form, footwork, performance, and percussion to embody and
tell stories, from classical epics to modern ballads, under the tutelage of
masters in the Jaipur and Lucknow traditions. Rajasvini received bachelor's
degrees in astrophysics and in interdisciplinary studies (social sciences and
humanities) from the University of California at Berkeley and a master's
degree in telecommunications/technology policy from the University of
Texas at Austin. She has also published, performed, and taught poetry since
1996.

The story of flat feet

16 years of longing
for dancing bells to snake up her ankles
and into her being
have led her to sleep and dream in
thak thak thun thunk dikda dikda dai
thak thak thun thunk dikda dikda dai

these days the dikda dikda dai wakes her at some very early hour
she sits up in her bed, hearing the white noise of chilly nights
in a jugalbandi with her lover's breath next to her

and wishes herself arches on the soles of her feet
wishes her flat aching feet to become untouched petals
for mundane walking or soaking

but these feet never formed arches
they were too busy crafting
ta thei thei ta
aa thei thei ta
before they ever knew how to walk

her little hands could wind ropes of dancing bells ghungroos up her
    ankle
before they ever learnt to tie shoelaces
the bells could wind tightly over red socks with feet cut off
some padding between skin and song

every morning since she was 3
her guru was her priest
leading her in a prayer of serious sensuality
crafted into motion

no she doesn't want arches
she wants the call of the earth in response to the smack of her flat feet
like hands on congas
tablas or pakhawaj
ta thei thei ta
aa thei thei ta

she remembers
when the child became a dancer
and the dancer moved her people
and her people became her heart

now grief travels from heart to shoulders and spine
her rhythm lives there
held in couplets
a daily ghazal of longing

thak thak thun thun
dikda dikda dai

so she writes poems about
saffron dissolved in warm milk
stirred with sweet jaggery
drink daily, guruji used to say
this fortifies a growing dancer
prepares you as a warrior
prepares you for rigor and beauty
you must dance in the face of derision

no this is not the dance of prostitutes, she must explain
this is kathak—we tell stories—we are storykeepers
we are griots, bards, we are seductresses yes
but then which story doesn't seduce

how could a story told through mudras and circles not
move, cajole, and turn the hearts
of men
and women for women
ta thei thei ta
aa thei thei ta

yes yes she's heard how kathak dancers
grow old and fat quicker than other Indian women
and yes her flat feet hurt sometimes
but after 10 years of daily riyas
rehearsing with the peacocks
on the old house rooftops in the desert
every morning at sunrise
after 10 years of daily training
sleeping with ballads that used to roll in like fog over these North
    American hills
thak thak thun thunk dikda dikda dai
thak thak thun thunk dikda dikda dai

how does one stop being a dancer?
clearly a choice has to be made
because a choice was once presented
ta thei thei ta
aa thei thei ta

when the text in books began to sit very still
words were captured in afternoon detention
having danced on the edges of appropriateness too long
the peacocks began to walk crooked
and the cacophony of sitars strumming at festivals
began to hurt her
even the ocean waves, irritatingly,
out of step with the next one
what kind of company are they keeping, she would wonder,
what happened to balance

between her feet and her ghungroos
a cosmic black hole lies gaping
and not her, she is too strong to be sucked in

so the girl becomes a woman
she keeps her flat feet
births infinite longing

and look, the ghungroos exclaim at sundown, your elders are dying
who will sustain their stories
have you noticed we are rusting
rusting

she shrugs her shoulders
it is not her responsibility
she cannot save the dance
the stories or the ancestors

she knows better
she moves on
she plans ahead
she invents words that dance
she surrenders to modern, jazz, West African, ballet
anything but stillness
home is nestled in the valley of
thak thak thun thunk dikda dikda dai
so in the meantime she finds home where she can

poetry exile longing music grief
folklore mother grandmother sisters

her flat feet don't let her forget
she is a ghazal in search of her refrain
she is a ghazal in search of her refrain.

Detine L. Bowers

DETINE IS A CREATIVE COMMUNICATIONS SPECIALIST LIVING IN NEW YORK City. She is the granddaughter of the late veterinarian William A. Thomas and his wife Naomi, creators of an early-twentieth-century interracial sustainable community in Brodnax, Virginia. She works on a range of communications projects that include motion pictures and independent films, media diversity advocacy, communications training, and eco-village communication and development. Harmony Blessings, her core project, is an evolving sustainable-lifestyle and diverse-arts community she envisioned in 1995. She holds a PhD in public communication from Purdue University and an MA in speech communication from Colorado State University.

Bearing Witness

Note to reader:
Awakened from sleep, this channeled piece came in the midnight hour during the Austin Project process. Over the years, I have had many conversations with Mary Lue and Major Bowers, William Lucas, Barry Brummett, Susan Paige, James Farmer, Jr., William H. Waddell IV, Molefi Asante, and Elisabeth Kübler-Ross about Harmony Blessings, out-of-body experiences, and death and dying.

I bear witness to the ages of genetically coded information that finds its
   place lodged deep within the cellular walls of memory. It is from this
   place that my ancestors speak of collective consciousness, of Isis:
The body is dismembered I weep, I moan, I groan with the pain of loss.
We groan and moan with the pain of separation . . . of loss . . . of
   detachment.
Dear Osiris comes and goes in the deepest places of my spirit.

I am an open vessel, a place of memory of those who have gone
   before, a channel to the past that speaks of golden places, of crystal
   stairways, of monuments to the supreme God.

We speak to nurture the soul, to uncover the sacred and the profane,
   to uncover what lodges in our feelings, our intellects, our rhythms, a

place where mother and father time meet and stand tall and firm, a place where we gather and wail for all that has pained us—all of our sufferings, all of our anguish.

We have waded in the water and we have returned to ourselves
We have come full circle, changing the tide of existence
We open our minds and souls
We pour out our hearts.
We call to you to remember who you are, to speak with clarity and conviction with the voice of memory only you can deliver, only you can nurture, only you can awaken for all those who must know, must feel, must deliver themselves to themselves and return to the living waters of existence.

We are the thoughts and feelings you imagine, we are your guides to freedom. We are the voices of love and longing here to be your guides of deliverance—to who we all are on this earth plane.
We speak, we feel, we know, we understand, and we honor
We bring the living waters to you
We return your memories of peace and tranquility . . . we return you to yourselves.

Osiris re-embodies himself, Isis as healer, collecting the pieces of ancient memory to restore what is stolen, what is real and true.
No more separation . . . we are a whole fabric bound together in time and space.
Hear us, hear us, through this clear, free, and open vessel
Love is the freedom we be together, collectively
Unknotted by time and space.

We bring you love—unbound, clear, free, and open.

Florinda Bryant

FLORINDA BRYANT IS AN INTERDISCIPLINARY ARTIST AND EDUCATOR. Florinda is the Artistic Director of the Austin Project Performance Company, sponsored by the John L. Warfield Center for African and African American Studies at the University of Texas at Austin. She has worked with the Theatre Action Project since 2004, and has mentored at-risk youth for over ten years. She currently serves as the program specialist for the

Theatre Action Project's after-school program. Florinda recently directed and performed in the award-winning play *HUSH* at the 2008 ArtSpark Festival.

Excerpt from *half-breed Southern Fried (check one)*

Digging

Planting

There is dirt on these fingers
ain't never gonna come off

Digging

Planting

There is dirt on these fingers
ain't never gonna come off

No slaving sharecropping working
someone else's land

There is dirt in these bones on these fingers in this blood
wasn't meant to come off

Blisters on thumbs from shelling peas, the pain hurts worse only when
you stop.

Dewberries, watermelon, peas, blackberries, greens, collards, tomatoes,
corn, ta'tas, and me.

Dirt

Held deep in my muscles screams fights what shouldn't be held down
deep.

This country dirt holds secrets that could set me free if I dig deep
enough.

What would Daddy/Aunt Faye/Uncle Pie say?

If they saw me back bent
in my back yard, on land I own.

Frozen

judging the quality of Kim Sung's work. My pedicure the only thing
    that catches my eye.

What would Uncle King say? Uncle Pie or Cousin Johnnie say?

If they saw me, all this blessing, and not one seed planted this season.

I pause

There is dirt in these bones on these fingers ain't never gonna come off

Something in me wars with this memory/blessing/shame.

And every morning when I wake, the birds sing and I pray. Maybe
    today will be a good day for planting.

.   .   .   .

Holy Jesus, father god bless her.

                            Holy ancestors, mother earth, bless her.

Stop trying to remember.

                                    Stop trying to forget.

There is only pain there.

                                    There is only pain there.

Holy Jesus, father god, bless her.

                            Holy ancestors, mother earth, bless her.

She wouldn't come to visit often. My father's mother, the one called
    grandmother. So much like her, it ran her hot. Come over here and

kiss me on my jaw. She was a very tall woman and in whispers I would hear how powerful she was. Not no more. A preacher now in the Pentecostal church. We sprinkle our own salves on each other when we think we aren't lookin. You just like your grandmother, ain't ya.

Check. transition moment playing with beat.

> Holy ancestors, mother earth, bless her.
> Stop trying to forget.
> There is only pain there.
> Holy ancestors, mother earth, bless her.

My best friend who was half-white and half-Pakistani had just left my house during one of her visits. Grandmother sat at the kitchen table, watching us doing the dishes. Once she had gone, my grandmother said, You sho is good with the white people, you know you get that from me. I just looked at her not sure what to say. My mother, who never left us alone for too long, tried to move the subject, yes, she sure is.

You get that from grandmother. I was always good with the white people. I was always nice. Remembered my manners, didn't come in there with all that loud nigga talking. You can't do that, they don't care for it. If you take care of your white people they will take care of you. You know a lot of white people, baby. They call you they friends. How bout the white mens? Is they nice to you. Hmm.

I could hold on to a position longer than anybody I know. Even if they wasn't no really nice people. I could get on in there and work hard, do what I needed to do, and they would thank me for that. Get little extra bonuses here and there. The white folks got they own way about doing thangs. You just got to know how to deal with em. Mind your manners. Don't back talk to em and they will take care of you.

You sho is good with the white people, you get that from grandmother. For the white girls like Nikki Dimitri
That I use to hang with.

> Sometimes I reflect on where I have been
> Exactly why you let me in

Accepted me as your only black friend

Macadamia nuts
Strawberry Hill
And acid

It was crazy cause even back then we knew
I could never really fit
And with each new moon that passes
I know better why it all came into play
Down to the way I called you MISS NIKKI
See for me
It was about already knowing and showing my position
As your Uncle Tom version of Topsy childhood friend
You had to let me in cause everybody has just one

Macadamia nuts
Strawberry Hill
And acid

But it was dope cause the Greeks had they shit too
For something to do
We would boost what you could afford
And in accordance with the unwritten wealthy-bitch rule
We'd skip school and climb houses
Tried flyin high off this earth

I used to think you had it made.
Too scared to say enuf and end it right now,
You had a maid and your daddy was paid
And I never saw so much fucking food in my life

Didn't know white girls had to worry about the feds
Runnin up in they house
Cause your daddy was up in it
That on the side white-collar crime
That thing that brings Americans pride.
But dad fits the profile
Would never look you in the eye
Said yes ma'am to a child

So we would get high and try to fly off this planet
That would never understand

Macadamia nuts
Strawberry Hill
And acid

Tried to find where the bees slept . . .

For white girls like Nikki Dimitri
That I use to hang with
Who never understood why I didn't mind you dating our men
Some even my kin
Even then I could see
The only thing you took from me was the opportunity
At misery

Took it back to the old South
Where every home was a whorehouse
Cause a woman ain't never been free
To do as she pleased
Truly realized that we were family
Miss Nikki and me
I recognized the wisdom afraid to be heard
And what a beautiful voice with so much to say of course
But after all it is all about choice . . .
To see no matter how high we'd be
The outer limits we would never see
TOGETHER

For the white girls like Nikki Dimitri
That I cried with when the maid died
And you didn't have to hide she was more
Your mother than not
And we'd get drunk til we passed out
Tryin not to notice what the world was about

We got older
The signs got bolder
Started lookin over my shoulder
For my visa for being white had expired

And no one wants an educated Negro

All this time we knew ours was a moment
And we could never be high enuf
Design enuf a way
To not see your soul runnin out with the fifth abortion
Knowing you would never take a black baby home

I wondered why you'd ever roam to my side of town anyway.
That was the day I had to look the other way
No need for words I didn't need to say

For white girls like Nikki Dimitri.

Monique Cortez

Monique Cortez is a performance artist, physician, and writer living in Austin, Texas. She has performed in *Broken Circles*, written by Omi Osun Joni L. Jones, and *half-breed Southern Fried (check one)*, written by Florinda Bryant. She has been a member of the Austin Project since 2003. She would like to thank her husband Steve Tseng, their four-footed companions Mari and Mimi, her parents Janie and Arturo Cortez, Sr., brothers Joel, Art, and Javier, and her large extended family for their love and support throughout her life.

Dancing with Memories

I walk into the room. How many of these have I been in? Hundreds?
    Thousands?

The smells of bleach, cleaning agents, and linens hang in the air.

Check the patient—quiet, resting, rise and fall of chest with breath.

Check the lines—IVs look good. One in the right forearm and one in
    the left hand hep-locked.

Check the fluids—normal saline, 1,000 ml bag, 500 cc left. TKO rate.

Check the meds—all bags empty. Names all correct. Joel H. Cortez.

No further meds due for 2 hours.

Check the pump—PEG feeds, 70 cc/hour. Per chart: no residuals.

Foley bag with clear urine. Excellent.

Lift the sheet. Heel protectors in place. Extremities warm.

The bed whispers as it rises and falls to prevent bedsores.

No clubbing/cyanosis/edema. Toes look good. Pulses good.

I refuse to look at his indwelling cath or the colostomy or the PEG.

What are you doing? Just say hi.

Can he hear me?

Will he know my name?

Does he remember me?

Is he even in there somewhere?

I'll do a sternal rub to wake him up. No. Just say hi.

Grandpa?

Grandpa? Wake up. It's me. It's Monique. Popo?

I never called him Grandpa when I was little.

It was always Popo.

I don't know where I got it from.

That's just who he was.

I remember his arms.

Working the Work

Carpenter's arms. Strong and long. Big hands. Long fingers

worn by time and tools and wood and steel and work.

I remember his face as it used to be.

Wide smile. Always smiling. Big, toothy smile.

You never noticed that his teeth were crooked.

Moustache for a while and then he shaved it.

It made him look younger.

Big nose. High cheekbones.

Eyes bright with untold mischief.

My brother Javier has his eyes.

Bald. I always remember him being bald.

He had this t-shirt that said, "It's not a bald spot, it's a solar panel for a sex machine."

He used to take me out on the dance floor with him at every wedding.

For weeks before he would tell me, "Get your dancing shoes ready, Mommy."

He always called me Mommy.

It was always a mixture of stress and excitement.

My grandmother wouldn't dance with him so he danced with me and Aunt Grace and Liz. They all danced better than I did. I could never do it right. I never really LEARNED how to dance until college.

I had to take a class to be taught to do what he did by instinct and sheer joy.

When we danced, he just went out there and did it.

And I was supposed to follow.

And he had these CRAZY moves.

He looked good, like a tall Fred Astaire
    and I could barely keep the beat.

The complete joy on his face was unforgettable.

I can still see his face.

Parkinsonism: a relatively common disorder that occurs in all ethnic
    groups, with an approximately equal sex distribution.

The most common variety, idiopathic Parkinson's disease,
    begins most often between 45 and 65 years of age.

One of the first signs of Parkinsonism is a tremor. Usually unilateral,
    it begins at rest and can be eliminated through effort or use of the
    affected limb.

In later stages, the tremor is persistent.

I know Parkinson's disease. I know it well.

I had seen it in my grandfather's father.

I watched it in my grandfather.

And it scares me to see my father's hand shake.

And when will mine?

Abuelitá

Pásale. Pásale.

Come into the memories.

Sweet tea poured from the plastic yellow pitcher stained from years of
use

into bronze glasses thick and heavy.

The scent of flour tortillas cooking on a hot sartén hangs heavy in the

air. I can taste them before they are ready.

Where's the butter?

Candles flicker.

In the dim light, a man on a horse sits in a frame on a small table
layered with crocheted doilies.

Water

Grass

for the horse.

Candles flicker.

Prayers whisper as she walks by.

The white sheet flutters over me

disturbed endlessly by the broom as it rushes past, over my face, my
hands, my legs, and feet.

Lying on my back, my lungs fill with the scent of incense burning in the
corner of the room.

I can hear the prayers but I don't understand.

The words seem ancient, spoken too quickly for a non-native

speaker to catch. Maybe that's the point. Chase. Chase

fast. Chase away. Soothe what remains. Calm.

I see her sitting in front of me.

She's gone through five names to find mine.

She places in front of me: Coke, flour tortillas, and carne guisada with
the gravy running all over the plate.

No fork. Extra tortillas.

Come sit next to me.

No one leaves Grandma's house hungry—even if you weren't hungry
when you got there.

She smells the same, a mixture of flour, canela, coffee, and sugar.

Her hands are thick like her varicose veins.

Her body moves with difficulty, worn by time, loss, grief, and a life of
picking cotton and cleaning homes (not hers).

Her heart is bound not by these burdens, lifted up by children,
grandchildren, great-grandchildren,

love, and riches that banks don't recognize.

She limps with arthritis but continues to walk forward, further towards
life.

It's cold and raining outside. We're all stuffed into and around her tiny
house. Uncles huddled

around the barbecue pit drinking beer and "barbecuing." Kids running around and through the house.

Aunts, babies, and cousins sitting and standing (you squeeze in wherever you can) in the house, drinking coffee and eating and talking. Oh the talking! The chatter can be heard for miles around and it permeates the night.

It is because of her that we all gather together.

Fireworks are outlawed but you'd never know it looking down the block.

The crumbled chocolaté measured in handfuls drowns in the canela and hot milk on the stove.

She knows it's my favorite. The whole reason I go home on New Year's Eve.

The scent fills her tiny galley kitchen stuffed with cousins, aunts, and noise. Through the hands, faces, plates, and food I reach towards her heart.

Geeta Cowlagi

Geeta Cowlagi is the founder and director of Interactive Peer Programs. IPP offers interactive workshops to explore dynamics of power and control in interpersonal relationships and in the workplace. Prior to her work with IPP consulting, Geeta served as the education specialist for the Voices Against Violence Project at the University of Texas at Austin where she founded the Voices Against Violence Peer Theatre Program. Geeta has also worked with nonprofit organizations and universities around the country to create awareness and change around the issues of interpersonal violence.

Betrayal

tiny little almonds
nestled inside the round soft of my belly
out of sight and out of mind
most of the time

bearing my stress
silently suffering the abuse
of my modern feminist quest

three jobs
one shelving books
finding my precious moments of peace
lost amid the dewey decimals in the library stacks
the second in a video store
wondering how we humans make
the journey from renting G to X
and the third a graveyard shift
which welcomed the dawn through
a motel check-in window
with bloodshot eyes

and the unending years of school
away from home and love
sustained on coffee and cigarettes

my tiny little shock absorbers
buffered the impact of the long moneyless days
when i lived for ideas and thoughts alone

aging before their time
they have moaned and groaned
and when i continued to ignore their whimpers
they sent a message to my mirror

a hairy chin and face stared back at me
trying to grab my attention
but i was too busy liberating myself and
claimed the hairy stubble to be a feminist revolt against feminine beauty

little tiny cysts now grow on those almonds
the years of neglect now has a medical name
polycystic ovarian disease

they now have my attention
and my grief

the place where life begins
lies dormant and barren inside me

i had thought my ovaries had betrayed me
but know now that it is i who have betrayed them

i wish it could be like old times
when mama kissed the boo-boo and made it all right
but i know this is no simple scrape

i ask for forgiveness from my body
as a batterer asks for forgiveness from the partner
knowing that this time around
flowers wrapped in a simple word of love or remorse
just won't be enough

we were made to take care of each other
until death do us part
but i did not keep my end of the deal
the damage caused is deep

it is not too late
i must make haste
i need to unlearn
and then relearn
to love myself again

D'Lo

DESCRIBED AS A "JOLT OF CREATIVE AND COMEDIC ENERGY," D'Lo IS A
Tamil Sri L.A.nkan-American, political theatre artist, writer, and music
producer. D'Lo is a teaching artist and has performed and held workshops
extensively throughout the United States, Canada, the UK, Germany, Sri

Lanka, and India. D'Lo holds a BA from UCLA in ethnomusicology and is a graduate of New York's School of Audio Engineering. In 2004, in New York City, D'Lo's first play, *Ballin with My Bois*, a queer, hip-hop theater piece, had a sold-out run. Since 2007, D'Lo has been touring with *Ramble-Ations: A One D'Lo Show*. For more information about D'Lo, go to www .dlocokid.com.

For the Young Warriors

The streets of downtown burn,
hot roads walked upon
soles of old Nikes keep callus peds covered
but skin tightens.
It is hell and young souls don't belong here.

Eyebrows frown in this heat,
as if sheltering retinas like awnings.
Sun makes brown skin shine back like mirrors.
Grey eyes are child's.
Reflections of innocent souls.

Glass tips for toast.
Another life goes
whispering its departure
in mist
ascending to the heavens,
to the future.
Some souls weren't meant for this life.
Not an accident they spent time here,
just sent down to investigate,
to witness the lay of the land.
They were told,
"This is what you're dealing with."
Come again, they must
be leaders here.

Medicated, those left
escape.
I, the observer, beg them, no,
please.

Beg them
to fight
for their lives.

There's a fucking war going on.
Please awaken.
Put down the blunt,
smoke it in a pipe.
Keep your third eye open.
It's yours to fight with—
against eyes closing.

I understand nothing, but expect the world
from the world.

Hand-woven threads kiss skin constantly
with reminding "hellos"
"my love, my dear"
"my love, you are taken care of"
"good day"
"good night, sweet dreams."
Understanding fatigue(s) can only be erased by this threaded armor . . .
Get out of other countries if you are there to fight.
Come back home, I support you,
fight for yourself.

My brothers and sisters are sick,
spreading infections to one another.
Vomit.
Wipe down.
Breathe two survival breaths.
Hand over someone else's heart.
Get them.
Don't call 9-1-1.
Mouth to mouth

has been the only thing that works.

Madre Tierra,
you speak to my stupidity
loudly.

No one wants to listen.
I still do not.
No excuses
I've lost my mother tongue.

Praying for clouds to lift
set adrift on concrete
praying for bravery
against ourselves
praying for dreams to stir the sedated
for visions to give the future hindsight
for love to be the root
for the tree to be the proof
praying for it to be done in silence
cuz loudness did not get us far at all.

Dedicated to Rene and raúlrsalinas of Resistencia and Red Salmon Arts, Austin, TX

Dulani

DULANI IS A WRITER AND PERFORMANCE POET BASED IN BROOKLYN, New York. A trans-identified Desi from a low-income immigrant family, his work uses personal narrative as a means for political discourse. Dulani holds a bachelor's degree from Oberlin College in a self-designed major, "Art for Social Change: An Interdisciplinary Approach." In 2007, he went on tour as part of Mangoes with Chili, a multi-genre traveling cabaret featuring emerging queer and trans performance artists of color. Dulani is a Kundiman Fellow and his work has been published in *SAMAR: South Asian Magazine for Action and Reflection* as well as on the Busting Binaries Web site.

Kindred strength

I

gold on wrist
laying on my back
in a
polyester hospital gown,

thirty-something pills later
my mother asked me
if I was gay

terrified
but still a smart-ass
my inner monologue said
well,
what is she gonna do?
kill me?

I looked at her
as my voice translated that to
a meek
two-word response:

"a little."

the minutes and months following that absurd moment
are a blur

all except for the heartbreaking, haunting words:
"sometimes you have to kill how you feel"

my mother's words seeped into my skin

sometimes you have to kill how you feel

made me bow my head
to mourn
all the death in our bodies

made me bow my head
because I cannot bear to look
into the layers
of why
why she spoke those words
so calmly

is that why ma was crying that Sunday afternoon when I called to
    say hello?

after finishing up the cooking and the cleaning, she didn't know
     what to do

guess you can't kill
loneliness.

for years, I told myself that ma was sad because we didn't live in a better
     house
with less debt
and new carpet

ma
had told my brother
that she thought I overdosed because
she didn't get me a computer.

funny how we wanted to give each other gold.

didn't understand that what each of us needed
was to be able to live in our bodies.

what were our mothers killing as we grew inside of them?
where did we find life?

2

a friend once said to me:
"sacrifice—that's all they know"

his words made me spiral
and think about how
ma's pain
and ma's love
lived in sacrifice

the logic of 'I love u' was
"I don't want to give my baby anything to worry about"

but the pain doesn't die, ma
it spreads in our bodies like a disease

and then

we don't want to live there anymore.

gold on wrist
laying on my back
in a
polyester hospital gown,
thirty-something pills later—

sometimes you have to kill how you feel

I was relearning
I'm not allowed to be broken.

3

Oloye Aina Olomo
said, "your life is your prayer"

my mother and I began living our prayers together
at a "pan-asian" restaurant in ohio

nineteen years old,
three months after
being in the hospital,
I sat across from ma
in the booth
and heard her,
maybe for the first time.

she said, "I want to be a part of your life."

slightly bitter from her silence around my queerness
I said defensively,
"well, I tried to tell you something in the hospital"

she looked at me and earnestly said, "you said 'a little'"

I almost jumped out of my seat,
"a lot, ma, I meant A LOT!"

not only did ma give me the gift of two coming out stories
(the first for being *a little* gay,
and the second for being *a lot* gay),

she began to live a prayer of honesty with me.

concealing pain
is a full-time
futile
task

no wonder it had been so impossible for us
to be present
with each other

I'm grateful you did not spare me your tears
that sunday afternoon, ma

I know they traveled a long, lonely path
to be set free.

gold on wrist
I'm listening ma.

I understand now
what I have been given
what I need to give back.

the gift
of being in my body
and finding something
other
than
loneliness

the gift
of finding solace
not in all the sacrifice
but in the breath
where the details

of our truths
find life.

the gift of seeing you
hearing you

gold on wrist
laying on my back
in a
polyester hospital gown,
thirty-something pills later

it was just the beginning

of learning what
each of us had survived

of knowing
kindred strength.

Amber Feldman

AMBER FELDMAN IS THE DIRECTOR OF CULTURAL AND PERFORMING ARTS
for the Mayerson Jewish Community Center in Cincinnati, Ohio. She is
also a staff member with KlezKamp, a Yiddish folk arts program in upstate
New York. Previously she was the director of education and literary manager
for the Jewish Theatre of the South in Atlanta, Georgia. She received her
MFA in theatre from the University of Texas at Austin, where she had the
great fortune to work with and learn from Omi, Sharon, and the rest of the
amazing women of the Austin Project. Amber lives in Cincinnati with her
partner Elisa and her daughter Shoshana.

The Second Hand

The most vivid memories with my dad take place in cars . . . don't ask
me why, but they do. As a child we spent more time driving than we
ever did sitting still.
I remember
driving to New York,
but I don't remember New York,

I remember
    driving to day camp,
        but I have no memories of day camp.
The car's eight-track tape selections alone are burned into my brain
and no matter how hard I try . . . I still hear those songs in constant
    rotation.

*"I write the songs that make the whole world sing, I write the songs of love
and special things."*

Daddy, can we listen to something else?
Pleeeease . . . I know we are Jewish but I'm kinda sick of the same
    eight-tracks of
Barry Manilow, Neil Diamond,
and Barbra Streisand.

My dad has this dry sense of humor . . .
we would be in the car and no matter how old I was he did the same
    joke: "I can't stop the car." I believed my father was the Jewish Bill
    Cosby.

This car thing . . . has been part of his whole life.
He always loved the idea of
leaving . . .
    going . . .
        not staying in one place long enough to get attached . . . even
        to me.

I never heard my father's stories . . . I learn about him through pieces of
    conversation
I collect at family funerals . . .
I met one of his girlfriends from high school at my grandmother's
    funeral,
and she told me this story about a Corvette my father had.

*"Amber, when your father was 16, he had this red Corvette. He adored
this car, I mean, he would not let a soul touch it. He got all the chicks in
this car. One day at school during lunch, some kid ran into the cafeteria
screaming, Teddy your car is on fire. The whole school ran outside . . . and
there in the parking lot was this red Corvette . . . on fire and melting."*

         Working the Work

He would never get another Corvette . . . but his obsession with cars
   never left.

There is a moment in life
when you
the child
becomes you
the adult,
one small moment
when all the fears about your own mortality are revealed.
Whether you like it or not, at some point God will slap you across the
   face and remind you that you are now an *official adult.*
You watch your father's mother or your mother's father pass away,
and the all too sudden passing of the torch takes place.

This is not a *real* happening but instead
   a surreal . . . almost film noir–like moment.
In my mind the lights go out, only a dangling light bulb remains on.
Shadows are all about
and sitting on a card table in an empty room in my mind
is the Polaroid of a torch.
Honest to God the moment is truly like this.

"Daddy, lift me up on your shoulders. I wanna be tall . . . please, please,
   please.
Daddy this is so cool. Oh, watch the door . . . I don't want to hit my head.
   Can you run?"

Memories are a powerful tool. They so easily erase . . .
My dad is only sixty-eight, but there he is . . .
The elderly man,
the distinguished-looking gentleman,
the aged person,
the old fart . . . that is my dad.

My dad has this couch . . .
The Couch . . .
he finally got rid of *The Couch* just before . . .
I spent nineteen years on this couch.
When I would visit my dad as a kid—for two weeks—every summer,

I slept on this couch,
in high school I spent all summer with my dad,
I slept on this couch,
on my summer breaks from college,
I slept on this couch.
I hated this couch, it was my jail sentence.
At the same time . . .
it is my most lucid memory of growing up . . .
each year my legs moved
further
   and further
      down each cushion
. . . 1 . . . 2 . . . 3 . . . until finally I touched the arm.
The Couch didn't turn into a bed, and my dad never bought me sheets
   because he said I wasn't there enough . . .
I can remember vividly the way this couch looked and smelled because
   it had the most heinous, beige, textured fabric that left marks all over
   me.
The fabric smelled of . . .
newspaper and cigarettes.
Oh, and the right cushion was always somewhat gray
from dad's weekly stack of daily newspapers.
I still see the small child with curly black hair,
balled up on this couch . . . crying for her mother.
I begged him to buy some sort of sofa bed so I didn't have to sleep
   on this thing. When I was thirteen I lived with my dad and after a
   month he agreed finally to *rent* me a bed.

My dad is dying.
I am told this is our last year.
Each month I hesitate turning over the calendar knowing that I should
   cross it off . . .
like a moment passing . . . each day slipping away . . .
my connection to *My* Jewish family . . . my history . . . will be gone . . .
buried in Memphis . . .
where stone-carved Stars of David sit memorializing the empty textile
   factory chimneys,
that rise up to envelop the sleeping.
I am anticipating and preparing my own shivah . . .

> mirrors covered
>> blinds drawn
>>> My shirt torn over my heart so the world knows . . .
I have died.

"Ms. Feldman, your father has developed Binswanger's, a slowly progressive
condition for which there is no cure. Patients with this disorder usually
die within five years after its onset. Basically, Ms. Feldman, your father's
brain is turning into Swiss cheese."

That is how the doctor described it to me.

Remember when you were a kid,
you thought your grandparents were soooo old.
I thought they were a hundred million years old . . . *at least*,
I would never be that old.
There was no way my parents would ever *ever* look like that.
The wrinkles were overexaggerated lines that looked like a comic book
    character.

Then one morning . . .
    not an unusual morning . . .
        just one of a million . . .
I realized my parents were *aging*.
First it starts with a letter in the mail, to my mother,
from the American Association of Retired Persons, the AARP.
Then I'm going to the movies with my dad and he says:
    "one adult and one senior citizen."
When did he become a senior citizen?
How had I missed the AARP Visa card in dad's wallet?
I was stunned.
How was it I was now the daughter of someone who is now seen by
    credit agencies as a senior?
You know what the root of 90 percent of Jewish guilt is?
Your parents,
and then your children . . .
neither of which will ever turn out the way you wish,
and no matter how hard you work over the years to make your parents
    into perfect
human beings that can be taken out in public . . .

---

they grow old,
and their worst traits seem doubled . . .
tripled . . .
even grow to four times their original size.
"Daddy, chew each bite, you're gonna choke."
"How are you feeling today?"
"Did you eat?"
    It is a lost cause.

I now look at my body in the mirror . . . tracing each wrinkle and line
    with my index finger . . . memorizing its shape.
    Who have I become?
I see my father's reflection staring out at me . . .
dark brown eyes, inlaid with soft skin . . .
large, sloped, Jewish nose . . .
my body . . . beaten up by years of self-loathing . . .
my mother's Anglo family called me *"little black sambo"*
my cousins yelled *"baa baa black sheep"*
I understood.

I am now my father's guardian. I had to tell him he couldn't drive.

My dad was no Ward Cleaver, but he's what I had to work with.
I am still a kid in my mind,
he is still the man that used to lift me on his shoulders and carry me
    around his apartment. The man that made . . . steak and boxed
    mashed potatoes every Saturday night.
The man I used to run to see the minute I stepped off the plane.

I can't do this.
I don't want to take care of him . . . I'm not ready.
He is my father for better or worse.
I saw him two weeks a year, slept on the couch,
and now I am supposed to become some sort of person he never was
    to me.
    I am no saint.
        I resent all of this.
I am this Jewish-academic-dyke,
I wanna just go on about my life,
and not have this huge father baggage hanging over my head.
I don't want a first date conversation to become

"So do you have children?"
"No, I have my father!"
Damn him.

Why don't they tell us this when we are born?
Oh, by the way, new life in this world,
you will someday have to take care of that person who forgot to buy
    condoms.

I just want to run away.
I don't want him to leave.
I want to be that eight-year-old girl
who grabs the pink wool blanket,
packs a box of cookies and a thermos of hot chocolate, and runs away to
    the backyard.
The backyard felt like a million miles away that day . . .
I felt like I had run so far.
I didn't care that it was only a few feet from the house . . .
    it was my great escape.
        I was eight and free.

Then my mother calls me back in from the cold and I run inside leaving
    the pink wool blanket on the lawn.
Singing.

This piece is dedicated to my father, Teddy H. Feldman, who passed away October
23, 2005.

Bianca Flores

BIANCA FLORES IS A CHICANA BORN AND RAISED IN SAN ANTONIO, TEXAS.
She now resides in Austin where she works as a diabetes nurse at a community
clinic. Working with youth for many years as a tutor, mentor, health educator,
and clinic coordinator, she has led numerous workshops on sexuality, sexual
health, sexism, racism, homophobia, and creative writing. As a health care
professional, she aims to provide and promote care that empowers and
values the health and well-being of individuals and communities. She feels
honored to be part of the Austin Project family, as it has helped her grow as
an artist, a person, and a nurse.

Me

Daughter   teacher
Granddaughter   dentist
Sister, Cousin, Niece   corporate executive
Friend
Lover   printmaker

Organizer, Educator   hip-hop emcee
Student, Nurse, Writer

Teen mom   busboy
Virgin   loan processor
Alcoholic   landscaper
Tecato, Crackhead, Stoner
Artist, Retard   bartender
Elder, Youth   handyman

Dementia-filled mind
Filled with life, laughter, history   housewife
Solitude   truck driver
Yearning   mechanic
Fear
91 years of being   work
12 children born   we work
2 children dead   to be

work   we work
we all know work   we are
work to keep
ourselves alive   Chicanita in
our family alive   their eyes
to know ourselves   Following the rules
to know each other   Playing the game
                                      The right distance to
                                          maintain the pace

work
                                      To keep a look out
used car salesman   But to stay in line with them
cotton picker
pecan sheller

---

factory worker

Bianquita in their eyes
Always inquisitive
Never too stylish
Keeping the family in mind
Carrying their pain
Keeping their secrets
Wanting to learn more

Woman in his eyes
Dedicated and constant
Uptight and frigid
Always afraid to let him in
Always loving
But not always showing her love

Keep the pace up
Where did she learn how to live?
How to work
How to be

Was it from them?
Is it a burden
or a blessing?

Güelito Chulo

I want a man
like my dad
I want a man
nothing like my dad

needs that others see
latest fashion on my back
food in my belly
and as long as I was an exceptional daughter
I made him shine

mija's smart
you know, she lives in Austin
goes to UT
pretty, mírala
chula la cabrona

emotional needs
that's different
how do I think?
what are my dreams?
who am I really?

does this man really know me?
can he really tell you
who I am?
can I
tell you who I am?

I don't know who he is
and definitely not who he was
I just know who my mom said he was
and he never tried to tell me different

he betrayed her
didn't betray me
but didn't love me the way I needed

he cheated too
found out later
later when I wasn't giving it on the regular
cuz I couldn't cum
cuz I took a life last time I came
but he still had to get his
whether or not it came from me

but I want a man who loves me like my dad
and I want a man who shows me who he truly is
but I'm afraid to show who I am

gone all day
missed the action

orderly house
food on the table
nothing bad to report
steady cash flow
when times were good

no jobs
notes from school
failing grades on report card
fights
dad home late smelling of beer and women
crying
screaming
shouting
screaming
crying yourself to sleep
when times were bad
when both parents were needed
when money didn't count
didn't help
and wouldn't make a difference

güelito chulo
mi güelito chulo
qué es lo que enseñaste a mi papá
qué significa ser un hombre
qué significa ser papá
un esposo
un rey
un rey en un mundo extraño
extraño porque somos extranjeros
¿puede ser?
¿para nosotros también?
extranjeros en un mundo en que nacimos
extranjeros y también nativos

dad
mi viejo
corazón sincero
corazón dolorido
mi corazón

hombre macho
hombre bravo
constantemente a mi lado
no me dejó
yo
te dejé
pero ni siquiera me explicó tus razones
y yo
no las pedí

brother
don't be afraid
strength
upon sensitivity
upon doubt
upon the will to love
one foot
in front of the other
walk your path
heal your pain
let the anger go
you have much to give this world

bianca
love
learn to love
open your heart
heal your pain
you can only give more
if you let others in
if you let them see you
if you discover yourself
and share it with others

güelito
viejo
brother
bianca
it's not too late to learn to love
to show your love
and live in truth

Theresa Burke Garcia

Daughter, sister, wife, partner, mother, educator. Theresa Burke Garcia's forays into the arts have oft been to further nurture and enrich her life in all these areas, particularly as an educator, where she hopes to further inspire those whose lives she's been privileged and honored to be a part of. She's grateful to Sharon and Omi for sharing the gift of the jazz aesthetic.

My work is not yet done

My work, facilitating the learning process of children as they engage in activities and discussions, is deeply involved in exploration and discovery, so that they might become facilitators of learning.

Imagine classrooms arranged so that children can flow in and out of learning spaces, interacting or independently delving into a passionate process of learning. I walk around watching, listening, questioning, evoking, and stimulating intrinsic motivation in the curious minds of the young.
Give me 5:
—Eyes on the speaker
—Mouth is quiet
—Ears are listening
—Hands are still
—Be here
Focus
Natascha is searching, can't find her folder, can't find her workbook, yesterday's pudding cup sits in the bottom of her backpack with last week's goldfish crumbs. There is disorder in her life and she is always two or three beats behind rhythm. *Eyes up, down, left, right, fidget, twist, fidget, twist. Backpack open, red folder out, workbook on yellow table, sit down and read. Five minutes.*

Johnny is having difficulty getting past the doorway because he is angry about a fight he had with his mother this morning. *Head lowered, fist clenched tight, face burning red, stomp, stomp, stomp, stomp, bang.* "I am the devil," he says. His body fills up with a rage sometimes too big for him to recover from on his own. We are working on releasing anger, *"10, 9, 8—breathe, Johnny, breathe—7, 6, 5, breathe . . ." Backpack open, red folder out, workbook on yellow table, sit down and read. Four minutes.*

Sierra stands halfway between the water fountain and the restroom staring into a space I cannot see. Which way will the pendulum of her mood swing today? Sadness creeps in and takes over this dreamy-eyed child made vulnerable by the fears she battles from being abandoned by a mother too overwhelmed by life and too overrun by four other children at home, one barely out of the womb. Her learning comes on days when she is not too frightened by the possibility of being left alone. *Blue-green eyes swimming in pools of liquid sadness she blinks herself back into uncertainty. Backpack open, red folder out, workbook on yellow table, sit down and read. Three minutes.*

Anthony is having trouble focusing because he didn't sleep much last night. He has made worry his bedfellow as he awaits the arrival of his mother who works late into the night, *the matriarch, head of household, sole provider.* He cannot rest until he feels her soft kiss and gentle touch, *"Mommy come home, come home mommy, mommy please come home."* Eyes half-closed, head bob, head bob. Backpack open, red folder out, workbook on yellow table, sit down and read. Two minutes.*

Tanya enters crying. She's hungry and the cafeteria is closed, dropped off too late again to eat breakfast, clothes still damp from a too early release from the dryer. She is starving for attention and I can only feed her a handful of animal crackers and some water. She gazes out bleary-eyed into the distance, tired to the bone, kept up by the sounds of late night partiers in the living room. She will spend the first hour of her day in the nurse's office recovering the sleep that had been stolen from her. *Where's her backpack?*

Imagine classrooms arranged so that children can flow in and out of learning spaces, interacting or independently delving into a passionate process of learning. I walk around watching, listening, questioning, evoking, and stimulating intrinsic motivation in the curious minds of the young.
Give me 5:
—Eyes on the speaker
—Mouth is quiet
—Ears are listening
—Hands are still
—Be here
Focus
My work:
Mistress of ceremonies in the greatest show on Earth, featured Act, No Child Left Behind. Watch as the children perform death-defying feats across a tightrope with no net. Their learning built around a curriculum pushing too much too fast. Be amazed as our children learn at the same ambitious

level at the same rate. Forget individual attention. Forget individual needs. Before your eyes the children's enthusiasm will disappear. Be astounded by the hurried pace students will have to maintain in order to keep up, "Breathe, Johnny, breathe." Witness as Washington imposes not just more tests, but also a whole new layer of regulations and paperwork, robbing administrators and teachers of time, creativity, and professional discretion. Hold on to your seats as more parents face isolation and persecution because they fit the profile and not the model. "At least I get them to school," says a defiant mother as she tries to hold on to the only thing she feels control over. She's been left behind too.

Our president put out the memo but it never got into the hands of the people who are still trying to catch up. It gives no regard to how drastically children's lives have changed because their parent's lives have changed.
Most are making less money and working more hours and more jobs, if they are even working at all. The district is too busy crunching numbers to appreciate the realities of our families' lives. *By the year 2014, one hundred percent of the nation's students will obtain passing rates on state achievement tests.* Papers pushed in invisible offices by invisible men who face problems with more paperwork.
My work:
I squash children for a living, pushing away all unnecessary issues and emotions that get in the way of education.
Leave behind your confusion.
Leave behind your anger.
Leave behind your loneliness.
Leave behind your fear.
Leave behind your sadness.
Leave behind your exhaustion.
Leave behind your hunger.
Where are we going?

Our hurried lives are catching up to us.
Imagine classrooms arranged so that children can flow in and out of learning spaces, interacting or independently delving into a passionate process of learning. I walk around watching, listening, questioning, evoking, and stimulating intrinsic motivation in the curious minds of the young.
Give me 5:
—Natascha
—Johnny
—Sierra

—Anthony
—Tanya
Focus

Kristen Gerhard

KRISTEN GERHARD WAS BORN IN KENTUCKY, GREW UP ON THE COASTS of Louisiana and South Texas, and transformed on the island of Hawaii. She has been dancing, writing, performing and producing, traveling, and gender bending her whole life. A lover of truth telling, peace building, improvisational music making, joy instigating, and serving the whole, she is deeply honored to be a part of the Austin Project.

Excerpted from "The Louisiana Chronicles"

I shared a bed with my older sister, but at least it was a big bed. After awhile, my sister and I got bunk beds. I think she must have liked not having to share a bed with me anymore, but I liked it because it was kind of like summer camp. Our cabins were full of bunk beds and when we were all supposed to be going to sleep, someone would start laughing or make a fart noise or a snoring sound and then everyone would burst into laughter and it would be hard to stop. Somehow it's funny to be sleeping in the same room with someone, but they are above or below you and you can't see them but you know they're there. My sister and I would play a game where I pushed my feet up into her mattress to make it bounce up and down and she would fling her pillows down at me. She was always ready to go to sleep before I was and I would get secret pleasure from shoving my feet into her back periodically until she was really irritated with me.

She also got annoyed by my need to have the closet light on. She liked total darkness and I had to have a crack of light, either from the closet or the hallway, which she called me a baby for needing. I almost always woke up needing to pee in the middle of the night, and even though the bathroom was right off of our room it felt like a sea of darkness that I had to cross to the toilet. When I reached the bathroom, the next problem was the cockroaches. My mom told me they came in from the heat, looking for water and coolness. But I did *not* feel sorry for them. I *hated* them. I certainly did not want to attempt to kill them though. I mean, they were almost as big as my pet gerbils, or at least as big as the baby ones. Anyway, they were big and their antennae reached out from their heads towards you when you turned on a light or made a noise. I wanted them to just go away but they did not care. I could turn the light on to one, two, three, four cockroaches on the floor, on the walls. They would just sit there, breathing, like they owned the place. So, I would flip the light off and race back to bed, being careful to jump out of reach of any monsters or demons underneath that might have tried to grab my foot. I fell back asleep to warm pee on my nightgown and sheets. My mom would be disappointed in the morning, but I would rather face her than the roaches.

I first broke my arm showing my dad how I could do a back handspring that I learned in gymnastics class. He had just finished mowing the yard and I said, "Watch this dad!" *Crr—ack!* He told me he could hear it from across the yard. It swelled up and felt funny and limp, but didn't actually hurt all that much. Since it was dinnertime, everyone sat down to eat before taking me to the emergency room while I cried on the couch. I didn't really feel like eating. In fact, I often didn't feel like eating. I would be the last one left at the dinner table.

My mom was always driving me everywhere. It seemed like I was late all the time. Or I would be the last one to get picked up, worried that my mom had forgotten. Soccer, T-ball, basketball, gymnastics, dance class—ballet, tap, jazz. I loved my jazz class. One time we did a performance outside for this festival at the capitol building that I was so excited about. It was different from performing on a stage because the audience was in broad daylight. I loved seeing so many adults paying attention to *me*. I felt very grown up. And our costumes, oh our costumes! All pink: pink tights and pink leotards covered with shiny pink fringe that shook and shook as we danced.

I wanted so badly to be a great gymnast. I loved to run and dance across the springy floor. I was often late, which my coach was never happy about. He was a big man with a booming voice and when he yelled his freckles took over his face and neck and he turned bright red. He liked to make examples of us when we made mistakes. The vault made me the most anxious. It just never made any sense to me to make myself run full speed at a solid object that I then had to flip over. Because of playing soccer, I was a fast runner and could really get up some speed in that short distance to the vault. One time, I ran hard as usual, jumped from the spring board, and, scared of my own momentum, forgot to put my hands down and just flew straight over, forcing my coach to break my fall. I was already terrified, but my coach proceeded to ream me out with the entire gym coming to a silent standstill. As I stood there with my long ponytail on top of my head, shaking, I wanted nothing more than to be swallowed into the floor mat so that no one could see me crying.

April Gentry—the first black girl I tried to be friends with. *You were tall, the color of hot cocoa, with a big smile that made me feel something I had not felt with a girl before. Your legs, strong and graceful—you were the best one on our team. The first time you were in our van, my dad driving us, we were shadowed by the dark road at night. I got nervous and my heartbeat quickened. I wanted to get closer to you, hold your hand in my palm and study your fingers that I had watched dance over basketballs. If I could only be alone with you, we could tell each other our secrets, run our fingers over scars. Why couldn't I get closer to you? I don't know what happened. I don't remember saying goodbye.*

I took a trip with my family to the beach when I was about six. It was somewhere on the Florida coast. Some of my dad's family came too, his brother, my Uncle David, and my grandparents. Uncle David is my godfather, whatever that means. He's the youngest of my dad's brothers and sisters. I really liked him because he was playful and he had big curly hair, the style for hippie dudes in the seventies, although I don't think he was really a hippie. He did drive a VW bug and took me on a ride one time. That pretty much put him at the top of the "cool" list.

My grandparents were really into playing card games, especially Oh Hell. I was so excited to get to play this game that had a cuss word for a name and involved making bids and taking tricks. Grandma played Yahtzee a lot with me, too. She *loved* playing Yahtzee. She would shake the dice in her hands and blow on them, like she was casting a spell, and when she rolled she yelled, "Hotsy totsy! I want a Yahtzee!" Then there were the times that she would grab my arm and pinch my skin if I wasn't cooperating or she would just get this really nasty tone that made me feel like I didn't know who she was. Grandpa was kind of quiet but he always wanted me to sit on his lap. Dad has talked about how *his* dad used to yell so much when he was younger, but that was not the grandpa that *I* knew.

Sometimes, when everyone was doing their own thing, I would go off by myself for a while. I would play in the sand dunes, study the plants, and watch the little critters. Other times, when I was tired of the hot sun, I would close a door behind me and lay down like I was taking a nap, but instead would have all kinds of fantasies that I knew I shouldn't be having. I worried that someone would find out somehow or that God would decide to pay attention to *me* at that moment (because God could read our thoughts) and then I would be a dirty sinner. But I did it anyway.

In one fantasy I was a stripper in a club, not as my six-year-old self, but as a woman with big, full breasts and long, thin legs. My audience was filled with older men in suits. They were begging for my attention, which they could only get by handing me money. I knew that I could make them do whatever I wanted, if I wanted to. But they could only watch and lust after my body, never touching me.

Erika González

ERIKA GONZÁLEZ IS A NATIVE OF EAGLE PASS, TEXAS, AND THE BORDER of Piedras Negras, Coahuila, Mexico. Erika is codirector of People Organized in Defense of Earth and her Resources (PODER), an environmental justice organization in Austin, Texas. Erika coordinates PODER's Young Scholars for Justice program and coordinates several environmental health, transportation, and juvenile justice projects. Erika has a BA in elementary education with a minor in psychology from St. Edward's University through the College Assistance Migrant Program. In her role as a teaching artist with the Theatre Action Project, Erika promotes socially relevant, interactive theatre and educational programming that ignites community dialogue and social change at elementary schools. She has also facilitated poetry workshops for Johnston High School students through Red Salmon Art's Save Our Youth program.

MIMA

you turned my sky
into a dream.
i looked at you
when it rained tears.
you looked for me
with watering eyes
as i grew into womn.
your reflection gave me hope.
i didn't understand that
you and i were one—
a piece of flesh separated by time.
i searched for you
in the womyn of my world
in communities
in the earth
in my-self.
you are everywhere
you are nowhere

i find you
in papi's song
the needle
playing tejano record
forever revolving
repeating
circular
movimientos of history.
you are a butterfly of songs
coming to me like i was your flower
in between cracks on sidewalks
ready to wilt away.
you were no warrior princess
or sun goddess of any tribe.
you are my vague memory of
chickens in the yard, fridge full of brown and blue-spotted eggs, kitchen
    smelling like frijoles con comino, a wave of black hair on my cheek, a
    muñeca with a black and red lace dress you sewed for me.
i taste you in my water
because water is what caused your death.
a gallon of *Agua Milagrosa* sold to you by a stranger
promising relief for your aching bones and arthritis.
Miracle Water said to have been blessed pure
from the Río Bravo.
you told no one.
drank a cup each day
like a ceremony
faithfully reciting
with rosary
prayers of *Santos, La Virgen*, and of the *Agua Milagrosa*.
"Dios perdóname por no estar cerca a mis nietos.
Dios perdóname por no confiar en tu fuerza.
Agua, limpia mi alma—mi espíritu—el artritis en mis huesos. Amén."
i taste you in my water.
wonder how much poison i can take
just to remember you existed
among the border that birthed you and took your life
like so many other women's lives
lost in between worlds never found.
but it's water that tries to show us how to survive
how to adapt to Mother Earth

Working the Work

trying to tell us something
is wrong—out of balance
is right—full of perfections.
is it our fault water is part of the cycle of life?
is it your fault you believed in miracles?
is it our fault that rivers divide countries
and that oceans feed and swallow civilizations?
Abuelita, you tried to tell me something with your death.
Papi, you tried to tell me something with your song.
Water, you tried to tell me something with your poisons.
Sky, you tried to tell me.
Earth, you tried to tell me.
all Grandmothers become water when they leave this earth.
all Water becomes us when we enter this life.
Mima, I still see you
I still drink from you
You hear that song, Mima, that's my song for You.
quiero verte allá en el Río
donde yo te conocí
podemos platicar, el mundo nunca será igual
como en el mundo allá en el Río
quiero verte allá en el Río
cuidando a todos para ya no sufrir
podemos bailar, el mundo siempre será igual
todos nos tenemos que morir
todos nos tenemos que morir para vivir.
adiós, Mima. adiós.
Tlazokamati
Ometeotl

Virginia Grise

VIRGINIA GRISE RECEIVED HER MFA FROM THE CALIFORNIA INSTITUTE
of the Arts, where she studied with Carl Hancock Rux and Erik Ehn. She
has worked as a curator, artist, and activist facilitating organizing efforts
among women, immigrants, Chicanos, the working class, and queer youth.
Her published work includes *The Panza Monologues* (Evelyn Street Press)
and an edited volume of Zapatista communiqués entitled *Conversations with
Don Durito* (Autonomedia Press). *Conversations* was recently translated and
published in Turkey. In 2008, Virginia's play *blu* was a 2008 recipient of

the Kennedy Center for the Performing Art's Latina/Latino Playwriting Award.

pineapple/full moon offerings for my nephew

pineapple/full moon offerings for my nephew is a performance installation that includes original photographs from Vietnam and footage of the Chicano moratorium. It should be staged on a series of altars in an act of public ceremony/healing/prayer. Italicized words are whispers.

> my father was a soldier. he served three tours of duty in vietnam. was awarded the bronze star and the air medal. he participated in more than twenty-five aerial missions.

> my father was a soldier. who refused to display his three purple hearts in our home. one night i heard him screaming. the memories of war that he once kept in boxes underneath the bed escaped and overtook him in his sleep. he found his best friend again with a noose around his neck hanging from the bathroom ceiling. all at once he must have remembered/must have seen their faces.

he must have remembered
cat lai

the large pineapple plantation was a buffer between saigon and
    cambodia
the pineapple is surrounded by rice paddies
soggy, slimy, steamy from the sun
flat, hot, and seemingly endless
covered with rice paddies, elephant grass, nipa palm
men always wet/throat always dry
guarded streams, rivers, bridges, and roads through paddy lands from
    vietcong infiltration

he must have remembered
long khanh

thick, wet, reddish-brown mud/caked on boots
rat patrol, operation strangler
enemy sympathizers were separated from those loyal to the republic of
    vietnam

24,000 men, women, and children processed in a tent city/issued i.d.
    cards

M-16 rifle training
helicopter assault training
light, swift, accurate
pacification, elimination, neutralization

baby san plays in elephant grass. he does not know there is a war

he must have remembered
july 16, 1969
when u.s. forces recovered 34,000 pounds of beans, 15,000 pounds of
    salt, 10,000 pounds of sugar, 5,000 pounds of peanuts, 2,600 pounds
    of rice

what will the people eat?

destroyed 3 hospitals, 200 bunkers, 115 pounds of medical equipment
enemy ammunition and weapons neatly stored in 55 gallon drums

the u.s. army leaves 100 newly-placed booby traps, orphanages, roads,
    bridges built/rebuilt and repaired,
    food, medical supplies, clothing, candy

he must have remembered
tet trung thu

the mid-autumn moon festival on the fifteenth day/eighth lunar moon
the colorful lanterns shaped like fishes and butterflies with candles
    inside
the dragon and flower dance
boxes of moon cakes filled with lotus seeds, ground beans, orange peels
bright yolk in center

he must have remembered
lost time with children
after the harvest season in the la drang valley they celebrated
under a monsoon sky/full moon, despite the war

he must have remembered

bottles, cans, dirt, sticks thrown in air
sky turns black
tear gas fired into a restaurant full of people
the shell hits rubén salazar
he dies of a brain hemorrhage
ángel díaz, lynn ward, rubén salazar—killed
40,000 people marched at the chicano moratorium
demanding we end the war in vietnam
riot police lined both sides of whittier boulevard
protestors beaten, tear-gassed, arrested
people came out of their homes
washed tear gas from strangers' eyes with garden hoses
ángel díaz, lynn ward, rubén salazar—killed
in the united states of america
killed for protesting the war in vietnam

aguirre, arredondo, castillo, galindo, garcía, gutierrez, iñiguez, rivera, santos,
   taillón, vásquez, martínez, pérez, ortega, ortíz

i haven't surrendered to the loss but i spend most of my time not being
   me
from inside out gaze at the headlines
my body wrapped around real bodies whose names do not appear in the
   newspaper
we get further away from the bones of it, the truth of it/the names
everything laid out in square/block/   columns
the people get lost in the in-between lines of the news
in the truth we do not speak

matthew

i can't seem to find the words to tell you little boy 16. i don't know what
   to tell you mijo when you say to me, you know, i've always wanted
   to learn how to fly. my nephew is 16, a junior in high school. he is
   failing english.

my nephew is 16. a junior in high school. he left his mother when he
   was 13 after he gave her an ultimatum, your drug-addicted, abusive
   husband or me. she chose wrong. he made it to north carolina on the
   greyhound bus.

my nephew is 16. a junior in high school. he has one more year before
he graduates and has decided to enter the air force. i always wanted
to learn how to fly, he says. not realizing he's always been flying/been
leaving.

i've watched you fly, mijo. i was there when you told your little sister
you'd be back for her. i fed you on ramen noodles and love for a
whole year while you waited for your grandfather to come back to
texas to take care of you. i took you to court when you had to explain
your frequent absences from school. helped you gather your clothes
from your mother's front yard when we asked her to sign the power
of attorney releasing you.

i was there when you told your brother, little boy 5, don't let grown men
hit you. took you to the hospital to stitch your lip when you followed
your own advice.

mijo
you have always flown. carried your four brothers and sisters on your
wings.

mijo
you have always flown. carried your four brothers and sisters on your
wings.

you never let anyone guide you wrong because you've always had places
you wanted to go and went no matter what anyone told you.

mijo
the world has turned backwards again

nicaragua *i haven't surrendered to the loss* el salvador *i spend most of my
time not being me* chile *from inside out* panama *gaze at the headlines*
north korea *my body wrapped around* vietnam *real bodies* cuba *whose
names do not appear* vieques *in the newspaper* puerto rico *we get further
away* kosovo *from the bones of it* afghanistan *the truth of it/the names*
palestine *the people get lost in the in between lines of the news* iraq *in the
truth we do not speak*

Alyssa Harad

ALYSSA HARAD IS A FREELANCE WRITER AND WORKSHOP FACILITATOR living in Austin, Texas. She has published essays on trauma, pedagogy, feminism, and perfume. Her contribution is excerpted from a longer piece, whose current shape was dictated by Sharon Bridgforth's emphasis on "getting back to the grandmother."

At Cost

Before my grandmother was dead, but after she had declared that it was time for her to die, I went down to Florida to help clear out her apartment. I hadn't seen her in a dozen or so years. No doubt you will want to know, before I tell you about my trip, what took me so damn long.

Well. Every family has its story, now doesn't it?

My own I can only claim to know in misremembered bits and pieces, held together with myths, jokes, and the occasional outright lie. It's a story that is true the way a recipe is true. The ingredients, a few directions even— these you have. But to get the proper flavor on your tongue? Sometimes adjustments are necessary.

You might say: Why not just ask some questions? What is so mysterious here? But I say, without meaning to be rude: When is the last time you talked to your family?

As a child, talking to my grandmother was a rare and exciting thing. Long-distance calls were reserved for holidays and birthdays or the settling of legal, money, and health matters. My mother's injunction to my father: *Honey, you need to call your mother.* After official business was over, my parents would hand the phone around to me and my brother. After a few moments of scandalous advice or outrageous complaint—*All right, darling, hand me back to your father*—it was over.

My family marveled over this juicy brevity, comparing her style to that of the other grandmother, who could talk forever about nothing at all. We said to ourselves, our eyes wide with wonder, our palms up, shoulders shrugging: *She doesn't like to talk on the phone!*

Even so, when I remember these conversations the whole perfumed, department-store world that was so much a part of my grandmother comes click-clacking toward me on its beautifully made heels with a full set of designer luggage (*always Louis Vuitton, darling, and it's not a knock-off either, I got it at cost*) in tow. The voice on the line was from Back East, while we, on the other hand, were very much Out West, not even in California, but in one of those states ending in a vowel which no self-respecting Easterner can keep straight unless they know how to ski. Back East was redolent with poverty and snobbery, work and stubbornness, and a mean, spiteful streak fueling successful ambition. It was a world whose taste ran to good bargains, name brands and big diamonds: things whose value could be easily calculated in the blow-by-blow accounting of money and things whose importance is not so easily understood by those from the softer, easier place where I grew up—thanks to my parents' industry, thrift, natural intelligence, and great good luck.

My grandmother's glamour, coming to me like an echo down the telephone line, was already an echo of glamour that had been, was supposed to have been, hers. It was fuelled, not by money, but by the sudden and terrible loss of money, followed, naturally enough, by a lot of hard work.

My great-grandparents had been wealthy Jews, immigrants made good, until they lost their money in The Crash. My grandmother, trained to be a rich man's beautiful wife, suddenly found herself working the floor of the women's department in the grand luxury department store her father had kept well-stocked with beautiful furs, and where she had shopped for pleasure as well as the serious business of social engagements.

From my comfortable distance, when I hear the phrase "lost their money in The Crash" I see an Old Hollywood montage in deep chiaroscuro: the black telephone, returned heavily to the receiver by my great-grandfather, who sits at his desk, head in his hands. My great-grandmother, her mouth set, thinking about her jewels. And my grandmother, slender and young but with a bustline to die for, in her daring at-the-knee coat, pausing on her way down the family brownstone's steps to adjust her cloche, as though she could feel the money disappearing in a sudden gust of cold wind.

And along with it—who can say?

My grandmother used her socialite training to project an air of authoritative chic that both borrowed from and bedazzled her wealthy customers. Trained to size up the buying power of prospective husbands, she could read the prospective commissions of customers as easily as the price tags they reluctantly fingered. Later, she became a buyer, previewing and selecting merchandise for the stores from the new fashion lines. It was a job she loved and one that she kept long after she had married. It allowed her to talk about fashion designers with a casual intimacy that made my mother roll her eyes while I hung on every word. *You know Ralph has gotten very successful but he's really just a nice Jewish boy*, she'd say, baiting me. *Ralph who, Grandma? Ralph Lipschitz, darling—oh excuse me, that's Lauren to you. Ha! Ha! Ha!*

My mother did not laugh at my grandmother's stories. Between the two of them lay a quiet but stubborn and long-standing enmity. My grandmother's snobbery was real, as was her iron will, and they had hurt my mother, in some undefined but clear way. It was an accepted fact in our family (my father was firmly on my mother's side) that my grandmother could be mean. My mother, on the other hand, had traveled far away from Back East and had developed tastes that made every gift my grandmother sent—mostly gaudy designer items she got at cost or for free on the job— seem a deliberate travesty. So, while I secretly enjoyed almost all the things about my grandmother that deeply annoyed my mother, I also grew up understanding that she was someone to be loved, but also suffered, best taken in small doses and at a distance. And to visit or be visited by her was understood to be a semi-heroic undertaking—a good thing, of course, but perfectly understandable if you were not quite up to it.

It is partly true that this way of thinking became an unconscious habit with me. But this is no excuse. It is also true that I lived, like so many careless, callous young people, as though I were something brand new, outside of History, and with no need for it, as though my life had come to me wholesale, free of debt. So that after I left home and there were no more family phone calls, I went for years and years without thinking of my grandmother except in a vague way, as someone who required thank-you notes for presents I had not asked for and didn't particularly like. I was content to know only what I already knew about her, which was plenty for storytelling, I thought, not wanting to be weighed down by troubles that weren't my own. And she was content, as always, to keep our phone conversations brief, having always, up to the very end of her life, something better to do than talk on the phone.

I didn't see then how absence, distance, and silence make their own kind of trouble.

But in my—not defense—but in my own honesty I must add that I believe now that part of why knowing my grandmother better, visiting her on my own, seemed so impossible is that it required travel not simply through space, but through time, and that this feeling came from my grandmother herself. I believe that was how my grandmother saw her few visits to us in my childhood—as a journey of almost unimaginable distance, Out West, back to a time of cowboys and Indians and horses, to a country with no Jews in it, no decent department stores, and who knows what else.

Time travel. It explains why she always got off the plane clutching huge shopping bags filled to bursting with provisions. Down the runway she would come to us, balancing on high heels in between the enormous bags like a well-tailored pack mule, trailing pungent, glorious clouds of garlic, smoked fish, pastrami, onion bagels, and bialys, enough to fill our freezer for weeks after she left with the salty-sour flavors of a world she was sure we couldn't live without.

All this I thought about, and a few other things too, when I got on the plane for Miami.

Amanda Johnston

AMANDA JOHNSTON IS A CAVE CANEM FELLOW AND AFFRILACHIAN POET. Honors include grants from the Kentucky Foundation for Women and the Austin International Poetry Festival's Christina Sergeyevna Award. Johnston's work has appeared in numerous journals and anthologies, including *Pluck, Callaloo,* and the *Ringing Ear: Black Poets Lean South.* She is an original ensemble member of the Austin Project Performance Company (tAPPCo) and is the founding editor of *TORCH: poetry, prose, and short stories by African American Women.* For more information, visit www.torchpoetry .org.

East St. Louis Still Life

PHOTO 1979

i
virginia slim poised between index
and middle finger, smoke escaping
from a dim ember caught at ease

her posture tense, frame out of focus
the kitchen blurs into the margins

ii
daddy kept a loaded gun in every room
in the house us kids knew how to hide lay low
freeze a .45 lays on the bed next to my sister

iii
mother's pale eyes see beyond our curled edges
a tangible tomorrow just waiting to be shot
captured in a roll yet to be developed

(Still Life—break)

(Still Life—continue)

iv

virginia slim poised between index
and middle finger, smoke escaping
from a dim ember caught at ease

v

we sit at her kitchen table sorting
frail photo albums and find a blonde
22-year-old image of herself leaning
against a tree in the backyard
of an abandoned home

Agent

for my father

I always thought you would be an FBI agent

I would have
believed so too
coming from he
who turned
playgrounds into
training camps

jump over that beam, now run to the sandbox,
pick up the monkey bars, now hit me as hard as you can

I'd ball my plum of a fist and pull back
holding the jab cocked in midair
desperately wanting him to believe
that I was strong enough to kill him

Omi Osun Joni L. Jones

OMI OSUN JONI L. JONES IS THE DIRECTOR OF THE JOHN L. WARFIELD
Center for African and African American Studies, and associate professor in
the Department of Theatre and Dance at the University of Texas at Austin.

She is an artist and scholar who produces performance ethnographies and scholarly essays around spirit, art, and identity. She is the founder of the Austin Project—a collaboration of women of color artists, scholars, and activists who use art for reimagining society.

The Right Bra

The basement was full of half-lit bodies, a tight round Afro nodding to the Dells in the corner, a hip and a hand twisting in conversation by the bar, beautifully dressed feet shuffling a rhythm on the concrete floor. A tangy tobacco smell thick in the air, the pressed hair napping up in a cool frenzy.

And me on the basement steps, peering around the corner as best I could, hoping to learn these rites of passage that I would someday cross, wanting to feel the force these adults conjured with such authority. The power of dancing thighs, of sweat on the neck, of fully parted lips, of toes that pushed so magnificently forward in strappy sandals—that's what drew me to my parents' Saturday night basement parties. Those were the details I needed to master so I could control my world and control others too.

I watched the bodies move and the music summon—the secret was there in the swirl of it all. Heat and skin, laughter and talking trash. Danger everywhere. A form-fitting three-button knit top sliding across a ripe lace bra, sturdy knees bent low low down pumping up the flow, sticky whispers licked into someone's ear. I ached for the spitty growl these fleshy pictures ignited. On Saturday nights I learned to grind, and all the traitorous moves that went with it. The Dells' "Oh, What a Night" provided the perfect blend of grunt and romance.

The deceit, the lies, the poisonous flattery, and mostly the lethal betrayals all moved through the basement like jealous lovers looking to get even.

Light-skinned, round-bodied Melba in her white hot pants; Eddy with her cloudy eyes—if she wasn't already too drunk to make it; red-headed Trina—the skinny temptress in capri pants and midriff blouse, and her bumpkin husband Dino; Percy who looked like a drowsy Santa and beat his howling wife on Sundays while we ate fried chicken and corn on the cob; the brothers Herb and Billy—raw and rowdy. All of them were there in the dark. Grown and stumbling in their new suburban lives. No bars to receive their passions like in The City, no street corners where loud talking freely lived and dissolved into the sky. The suburbs were neat and contained, so their most unclean urges had to find the right locale. And my parents' basement on Saturday nights was it. They gathered at our house full of a potion that looked like desire and sometimes even love, but was laced with a sinister manipulation and a ferocious competition for conquest.

The women came to the basement to be lusted after, and the men came to lust. The room throbbed with its own sloppy need as the stereo pulsed with "Wang Dang Doodle." The full breasts that dared anyone to touch them. The red eyes that licked their lips as they looked. The hands placed casually, strategically on the crotch or a thigh. This combat had no rules. Loyalty and respect were checked at the basement door.

I sat on the steps and watched what I could from around the corner. Daddy danced with Trina—familiar promises were in the hands that held each other too long. And everybody danced with Melba—just ride that booty, just reach for those titties, play the game recklessly, watch her hot pants rise up higher, wet in the seams from sweat and juice, and howl at the nastiness of it all.

And Momma was sitting or talking or doing her own bop—that sweet countrified two-step swing she did. Her eyes torn between rage and regret. Every Saturday this contest, and my mother always on the losing team.

My heart bent when I saw Momma trying not to see Daddy, pretending everything was just fine. My own desire warped like a 45 left on the dash of the Electra 225 when I saw Daddy press against Trina and laugh his full man-laugh in her ear. I learned that lust was best when you could crush someone in the midst of it; passion was most sweet when you could be unflinchingly cruel. My heart craved these dirty truths. I fed on them, worked them into my child self, and made them the necessary ingredients for my own satisfaction.

I think it's the little things in childhood that cut us the deepest. To others it may seem inconsequential, downright mundane and trivial. But to the open heart that receives the wound, the damage is profound and can last a lifetime. And as time moves forward and back, circling to hold a piece of a birthday party, a bit of a Platters song, the best line from a well-worn story—the original wound is mostly forgotten, appearing only as ghosts at inopportune times—butterflies in the shoe store, nausea at a lover's touch, sadness at the smell of Momma's baking biscuits.

Working the Work

Real women were vain killers; weak women were pathetic victims complicit in their own abuse; men, even the best ones (Mommy always said, "*Your Daddy is a good man*") were rendered unaccountable in a room full of perfume, push-up bras, and Johnny Walker Red.

Secretly in my bed I come in my own hands, those images of twisted lust pushing me to a trembling climax and creating a perverse formula for release.

And now I work to undo these lessons, to unhook my desire from distrust and conquest. Now, I try to stop the home movies in my mind and feel each sensation anew.

Angela Kariotis

Angela Kariotis is the author and performer of the shows *Reminiscences of the Ghetto & Other Things That Raized Me* and *Say Logos-Say Word (exploring the other-side of my hyphenated self)*. She graduated with an MA in performance studies from the University of Texas at Austin. She is an artistic associate at Plays for Living. She currently lives in New York City. For more info visit www.angelakaRIOTis.com.

Mother Tongue, a Herculean Effort

I say *Yee-rro*
You say JY-ROW
I say *Baahk-la-vaah*
You say BUK-LAVA

Let me get this out of the way
I saw *My Big Fat Greek Wedding*
not because it best exemplifies the trials and tribulations
of the Greek American experience
but because Greeks will support anything with "Greek" (or at least a G)
    in the title
name brand ingredient et cetera ad infinitum
It's no longer geeky to be Greeky
Scores of abbreviated celebrity Greeks are reclaiming their ancestry
in this Grecian trend
Billy Zane (although we hate to admit him)

Jennifer Aniston
George Stephanopoulos (never could hide with that name
and makes us proudest since he worked with *Presi*dent Clin*ton*)
Finally something Greek to get excited about
But a small footnote to what my Greek compatriot had begun

Lest you enjoy too much hearty laughter
at this revitalization of a culture a few thousand years old
The birthplace of civilization relegated to dusty textbooks
and classical studies majors
Ancient
Classic
Archaic

But the crooked bend of my nose
knotted, being born from Zeus's skull, holds the wisdom to ascertain
the trippy staircase of my last name
Walking bridgeboard consonants across the seas
a bunch of us landed in Astoria, Queens

A social studies map dramatization of the Ottoman Empire
has it stretching longer-tude than page margins
and boundary lines could accommodate
but the four hundred years of slavery endured

by their Aegean neighbors was not drawn to scale
The virgin oil drained from cut-open wombs
is not a metaphor

The snapped necks of holy men dangling from fig trees
decay into sweetened soil eternal
Dust rises with the winds in these modern times
revealing the residue of last hymns sung
static clinging to the blood memory of an inner ear drum
kirie eleison
kirie eleison
kirie eleison

Revolutionaries with only courage as a plan
Unheard syllables like Theodoros Kolokotronis

Working the Work

but as history repeats there is no such thing as finally free
The declarative remains theory

Lord Elgin in 1840 forcing his foreign body upon the Parthenon
Breaking bits of hymen
scattering pieces of my after-birth-right across the continent
immortalized behind glass cases and "Do not touch" signs

It's called Ancient Greece, as if the land had no future, no heirs
A loophole absolving their looting sins
"We cannot surrender the pieces," the British museum muses,
"It will be left impoverished"
But I no longer believe in mythology

I float somewhere between the classical and this modern me
Questioning the designated beginning of my history
I walk tight steps on this roped timeline

The togaed foot of Peitho in London
The arms of Aphrodite in Venice
My left eye shelved in a jar
Tongue caught in a drawer
Head dusty with memories of a past life
explains this inexplicable longing
Reclaiming with the stiff hair of the brow
A plump end of a nose

The tilt of a vowel sound
I ride a cloud
picking up question-mark dots and exclamating points along the way

These ancient people of the New York City hot dog stands
glossy tourist pamphlets and recipe books
Spawned from a seed rooted in all your words
The swallowed footprints in a glass of wine
Maria Callas's features reverberating echoes

Hesiod did not write the *Theogony* of will
Never foreseeing the need of his people to evoke the deity
Will is an Oceanid born of the Titans
I offer libations to her annually on the Island of my Discontent

Casting a muddied reflection into the rolling sea
Only to reel in a broken piece of wave
I lick the preserving quality of will from the salted creases of my lifeline

The olive of my skin eclipses the pupil in my eye
The eyelid shuts hard on the pit
Chokes lashes
Spasms my eyes opening wider
to transcend the threshold of vision
and witness the lineage of me somewhere beyond that
and beyond that

In a dream
I gasp for clean air
in the midst of a polluted ring
asphyxiating the Acropolis
Marble turns to gypsum
Historical evidence washed away with the rain
I pray for drought *Thiemou*
Theo
until I return again

For now
I keep a mirror close by
Get my hand stuck in my hair
and practice breaking Greek in the kitchen

I take fierce notes of the songs spilling from Mother's tongue
The language is the remaining thing that makes me feel fluent in being
    Greek

*ise numizys pou to lathos ine mi sena yati les then xeres ta Englesika arkyta
    kala*
You think the fault is with you because you say you do not know
    English good enough

But *igo lego* that *logya then mas ftan outy inglesika outy elinika*
But I say that words are not enough neither English nor Greek

Tu alphabet y hellenes to kanan
The alphabet Greeks developed

Working the Work

*Tu alpha ky tu omega then borune na kratisune tin agape pu astanome gya
    sena*
But the alpha and omega cannot hold the love I feel for you

Te les kale?
And what are you saying?

*Tu ponum ya tosa hroyna itan monu pu then borusa na si milisu etsi pou
    ithyla*
My pain for all these years was only that I was not able to speak with
    you the way I wanted

Ya ti then iha ta logia
Because I did not have the words

San alitis emina munahyam mestimes to thromu
Like a bum I remain alone in the middle of the road

Tu alphabet etrihy sa niro apu tu stomas
The alphabet spilled like water from your mouth

Adi pos then ixira na tu kratisu natu pyasu mi ta heryam
And how I did not know how to hold it to catch it with my hands

Lipone kitaga pos to nirows crystalu aptu Theo etrihy apta thaktilam
Therefore I was forced to watch how your water crystal from God ran
    from my fingers

Ta heryam eglifa na zvihsy tin glossam pou kegotan
I licked my hands to put out the fire burning on my tongue

Prin na kimitho lego mesa tu myilom milow mi tu Theo
Before I go to sleep I say in my mind I speak with God

Tune rutow Thiemou na ehis ti manam na ine ghiry ki sitherenyo
I pray God keep my mother to be strong like steel

Monu afto lego stan elinika
Only that prayer I say in Greek

Note: Italicized words above denote phonetic spellings of Greek words.

Ana-Maurine Lara

ANA-MAURINE LARA'S WORK HAS APPEARED IN NUMEROUS LITERARY journals including *Blithe House Quarterly*, *The Encyclopedia Project*, *Sable LitMag*, and *Torch Magazine*. She's received awards from the Barbara Deming Memorial Fund, the Puffin Foundation, the Brooklyn Arts Council, and PEN Northwest. Her debut novel, *Erzulie's Skirt*, was a 2006 Lambda Literary finalist and her unpublished second novel, *Anacaona's Daughter*, won third place in the National Latino/Chicano Literary Prizes. Ana-Maurine is a Cave Canem Fellow, a member of the prize-winning Stamp Lab Theatre Group, and a member of the Austin Project. She also coordinates the Magicians, the Path Breakers, and the Dream Makers oral history project, which you can visit here: www.themagicmakers.blogspot .com.

The Dancer

THE SEED BEARER STUDIES THE SOIL

First, you wait for the sun and the rain, the wind and the fire
to tell you it's time.
How do you know you're ready? you ask.
You're born ready, they say.
But then there's also the grandmother, the rivers, the earth,
the forest, and the sky waiting to tell you it's time.
That's when you're ready, they'll be there.

First, you wait for the sun and the moon
to face each other across the plains.
You wait for the clouds to gather along the edges of the canyon,
the valley, along the peaks of the mountains.
You wait for the rain.
You wait for the wind to pick up and carry the seeds
over to where they need to be.
You sit under the light of the moon, wrapped in your shawl,
lighting a fire to keep warm, to pass the time.
Til you're ready.

And in the light before dawn, you gather
the deer hide
the beads

the sinew that you've made into thread.
You wait for the ancestors to speak through the fire and
feed the pattern into your hands.
For that pattern to pass through from your hands to your heart

and down to your feet.

The Seed Bearer Rubs the Soil between Moistened Fingers

When it's time, you pick up and go to where the others are waiting.
That's how all the tribes are gathered.
By the moonlight rising over ridges.
In cars and bicycles, buses and planes.
Some even walk.

Most of us don't use our feet to get to where we're going,
but that's what you're going to do.
You don't know how, but somehow,
you're going to find your feet again.

When you see their faces, you know that
somehow, they've all been called to gather.
Somehow, it was the right time.
The sun was at the right angle,
the rain stopped just long enough,
the wind had become a cool breeze and
the fire had died down just enough to warm them.
And so they gathered, you among them.

Everyone sat.
Nobody spoke.
And then light broke through
and it became part of the pattern
passing through the fire
into your hands and down to your feet.

It is then that you realize you are in a circle.

The Seed Bearer Tastes the Land

First it is the drum that speaks.
It is there when you arrived.
It is slow moving.
It calls you in
and you and everyone sitting
are larger than that circle.

Then elders shed their skin
and in the shedding
reveal their stories.
Along the ridges of their flesh they show you
prisons and guns
hunger and death
suffering and violence:
all the things you bear
even when you're not looking.

This time you choose to witness
because the other option
is not possible any longer.
Not when your elders are dying.
You witness their skin
their survival;
they reveal their weapons.

One by one they undo their hair
and before you is light.
The same light that comes down
from the mountains at dawn.
The same laughter that plays
between leaves in the forest.
The same love that makes
the fire jump between you.

You see how they are made of flesh and blood
and when you look at their feet,
you see that they are hidden in the dirt.

From a darkness full of heat,

you feel the pattern taking shape in your mouth.
You feel a smoky fire escape from your lips
and become sound.
You breathe life into words.
Allow them to take shape in the circle
between all that has been said
and all that has been left unspoken.

It is truth, your truth that you have come to find.

You dream of them,
these elders,
watch them become ash and tepid coals.
In the dreams you are all dancing
like the tips of flames licking at the night air.
Right foot forward,
left foot back,
right foot forward,
left foot back,
fall
back.

The elders turn in your direction.
Their lips move, but
you hear only the drumming
and the hum of bees
circling around your head.
The bees dance in and out of your hair
before rising in one wing
up towards the mountains.
You feel the mountains breathing.
Slow breath echoing.
You see your elders.
Their lips no longer moving,
their voices reach you.

What have you to say for yourself? they ask.

You squint,
your breath quickens.
The beads in your lap

spill onto the ground
forming a river before the fire.

You stare at the river at your feet
and at all the kin
rising before you.
They dance around you
their hands becoming the dawn sky,
their feet masked by the fire.
They bend over you,
shaking their arms that rattle like rain.
They say,

Listen. Listen to what we are saying.

You put your hands in the river
over the beads to feel
their heat,
their pulse,
their movement.
They gather the waters in their mouths.
You watch as they
swallow clouds whole,
drink down deltas,
become as big as the oceans.
They grow large like the mountains.
You take the beads in your hands.
They turn into glass.
You gather them into your skirt,
kiss them with your dry lips,
hold them in a small cloth close to your heart.

The Seed Bearer Smells the Land

You are the shoemaker
sitting in the northern sun
your shoulders are forests
that glisten with pine
and oak, maple
and thunder.

You sit across from the southern sun,
the old weaver
bent over threads of
gold and stories
patching the earth together.

To the east are
the plains
where the seed bearer
sows our crops
while the wind plants
seeds in her hair.

To the west
are the mountains
guarded by the elders
wrapping their hair
and the elders
who have yet to come.

In the center is the fire
tended by the keeper
who watches the dancer
become the dreamer.

THE SEED BEARER TILLS THE SOIL

The air is deeply silent,
punctuated only with the sound
of fire snapping in the crisping air,
of water running under the earth,
of earth shifting so that you may sit there.

You listen.

You feel your own breath catch.
You pull your hands close
wait for the dreaming to tell you what to do.
You hear the first story.
It's the weaver's story.

I am the weaver. My work happens in small pieces. Sometimes my carpets are no larger than my thumb. Sometimes they are so big I can't even see them. My hands are big. Back then, before I came here, my sisters used to joke about them. "It's not the size that counts," they'd say, laughing as we squatted over the river washing the excess dyes out of the cotton and wool fibers. "No, it's not the size . . . it's not!" And their laughter chimed in with the sound of the water. Of course we were talking about our hands; they believe fine hands make it easier to weave the threads in and out of the loom, and big hands make it easier to spin. I was only s'posed to spin. But I'm not here to do what one's s'posed to do. I am a weaver and on my hands are the lines mapping out ancestral lands. Out of those hands come the stories that I weave into the carpets. Stories that once, a time ago, I used to tell to my sisters under the light of the Dreamer. I'd tell them: "And there is Dancer of all creations, her face as wide as moon, she dances in full circles. And when she dances she is golden, shining out so plants can breathe. Keeper sits and patiently waits for Dancer to turn into Dreamer. Keeper would look for Dancer herself, but her vision is already gone and so she can't really see her. She sits by the door of the lodge where the dance was created, and waits. When he feels like it, Coyote comes outside licking his lips and howling. But Keeper just ignores Coyote—where's Dancer, she asks, because she begins to feel cold. Coyote stares at Keeper and soon he gets bored and so he looks inside the lodge and sees that Dancer has become Dreamer, and she is dancing deep in circles. She can never stop dancing. Cause if she stops, we wouldn't have babies or flowers or the light of the moon to weave by. It's when she's dreaming that we can look at her, admire her. Thank her. That is our time. And in a chorus, my sisters would turn to face Moon and thank her for each other, for their dreams, for the fruit that made them full of life. That was then, when I still told stories. Now, I just weave the stories in colors: blue like bird feathers, purple like Dancer's back, blinding white like Dancer's eyes, yellow like the first light that came out of Dancer's steps, grey like Coyote, pink like baby's breath, and orange and all sorts of other colors. This one, this carpet I have before you right now, has these colors: the green of old copper, blue of lapis lazuli, yellow of saffron, red of blood, and black of jaguar. This one I will weave until it's done. That is my story, sister.

Working the Work

Jacqueline E. Lawton

JACQUELINE E. LAWTON RECEIVED HER MFA IN PLAYWRITING FROM the University of Texas at Austin, where she was a James A. Michener Fellow. Her plays include: *Anna K, Blood-bound and Tongue-tied*; *Deep Belly Beautiful*; *A Delicate People* (Journeymen Theater commission); *The Devil's Sweet Water*; *Lions of Industry, Mothers of Invention* (Discovery Theater commission); and *Mad Breed* (Active Cultures commission). Ms. Lawton is a three-time semifinalist for the Playwrights' Center PlayLabs and a recipient of the Young Artist Program Grant from the D.C. Commission on the Arts and Humanities.

Cinder Blocks (an excerpt)

SCENE ONE
(*The stage is dark and empty. The sounds of scurrying feet are heard upon the stage. A little black girl not yet visible crosses center stage. She stops, and laughs so loud the angels hear her and laugh back. Lights up. Little Girl jumps in circles around and around, until she's dizzy and breathless. Catching her breath, she smiles.*)

LITTLE GIRL:
I'd like to tell you a story about little girls who dream big on beds held up by cinder blocks. Cinder blocks. Cinder blocks. Cinder blocks!

(*She tosses pennies high in the air. They fall. She counts them out loud, then stuffs them in her pocket.*)

LITTLE GIRL (*taking on "Mama's voice"*):
Baby, I'm sorry, one day you'll have a real big bed.

LITTLE GIRL:
Mommy, Mommy, I don't care. I sleep good at night and I'm never cold. Not even in the winter. And my belly's always full. One day I'll be fat, just wait and see. (*Beat*) But still Mama says, "One day we'll have better." But for now the Sears catalog is her Christmas wish book and we browse all year long. But little sister will one day turn away and frown, "We're never going to get any of that stuff, so what's the point?" But I don't mind, I don't mind! Dreaming's never hurt my soul, only people do.

(*She makes up a tap dance routine. The sound is raw and unmelodic, but soon she sings and evens everything out.*)

LITTLE GIRL (*Singing in a jazzy melody*):
Baa baa-baa, baa-baa, baa baa-baa, baa-baa, baa baa black sheep, have you any wool? Yes sir, yes sir, three bags full. One for my Master and one for my Dane and one for the little boy who lives down the lane. Baa baa-baa, baa-baa, baa baa black sheep, have you any wool? Yes sir, yes sir, three bags full.

(*She jazzes up her tap piece a little bit and makes up a little tune for her next speech.*)

LITTLE GIRL:
What's a Dane? I don't know. I'll go down the lane to a picture show? What's my name? I don't know, but Mama's home . . . So! Here! I! Go!

LITTLE GIRL (*taking on "Mama's voice"*):
Stop that singing, your father's trying to sleep. Stop that tapping, and give me a bit of peace. Stop that whistling, now go outside and play. Stop that dancing, you've got work to do today.

(*Little girl stops dancing.*)

LITTLE GIRL:
Mama took her language from what she knew. From what her Mama told to her. That's how we get the words we know. Our Mama's put 'em there.

LITTLE GIRL (*taking on "Mama's voice"*):
You've gotta get yourself an education. If they see you can sing . . .

LITTLE GIRL:
Well, you just heard me sing, so there's no harm in that.

LITTLE GIRL (*taking on "Mama's voice"*):
If they know you can dance . . .

LITTLE GIRL:
I wouldn't call trying to imitate the steps drawn in my World Book Encyclopedia really knowing how to dance, but okay!

LITTLE GIRL (*taking on "Mama's voice"*):
Baby, just listen to me, if they see you can do those things, like singing and dancing like that, that's all they'll ever let you do!

LITTLE GIRL:
But Mama, I like to sing and dance and whistle and snap! So if they let me do it I'm going to do it!

LITTLE GIRL (*taking on "Mama's voice"*):
Girl, don't you back talk me! Get yourself in your room!

LITTLE GIRL:
But Mama, I have a dance in me that I'm going to dance. I have a song, the words aren't all there yet, but it's coming and I'm going to sing it. And that's not back talk that's what it is! That's truth!

(*Beat*)

LITTLE GIRL:
And Mama would raise her hand real high and I'd cry knowing the hurt coming out of that love. Knowing the hurt before it hit, because she knew it before it came. That kind of hurt came out of her Mama's love. Even though I never knew her Mama, cause Daddy was Methodist and Mama was Catholic. You see when Mama graduated high school she wasn't married so she went into the military and she bled for one year straight. Mama bled out all her hurt and gave me some and gave my sister some and even gave my brother some. But that's okay, because when my Mama bled for one year straight, she prayed we wouldn't get hurt. So the hurt from my Mama from her Mama wasn't hurt at all, it was love bled for one year straight. And that love is the kind of love that brings Catholics and Methodists together. So I don't have to know her Mama to know my Mama, because now I bleed once a month. And what you don't know, Mama, is that it's the same blood that bleeds your love and disappointments into my soul. So Mama, I gotta dance. Mama, oh, Mama, I gotta sing! Because your Mama told you not to! See, I'm just doing what you didn't have time to do!

(*End of scene*)

Polyphony

Krissy Mahan

KRISSY MAHAN IS AN ARTIST AND WOODWORKER. SHE HAS BUILT LYRES, folding chairs, and cabinets. Krissy has been a part of progressive creative communities in New York and Texas. She has been helping vulnerable communities—such as queer, poor, non–English speaking, and rural peoples—make records of their lives for twenty years by photographing them and making videos about them. Krissy was involved in volunteer efforts with people evacuated from New Orleans after the flooding. She is interested in using the arts to work towards a better world, and is committed to using her skills to help the widest variety of voices contribute and be heard in that discussion.

Untitled

when the doctor said, "you might not walk again," i heard, "you can't be a butch dyke anymore."

in the autumn of 2005, i spent two long months in the hospital fighting both meningitis and encephalitis. i'm still recovering.

i got called a "lezzie" since i was in second grade, although i didn't know i was gay until i was twenty. it was fine with me, since i usually got called it for hitting a home run, making an incredible catch, running faster than anyone, or beating the crap out of some kid at school who deserved it. when they told me i would be disabled, i freaked out because i don't know who i am without the things my body does. no matter how bad my grades were, or how many times my "winter boots" were made of bread bags inside my sister's last year's shoes, when i got called "lezzie" i knew i was doing something right. it wasn't until like fifth grade that i found out that "lezzie" was a bad thing. "tomboy" meant i played games that involved bodies, rather than words, and there was no shame in that for me. my family's first language was WORK. words came much later, and i've never felt quite fluent with them.

DEPARTMENT OF ASSISTIVE AND REHABILITATIVE SERVICES

Disability Determination Services
Form DDS-99M revised 11-05 Daily Activity Questionnaire

Question #1: Do you have mental or emotional problems that limit what you are able to do? Yes / No. If yes, explain.

if you wanted to be a hero, like the people in the IRA, you had to be ready to put your body in physical danger. the uncles and cousins who came back from vietnam went there to answer america's call, and to put their bodies on the line, and that was the kind of person i wanted to be. physically ready to defend anyone who could hurt the people i love. they said we'd all be speaking russian if my grandfathers hadn't gone overseas.

where i'm from, it's where your body is, and what it's doing that says who you are. when those women's libbers were burning their bras, my mom was already practically running the hardware store down the street in the only bra she had.

Question #8: What difficulties, if any, do you have caring for your personal needs (for example, bathing, brushing your teeth, dressing, picking the right clothes, etc.)?

that's one thing my town's got right and wrong. my family judges a person on where their body was, not on words. that went equally for women and men. they are so crazy about sports that every girl had to play ball. it wasn't until years later that i saw a girl throw badly (well, except the finnegan girls). my dad was a minor league baseball player and i was his team's ballboy as soon as i was let in the dugout. they called me "pedro." i guess that was my first sports name.

girls had names that described their appearance, usually, except for my aunt toots. she is so mean that everyone had to say "you'd best hold your tongue, toots," so many times that they just started calling her "toots." her husband, my uncle skeets, was a prizefighter. he wasn't very big, but he was quick like a mosquito. they still call him "skeets" even though now he's a grumpy old man with heart trouble. if i was disabled and just sitting in a wheelchair, i'd never be able to BE anyone except that. the only time i saw a wheelchair in a bar, it was in the bar at the VFW, not a queer bar.

Question #10: Does anyone help you with shopping? If yes, how do they help you? If no, what shopping do you do?

you could tell who your friends were by the name they called you, and the names usually had to do with what you DID. when i first came out, my name was "gambler." i was working as a janitor and usually very broke, so i would play pool for drinks and take any dare. enid, who loved basketball was "hoops" and lisa was "argyle" for the kind of socks she wore to play rugby. dykes play sports. if i can't play sports, or at least look like i could play them, then i am not sure how to be a dyke.

i was thinking of these things in the hospital, and now that i'm trying to get back to work i am feeling a sense of panic about it.

most every butch i knew had a nickname, except for my friend katie. she had a five-syllable-long last name which would have been easy to make into a nickname, but she hated it when anyone said anything about her last name. she was my best friend, even though she often slept with the girls i was dating. we played softball, got high, drank, and secretly drummed together, which at the time was not cool to do. she and i bought a video camera at a garage sale, and taught ourselves how to make movies, which we also didn't tell our team. katie worked at a print shop that made maps. we'd get really high then look at all the names of cities and roads. she blew her head off with one of her stepfather's hunting rifles.

i've got nothing against hunting rifles, and i am a pretty good shot, too— even before i was in the army. so i don't mind hunting rifles, but man i wouldn't have kept them around the house with a suicidal daughter living there.

Question #16: What difficulties, if any, do you have getting along with family, friends, or others? Please explain.

katie took her life, but not her body with her, when she was twenty-eight years old. katie was the only person who lived more recklessly than me, that's why we were friends, i guess, because we'd get ourselves into bad situations. katie didn't know when to knock it off. i'd end up getting her out of trouble and home safely. i guess she was braver than me, or maybe i just had more of a sense of self-preservation. i don't know. i didn't pick fights i wasn't sure i could win. and i didn't drive drunk or high because people on my softball team worked at group homes for the head-injured. they joked about the people there.

the only clue i got about why katie did stuff was once we were out after a game and some man walked into the bar and she got all rattled and said "we're leaving" which was very not good because i was finally talking to this girl i'd had a crush on all season. so i left of course—you don't ask why when your buddy says, "we're leaving." but when i told her it was super-bad-timing, she said that man was the "friend" of her parents who sexually abused her all those years. "that sonofabitch will never even get to put his EYES on my body again."

Question #21: What upsets you and what do you do when you are upset?

i saw that man at katie's funeral, can you believe it? i almost threw up. he was sitting there in one of the first rows, making small talk. i wish i would have clocked him in the face with a folding chair. that's what my brothers would have done, just ask any of my sister's ex-boyfriends.

it was katie's funeral, but the person in the open (yes, open) coffin had her hair dyed all the same mousey brown (no blue streaks) her piercings had been spackled shut, tattoos covered, and she was wearing a dark blue pantsuit with gold buttons (with anchors on them, even though they weren't "navy people"). i was afraid i'd embarrass myself by falling down if my knees gave out.

Question #23: What do you do when you feel stress or pressure?

there was a bulletin board with photos of katie with only male relatives and friends. she was usually wearing a dress.

Question #24: What do you do when someone criticizes you or tells you what to do? Please give examples.

i thought about finding that guy and kicking his ass. but instead i worked out for like three hours a day for the next few months, which increased my batting average by like 150 points. but i wasn't really into softball that summer.

Signature Page: Is there anything else you wish to tell us about your condition? Please use this space.

last week i took a job at a cabinetmaking shop here in town. i like working with wood. i think i might not be well enough to do it, but i can't quit because i want to do the work i like and am good at. the scarlet "d" i wear on my hat is for "big dyke"—if i am truly disabled, i might turn into one of those "wannabe butches" who can't do anything but still think they're all tough. that's not me.

Rosalee Martin

ROSALEE MARTIN HAS A PhD IN SOCIOLOGY AND IS A THIRTY-FIVE-YEAR master teacher at Huston-Tillotson University in Austin, Texas. Dr. Martin is a writer of professional articles, children's books, pamphlets, self-published poetry chapbooks, and was a contributor to two grassroots newspapers. She was recognized for her literary works in 1984 and 1994 when she received Outstanding Authors Awards from Delta Sigma Theta Sorority. She participated in the Austin Project three times, where she worked on her chosen art form—poetry. Dr. Martin is an activist and HIV/AIDS educator and works on issues related to social justice in Austin.

A Tapestry of Wholeness

The year is 2005.
Looking at him from the back,
five-eleven statue bent
bones protruding
meat wasted away
hair scarce, turning gray at the edges
physique has no resemblance to years ago.
He turns in his wheelchair
no feet
ankles missing
blanket covers stumps
hides torso
only a trace of a former life.
My eyes meet his sockets—hollow places;
pupils dilated, straining to see.
Smoothness of skin replaced
with sores in different stages of oozing.
Nose half-eaten—amputated to allow breathing,
leaving one nostril; he won't wear the prosthesis.
Mouth ajar to whisper inaudible words
"I'm sorry," I think he said!?!
Teeth missing
open cavity reveals diseased gums.
Face gives scarecrow a run for its money.
Breath shallow.
Laboring, difficult.
Oxygen minimal.

Shaking.
Extended hands
thin with veins pronounced,
flesh absent.

My mind went back to 1965
to my years with him as husband and wife—twenty years!
I was 21 and he was 23.
I was a virgin, believing God's word and
trusting him to do the same.
Placing him as the head of my house.
Submissive
committed to us and three children yet to come.
He and I became one under God—so I believed.
He was ordained, a man of God
called to a church. I followed
and moved forward not knowing
not suspecting
ignorant of his ways
til life happened and scales fell from my eyes.
Questions were raised
lies were told

1984 I filed for divorce
I raided the attic for evidence of his sexual indiscretions.
My heart raced—skipped beats.
Breathe
breathe deep.
The room spun
my palms sweat
as I picked up letters sent to his P.O. box.
One by one I read them through unfocused eyes:

Letter from William, August 24, 1974, from New York City:
Hi There
Thanks for calling . . . I would like to tell you something nice. "I think
    of you often" . . . If I write too often the next time you call let me
    know, ok. . . . . If you had planned to spend Thanksgiving with your
    family I guess we will postpone until a later date. I think of you so
    often I wonder if it's right. And if I should get so deeply involved
    and if my feelings toward you are mutual . . .

William, October 8, 1974:
I am blessed with a restless night and you're on my mind . . .

William, October 30, 1974:
Hi:
Thanks for writing. You don't know what a pleasure it is to hear from
    you . . . P.S. Bill, I guess I love you. I never felt this way about
    another human being . . . But we have one life as we know it and
    feelings should be expressed to continue the principle of pleasure.

A letter from Lee, October 30, 1974, from Mississippi:
Dear Love
I know that a lot of things have been running through your mind as a
    result of my not writing or calling . . . Take care of yourself and give
    my love to yourself.

The room spins.
I couldn't believe—letters from William and Lee on the same date
—love letters—missing him letters—from NYC to Mississippi
Still more.
Can I continue
should I continue?
Couldn't stop now
"Snoopy" was too close to home—he was in Austin.

From "Snoopy," alias "L & S" (Licks and Slurps), August 1977:
Dammit,
how cruel can you be? Repeatedly,
just about the time I figure you've forgotten me,
and have convinced myself to forget you,
you resurface . . .

Just as you did with that phone call last night!
And it's always with a request for something to satisfy YOUR needs.
This time, it was for something in your *MAIL BOX.*
Well, friend, I have needs too . . . like a *MALE BOX*!
In my . . . oh well, what good does it do to bitch?!?

Maybe I just expect too much. It's not your fault that
I went and fell in love with an individual whose apparent desire
is only for an occasional hole to punch.

Working the Work

But tell me, kind sir . . . what's a fella to do? I don't want to hit the
    streets;
I've been spoiled for all others;
Yet, I'm climbing the walls in need of satisfaction.

Crunch! When you asked for something in your new box,
I'm sure you weren't opting for anything this heavy.
Perhaps at some future writing I'll be a bit lighter 'n'
brighter; perhaps by then I'll have some reason to be.

Meanwhile, consider me for what I'm worth and know
that you ARE loved.

From "Snoopy," 1977, card with handwritten note:
Let's burrow together again soon. I like the way you dig my hole.

MORE LETTERS

Letter from Ron, May 8, 1978, Compton, California
Letters from nameless persons, 12/21, 11:15 a.m.
Letter, no name, no date, Austin

I slept with these men too
He brought them into our bedroom—into our bed—into my body
no condom—no dental dam—no female condom!
My vulnerability left me open to diseases.
My choices were taken from me.

Letters to him from the Texas Department of Health should have been
    sent to me as well.

**March 8, 1978, form letter sent to Bill indicating that he was exposed to
    syphilis:**
Go either to private physician or public health clinic. Appointment
    scheduled for March 14.

Follow-up letter:
I have notified you that you have been exposed to a communicable
    disease . . . you have not responded by having a medical evaluation.
Please let me know what arrangements you want to make concerning
    this urgent health matter. I will shortly have to report this fully to

the health officer. Under Texas health laws, he does have authority to cause you to be held until you consent to examination or until he can determine you are not infected.

March 23, 1978:
Mr. Smith, because of the possibility that you may have a serious contagious disease with implications for you and others' health . . .
It is my duty and legal responsibility to require you to cooperate with the law of the State of Texas. If within ten days of the receipt of this letter, you do not make arrangements, . . . I will be forced to send a police officer to insure compliance with the law.

March 22, 1979:
Bill Smith, the results of a recent visit you made to this clinic indicate a need for additional follow-up . . .

I flipped through the letters. Tears flooded my being.
My stomach reacted, with acid flowing and churning.
Doubled over in pain, now knowing the depth of his betrayal!

Pulled back into the present my stomach churning even now.
Hi, R os e M a ry y y name slurred
my knowing eyes fixed into his.
Anxiety raised from my gut.
Didn't know why.
Twenty years later
my last chance
MUST know!
Questions cried for answers
would he remember?
Would he tell the truth?
Questions took on a life of their own
rammed through attempts at silence.
Reframe them
a voice came from who knows where
through my mouth came sounds alien to my ears.
He leaned forward as if to hear
brows lowered making slit for eyes
mouth opens
then shuts
making what appears to be a smile.

Working the Work

Fingers moves across lap
reaching for mine
drops before we connect.

I saw the shadow of what he used to be.
Questions dissipated
answers were written in each wrinkle on his skin.
On his amputated nose and feet
on his red inflamed gums
his last bout with pneumonia.
Answers were clear.
He made his "cooling" bed
invited death in
no longer wanting to fight it.
I sat shaken.
Emptied by the space no longer occupied by questions
I must let him go.
Pieces I held for twenty years
more like forty.
Anger, distrust, sadness
must let them go.
I sighed, breath rushing out
rain rushing from my eyes
spilling over my body
sighs became thunderous
as if lightning was tearing me apart.

Then calmness came over me.
Forty years of tears
a washing
from the hurt and pain
of disrespect, of not being valued, of being used and unloved,
of being cheated on.
I embraced this cleansing
relaxing the water from above
feeling its coolness over my extremities
fixing on its rainbow.
New colors to weave with textures of silk
soft to the skin,
highlighting my goodness, at last,
creating a tapestry of wholeness!

And I looked at him,
took his hands and wished him well.

Carole Metellus

CAROLE METELLUS IS A HAITIAN AMERICAN WRITER, ACTIVIST, PER-
former, and cultural worker from the East Coast. Her poetry has appeared
in *Chariot on the Limp*, a collection of Haitian American poetry; in *Affirming
Flame*, an anthology by progressive Texas poets in the aftermath of September
11; in the *Lambda Literary Review*; in *Mother Tongues*, a compilation
addressing the theme of mother-child relations; in the *Austin International
Poetry Festival Anthology*; and in *The Tenth Anniversary Poetry Ink Anthology*
in support of Robin's Bookstore, in Philadelphia, Pennsylvania. In her
writing, Carole works to combat oppression in its numerous forms: world
hunger, domestic violence, racism, sexism, homophobia, and child abuse,
to name a few. Under the tutelage of acclaimed poet Sharon Bridgforth,
Carole has sought the dormant voices of her native people summoning her
to her pen's task.

Ti Jean's Woes

That's! for letting the neighbors see you
playing marbles on the corner!
That's! for vagabonding
when your school work
and chores weren't done!
That! and that's!
for leaving the broom
at the corner of the room
and the dust pile
in the middle of the floor!
Don't you know that brings bad luck?
Do I need any more bad luck than you?
And that's! for missing the crumbs
under the kitchen table!
What am I, hosting a vermin hotel?
You want the rest of your species here?!
And did you cover the trash before putting it out?!
That's! for letting the neighbors see
that I cooked *mayi moulin*, yesterday!

She already made me tell her we had chicken creole!
Take that! that! and that!
for disturbing my good demeanor!
You miserable piece of shit!
Don't you dare cry!
Don't even moisten your lids!
You failed abortion, miserable pest, used Kotex!
And that's! for disturbing my sleep
with your whimpering the other day
Things are hard, and I have reason to whimper
but do you see me whimpering
in the middle of the night?!
And that's! for wetting the bed!
I keep telling you not to do that any more!
I went all the way downtown
to get you a night bucket in the *marché*
praying the whole time
that the maid next door wouldn't see me.
What's a woman like me,
doing in the *marché* downtown?
You ungrateful manure!
That! that! and that!
Why are you crying?
To make the neighbors think that I'm torturing you?!
With all the tortures you've brought me!
You filthy trash!
Look at your grades at school!
That's! for not bringing me the right grades!
For all I do for you?!
And that's! for having the teacher
call me into her office!
What were you doing in the foyer, anyway?!
That's! for being in a place
where you had no right to be
when you already know you're dark!
You ingrate, scum of filth!
I took time to drop you
when I couldn't go to school
you, with the chance to go,
you're reciting poetry!
You ingrate!

And that's! and that's!
for not staying in the country fields
with your species
on the ground where I dropped you!
And that! that! and that's! for the time
your father turned over
when I told him to leave me alone!

Première Dame de la République

The First Lady
was properly trimmed
in French couture
and Italian slippers
with Créole scarves for color
She was fire
She was ice
She was the darling
of her pompous class
Ale! Fout Koshon!
They say her mouth
was filthier than hogs
for a Lady Aristocrat
Her beauty noted
among her rivals
as she roamed
with well dressed hogs
Bann kaka n'a jwen anko!
For all the progress
she made for women's stead
for children to read and be fed
her people remember most
her furs, her jewels, her extravagance
They will not understand or forgive
her marriage to wealth
the poor vision
the oppression
and grand indecency
between the haves and have-nots
What her people may not know
or wish to understand

that in her palace,
in her bedroom
there,
she fought
alone.

La Devineuse

She is a seeing woman
a piercing clairvoyant pool
with eyes of the Spirits
within her
Speaks in tongues of ancestral visions
to voice predictions on course
She moves undisturbed
like time
Smiles at the children laughing
Laughs at the people crying
Lives beyond her touch
Her body is a vessel
cleansed for visitors
tending services
to lost souls
She can offer you gold
She can find you a lover
Then set your lifetime path in your eyes.
Cross her,
she can snuff your breath
without your feeling the pinch
cut you without a knife.

Lisa L. Moore

LISA L. MOORE IS ASSOCIATE PROFESSOR OF ENGLISH AND WOMEN'S AND gender studies at the University of Texas at Austin. She's the author of *Dangerous Intimacies: Toward a Sapphic History of the British Novel* and more than thirty articles, essays, and reviews on eighteenth-century literature, queer studies, and feminist theory. She has been a grateful member of the Austin Project since 2002.

I

All morning
all weekend
all my life
I have feared the words I am speaking now.

Sounds gather like bees
around my mouth
and the taste of blood
eases my jaw open.

II

A child on a swing
I pump high in the air
daring myself to jump
from the top of the arc.

Eyeing the patio
two floors below
I'm laid out flat
on the peak of the roof.

Red shingles warm
my chest and thighs.
If I jumped, would I die?
Or just break a leg?

Strong straining legs
push pedals up and down
lifting me on my golden bike
up the street to the dam.

Sweet cool air
stretches my ribs apart
surprising a little ease
out of the painful effort.

III

Shamed and cold, I stroke the brush
across the horse's back
the spine almost too high
for me to reach.

The mare sighs
shifts to yet another leg
groaning a little
as she settles into the stroke.

Back and forth
girl and horse
pass the breath
the mare's flank
rising, falling
beneath my thawing cheek.

The indrawn breath
if held too long
chokes, and leaves a subtle mark.

IV

It's written all over me.
All you have to do is look.
All you have to do is listen.
You don't even have to ask.

I cry too much.
My tears say:
don't make me go home.
My tears say:
don't make me say why.
My tears say:
let me know you already know.

It's written all over me.
My broken glasses shine with it
it shimmers off the slick green poly

of the too-tight top
that doesn't keep me warm enough.

At school, I avoid my brother's eye. He looks away too.
His thick glasses and shamed, shuffling walk
bear a family resemblance we cannot afford to claim.

It's written all over him.
All you have to do is look.
All you have to do is listen.
You don't even have to ask.

He got tough, rigid, stopped crying.
I cried more than ever.
"Squeaky clean" the doctor said
after listening to my heart.

V

At my house
my dad is a vet.
At my house
we don't have any pets.

At my house
I crouch in front of the hot-air register
at the foot of the stairs
to get warm before school.

At my house
my mom cries at the frying pan
while my brother and I
hug her legs.

At my house
he might come home anytime.
You can hear the garage door open.
You have a minute to get ready.

At my house
the stairs are really steep.

The roof is really high.
You could fall down and die.

At my house
it's no snacks between meals.
Dad gets the biggest piece.
Mom shouldn't take seconds.

At my house
I'm the oldest.
I should know better.

I should already know.
I should have realized.
I should have thought of that.
I shouldn't have asked.

At my house
my dad pulls my panties down
and spanks my bare bum hard.
But what really scares me
is his breathing in the dark.

At my house
I'm not allowed to lie.
At my house
I'm not allowed to tell the truth.

VI

At twelve, I count the years to eighteen
contemplating the red-shingled rooftop
wondering if I will still be alive
by the time I am old enough to leave.

Courtney Desiree Morris

Courtney Desiree Morris, 25, is a recovering community organizer, writer, and a proud alumna of the Austin Project. She is currently completing her PhD in African diaspora studies in social anthropology at the University of Texas at Austin. She lives in Austin with her partner. You can read more of her work at www.creolemaroon.blogspot.com.

Becoming Oya

I

I decide to live alone.

It is the year that I decide to reclaim my mind and body and stop casting my pearls before swine. Living alone, I learn to become comfortable in my own skin. I take hot baths in the middle of the day, eat cereal in my underwear or nude. I wake up in the morning, open windows and curtains wide and enjoy the sunshine in silence, listening only to my own thoughts.

Two months of this and I feel light, I feel strong as though the world sits weightless between my hands.

I marvel at the shine of my skin, the kinky, blackgirl texture of my hair.

I begin to learn to love myself.

2

"Hey! I said 'I love you!'"

Chest tightens
ears draw back
shoulders stiffen
eyes dart both right and left

Nowhere to run
if this alcoholic man decides he wants to show me how much he loves
me.

Could dart into that convenience store but perhaps he'll simply wait me
out.

Look back, he's slowly walking away, distracted by something or
someone else.

The longest seven seconds of my life.

3

I feel stronger
more sensual
as if light were pouring out of my skin
bursting between my lips.
Is that what Zora meant by being drenched in light?

I am not the only one who notices.

The light, it seems, attracts both the righteous and the unholy.

4

Six years old

Pinned down on my back by a nine-year-old foster kid that my
grandmother, now a widow, decided to give a proper home.

His name is Curtis and whenever I enter this room, the musty back
room off the kitchen that my father shared with his brothers nearly
two decades earlier
I am initiated.

I go partly out of curiosity, partly out of fear.

I do not like how Curtis smells or the way his sister, Felicia, looks at
me.

They all smell like poverty.

Curtis hoists himself on top of me and jerks around.
I watch the ceiling wondering when he will stop and let me leave.

When my grandmother finally catches us, I am afraid but relieved.

I will never have to let Curtis lay on top of me ever again.

5

I rarely feel safe anywhere.

I move about the world not because I am brave
but because I know that I have to learn to move beyond that fear.

As Audre Lorde reminds us, we are afraid of so many things:

*When we are loved we are afraid / love will vanish / when we are alone we
are afraid / love will never return / and when we speak we are afraid /
our words will neither be heard / nor welcomed / but when we are silent /
we are still afraid* [1]

To which I would add:

*When we are safe we are afraid / we will be violated / and when we are
violated we are afraid / we will never be safe again*

6

When I am nineteen, I date.

I see a man who is ten years my senior, a graduate student in the
Department of Economics. One night in the middle of conversation
he leans in quickly, crushing my lips and pinning me to the sofa.

Startled, I feel my body react in fight or flight mode. I tense, shoulders
tighten, breath quickens, and my eyes flutter in alarm as he squeezes
tighter until he notices the fear lurking in my eyes and pulls away

repulsed by my fear.

I can still see him, confused, wondering what it was I saw in him that
he simply can't acknowledge.

I hate who I become when I am afraid.

I am afraid and disgusted by what I transform men into with my fear.

There is no room for trust.

All lovers are potential thieves wooing me into an illusory state of
    security
So they can break into my home and ravage my belongings . . .

My fear turns both of us into monsters.

I do not see him again.

7

Shit that scares me:

> *I. Inexplicable noises in the middle of the night*
> *II. Losing my mind*
> *III. Dying young*
> *III. Death*
> *IV. Disappointing my father*
> *V. Drunk men downtown who get handsy after a few drinks*
> *VI. That I'm really not as smart as people say I am*
> *VII. That I'm really not as strong as I think I am*
> *VIII. Maybe all this shit really can't be changed . . .*

8

I live much of my life in fear.
Afraid of how I feel
who I am.
However, in the spirit of the twins,
this is truly only one side.
I am not always afraid
and each day I fight to be courageous.
As a child my favorite color was 9
and my Creolemaroon alter ego refers to more than my family's
    diasporic heritage.
I am a daughter of the Baptist tradition.
I know no women models of how I might release my fear
and dream myself a warrior.

These are my visions of myself:
Rebel writer
passionate organizer
fierce in love and struggle.

These visions belong to Oya
I am neither religious nor spiritual in any meaningful way
but the ancestors, wherever they are, linked my dreams to Oya.

9

The only emotion that I feel that is stronger than my fear is my anger.
And anger *always* trumps fear.

When angered, I am that woman my family always feared I might
become. I channel my grandmother's rough tongue, my father's
fierceness, and my mother's tenacity. I become Oya, speaking truth
to power, exorcising evil with the strength of a prophet.

9

I am not always afraid.
Sometimes I am brave.
And more often than not I am angry and seething with a rage that
threatens to burst through like a flooding dam.

Female rage is a powerful thing. Make no mistake, if I voice my anger,
you will be simultaneously freed and punished. Such is the nature of
Oya.

This is the lesson my father tries early to plant inside of me, written on
my flesh. Perhaps more from knowing the place in the world carved
out for little black girls, my father attempts to save me by teaching
me to never place myself in harm's way by being too loud. Which
presupposes the notion that there is any safe place in the world for
any black woman, any black girl child, anywhere.

There is not.

I have a recurring dream/daydream in which I am delivering justice.

I open my palms, lightning bursting from my hands, setting the captives free.

Oya.

My soul is heavy with age

She's crossed this
Earth
9 times.

9

Nine.

It always was my favorite number.

A Maroon woman who has walked
this Earth at least
9 times.

My life, it seems,
is a field of violent thunderstorms
dancing nines
with righteous fury.

An unruly woman
sits atop my
Crown.

9

I scramble to learn more about Oya, the warrior goddess who bends weather to her will and demands justice above all else. She is the type of woman I seek to become and a model of the type of life I am attempting to build. A life dedicated to active political struggle in whatever form, be it subversive resistance, outright rebellion, or being true to the most difficult and intimate revolutions that take place in our hearts and the corners of our minds.

I am expelling my fear.

I am becoming the woman,
the warrior,
that I was born to be.

I am

Becoming Oya.

Jane Chi Hyun Park

Jane Chi Hyun Park is a lecturer in the Department of Gender and Cultural Studies at the University of Sydney with affiliations in the Asian Studies Program and the United States Studies Centre. Her first book, *Yellow Future: Oriental Style in Contemporary Hollywood Cinema*, will be published by the University of Minnesota Press in 2010.

Amnesia

It is about speaking the language
Of the people
Who stripped, beat, and killed you

And learning to love it

Telling yourself
This is the only language I have known
This is the only way I have walked in this body
   In which I have lived always
And this town, these people . . .

It has never been otherwise.

But something in your bones remembers
Another tongue   throat   song
Curves of another landscape
   Tributaries of tears flowing over and through
      A rough terrain of dried-over scars, wrinkles, corpuscles

Memory etched in body

The grace of strong, gentle hands tugging at roots
Underfoot, white fur rustling in moonlight

From below somewhere
A slow low moaning, soft
At first then reaching the pitch
Of scream so high
No one hears it

Its echo catches in the trees, falls into
Velvet pools and drowns
As the night gradually sets and
    You wake to morning

Wrapped tight in a
Blanket of bright white

Tongue swollen and thick

The sound of grinding then
The swirling rich bitter aroma
    Of quick caffeine forget

Education

ENGLISH

The letters in the picture books come alive and crawl across the page. My eyes try to catch them but they sprout wings and fly into my head and their buzzing drives me crazy. I study English diligently. Because no one talks to me or plays with me at school and a nasty little boy named Jeremy in thick glasses with a potbelly chants Chinese Noodle at me over and over near the tires on the playground. The others join in and I stand there naked with no language. Because I can't go to the bathroom and my bladder is in constant pain because I don't know how to ask permission in English and I am too ashamed to tell my parents. So my bladder is heavy for six weeks while I work very hard on Dr. Seuss and smile pretty for the teacher and try to stop the buzzing in my head.

MATH

I am *always* voted Most Studious and Most Likely to Succeed because I have black hair and slanted eyes and I never talk. But I'm getting increasingly bad at math. In eighth grade we move from Baton Rouge to Akron—world capital of polymer. At Litchfield Junior High I enter my first day of Algebra II/Trig. The teacher is a former marine drill instructor, a bald old man named Mr. Barrett who looks like a cross between Yoda and a fat bullfrog. I scan the room and notice one other Asian kid. He's shorter than I am, wearing a sky blue sweatshirt, pants cut off at the ankle, and bottle-cap glasses. His hair sticks out in tufts, like duck feathers. "Walter, would you like Jane to sit next to you?" asks Mr. Barrett. Winking at the uncomprehending FOB boy from Hong Kong, math genius extraordinaire, "Walter, do you know about the birds and bees?" The class explodes in laugher. I vow never to speak to Walter Lee. I get worse at math. I hate quadratic equations. My father tries to help me with my homework. In that infuriatingly patient voice he says, "A person of normal intelligence could solve this equation in five minutes. It took you ten minutes. That means you have to work twice as hard." I start reading Camus.

ART

In sixth grade I find refuge in Greek and Roman mythology. Latin becomes my favorite subject. I write short stories during lunch period about slave girls killing their masters in their sleep. For the National Junior Classical League Convention I make a huge mosaic of one of these slave girls out of aluminum foil, candy wrappers, and bits of pink cloth. It's hideous and wins third place. I start drawing faces. In tenth grade I take an art class with Ms. Paris-Krummel whose mission in life is to teach us how to draw with the right side of our brains. One day, during the self-portrait unit, she motions to me to come and stand in front of the class. I obey. She clears her throat and asks everyone to look up from their oil pastels. "I want all of you to look at Jane's face. She has the typical Oriental face. Flat eyelids, small eyes, round cheeks, soft jaw . . ." The room spins, a kaleidoscope of staring eyes. My body goes numb and my eyes turn fish-gray. It doesn't bother me, I chant inside. I will forget this. I will forget this. I will forget this. I will forget this.

But I don't. It keeps coming back to bite me in the ass.

GRADUATE SCHOOL

I am twenty-nine and in my second PhD program. I have decided to wreak revenge on those who made me feel small, ugly, and unwanted with my ever-increasing stash of cultural capital, official pieces of paper legitimating my cerebral superiority, and a practiced ability to turn a phrase quickly.

But it's not enough. I need a new language—something that comes out of my own body, this strong, cracked vessel whose surface reads like an Etch A Sketch map of pain. I'm tired of borrowing inadequate terms from French critical theorists and British cultural workers. Marx and Freud were crabby white grandfathers telling clever stories by the fire.

I want to tell my own stories. In a language that doesn't contain. That doesn't sort and compartmentalize and peer into my mouth with clinical fascination. I am tired of being dissected and dissecting myself, of turning myself inside out. I am tired of performing poodle tricks for invisible robots in white lab coats who take methodical notes behind the mirrored window.

> A messy language.
> To articulate
>   through art
>
> the art-ificial real
>
> The art-ificial—imagination.
> Becomes real.
>
> If only momentarily,
>   through art,
>
> the hovering place,
> the art-iculation of language
>   —as song—
>
> and myself,
> its non-hyphenated, non-modified
> Subject
>   with a capital S.
>
> What does it mean for a little Korean girl lost in the Bible Belt
>   to claim the space of universal voice?
>
> What is the punishment for screaming?

Anime Wong

My friend in Los Angeles says I look like a cartoon character
Like I could have leapt out of a *terebi manga*
Like I could be Speed Racer's girlfriend cheering on the sidelines
My hand demurely smoothing down my skirt, my mouth
    A perpetually sweet, pornographic O

It's creepy, she says

That under the
Cute and Innocent and
Terribly Funny exterior
Slurps

A voracious, glutinous,
Pink jellyfish of a
Mind

Sucking in steel and spitting out
Shiny, sharp-pointed stars

Piercing porcelain blue neck skin

Digging

  And digging

    And digging

      Dirty long fingernails

Until they strike the

  Clean white bone.

Plane Trips

> *anyoung haseyo*
> *juh nun bak ji hyun ibnida*
> *gu wul eeship chun gubek chilsam nyun eh seoul eh suh tehwuhnasubnida*
> *jeh ga neh sal ddeh*
> *ooli bumonim wa nam dongseng rong*
> *miguk uh ro imminwassubnida*

HONOLULU, HAWAII, 1978

I am lost in a sea of urgent brown faces at the airport in Honolulu.
My introduction to my new, adopted nation
    a pit stop in one of its ex-colonies.

I am staring into a security guard's hard belt buckle.
My face is squeezed tight to hold in the fear

I feel choked by the velvet red ropes that encircle me.

When my mother comes to claim me, the airport personnel tell her
    I am a brave little girl
    I didn't cry.

TAEGU, KOREA, 1988

I look down, shocked at the intense green of the rice paddies that dot
the Korean peninsula. Kimpo Airport smells faintly of fish. We visit our
grandparents in their Japanese-style house with paper walls and cool wooden
floors. The little boy next door watches me undress through the window in
the backroom. I wear a pale green T-shirt and a white cotton training bra
with pink ribbon threading. I have braces and I'm growing out a bad perm.

SEOUL, KOREA, 1990

Everything buckled in the summer heat. Playing cards wilted in the
heaviness of the air, of summer monsoons about to break. Raindrops pelted
the blue roof of my grandmother's house like giant pebbles.

When I wake up from my nap, she is making *sam-gye-tang*.
Already the cancer is spreading through her brain.

I ask her about the white sweater she knitted
  when she lived with us in Oklahoma.
Her face registers nothing.
She tells me I should marry a Korean man.

JANUARY 1994

I sit for seventeen hours in business class, crossing the Pacific with my
    father.
I am *en route* to junior year abroad at Yonsei University
He is returning to Taegu after the annual family reunion in Texas

We are *so* diasporic.

My haircut is a sad cross between bowl and butch.
We're drinking scotch.
He confides in me that I'm named after Tarzan Jane, as much as Eyre
    Jane
        the sensible sparrow of a governess who lands
        financially stable Rochester
            (albeit old and crippled)
who locked up his mad Creole wife in the attic
and watched her burn to ash
in the fire of her frustration.

JULY 1999

I am flying back to Dallas, my high school home, land of big hair and
    Neiman Marcus, after a year of playing liaison between warring
    parents, a tired orphan.

I remember Korea as a stranger who looks like my mother in a recurring
    dream.

She passes by me, not seeing,
    as my eyes plead.

I pull up the shade while everyone is asleep.
It is impossible to say whether the sun is setting or rising.
And strangely, I feel at home there,
    hovering between morning and night,
        in the in-between space of wide awake.

Assimilation

You were forced to submit so
You revised the primal scene
Muffled the internal scream

You remembered it differently

   You must have

     Wanted it,
You must have

   Asked for it

In this way you kept yourself together
Maintained control

Kept your face from reflecting the shattering inside

Success kept you from trusting yourself
Trusting how you record,
How you see.

The last boyfriend said you gave off mixed messages

   Ran hot and cold
   Beauty and Beast
   Madonna Virgin Whore

It must be hard to be an attractive woman
With a brain, he said. And you said
With an ironic smirk
Yes, it's a real bitch. As you mixed another
Extra dry martini and slipped
Into his lap like a pretty lap dog
With a pedigree.

Pretty is a cursed blessing.
It is what
   Yebba yebba

He was chanting as he entered
Your mute and trembling
Five-year-old body

It is what you didn't want.
It is what you wanted.

So now with perfect posture
Some twenty years later
You want a man to tell you
You are pretty, pretty, pretty
As he strokes your hair
And traces down the length of your neck

It makes you hate yourself
Because inside
Of course you
Don't want it
Didn't want it

How could you?

Your grandmother
Knew what was happening
Told your parents
Who asked you

And you lied
Betraying her
The way he betrayed you.

When it is in the family
You cannot speak it

To speak it
Would be
To make the shame real
To give it body
It doesn't deserve.

But the silence

Working the Work

Made you
Phantom
Conditional
Un-present

At the point of shattering
You were caught in emotional deep freeze
No warm lips could kiss you
Out of the ice glass coffin

That was your body
Your face
The words you mouthed
The gestures you pantomimed

You walked the pretense
Numb, unseeing, dead

We walked together, you and I
Unable to face each other

Unwilling to free
The warm blue thing rattling
Inside our cages of sharp bone and
Slowly rotting meat

Not daring.

deisi pérez pérez

TAÍNA NEGRA BORICUA. BROOKLYN BORN. JERSEY RAZED. REVERSE immigration to Puerto Rico when English was a curse word. *El diario, la prensa*, Spanish rolls off the tongue. Trilingual triculture maremoto. Lands in the technical world of television and film. Storm settles into the world of art words and massage therapy. At present living in Puerto Rico. Bonafide certified Puerto Rican artesana, massage therapist, trilingual word mis.stress. Published works include *Brick City Blues, A Play on Words* and a chapbook titled *Enboricuada*.

abuela

coro: eyes roll tongue cluck roof of mouth four eyes on arm two nails pick gnats
heh heh heh heh heh ahah ahah ahah ahah
ma fa ma fa ma fa ma fa oh no oh no oh no oh no uh huh uh huh
hands on hips one able body circles table round chorus
say it one mo time ama take out my gun an shoot ya mafakinass
morir soñando now that's a thought
jugo de china con leche gots ta mix it just so pa'que la leche no se corte
wake up despierta boricua
white pillow white wall white teeth white sheet
time to pee can't see
white seat white towel white soap white sheet
1 ply 2 ply comply sin ply same shit
sheetshitsheetshitsheetshitsheetshit shit shoulda shit first
ivory fresh viejitos
limp drag step walker wheel in community room gather
sit drool speak utter mutter curse hit smack bitch slap mute tv watch
mindless games of bingo roll off tired tongues
as abuela questions why
her clear mind sits with minds lost to time
waiting for someone something make time count
seconds tick minds click the mouse ran up the clock and now it's not
time to eat institutionalized food forced fed on military time

time forced to coincide with clock works of underpaid overworked care
givers takers
living color in white shirt white pants white shoes white gloves
trays full white milk white eggs white sugar white bread
coro:
sacame de aquí voy a morir despierta
suave abuela abuela's skin was smooth
porcelain ponds cold cream suave smooth
tight cellulite free tight
pero when she got mad una ciruela
big albino prune
she loved fruits not prunes
cause they looked like cucarachas
in pr cucarachas fly
ate 5 a day killed that diabetes
fruits not fruit flies

cucarachas fly
fruit flies prunes fly fruit flys they fly we fly
mad dash round chorus
through white double door race down white halls
pass mad stalker lashing out to imaginary wife
a rage he fits cause abuela's got her wits
lasher slasher whisked to third floor shrink
we mad dash into room abuela shares with doña ana
who depends on depend
sips lunch through a straw
life clocked by shifts
passing thoughts
passing days
passing gas
passing love
thru
love filled
love lost
love me
eyes
como estas doña ana
she smiles nods
i look at abuela abuela looks at me
roll table out she wheels up I pull in
grab a pad domino time
for hours in silence we play
abuela was a damn good domino player
betcha nobody knew that
abuela mamá comandante
gots ta look real hard ta see love in armor
today we trip to la finca
recogiendo gandules albahaca pimiento ají
maiz pa los pollitos los gordito pasopao
huevitos del pais pa'desayuno
ayuna would kill her
40 years diabetic 20 nails intact 85 hair black
memory sharp tongue sharp as la cuchilla on that bára de bamboo
tumbando
papaya pa dulce chumbo pa pastel hojas pa envolverlos maduros
pa'cornflake
china pa morir soñando

u won again abuela!

chi bi ri bi ri po ro pom pom vamos pa la playa calienta el sol

bajo un palmar en piñones sabana de cuadritos abuela spreads

abuela spreads fried chillo batata asa dulce de coco con jenjibre

sippin agua de coco thru bendable plastic straw

sportin polyester shorts

80 years first time abuelas en pantalones on a beach en piñones

silla playera gafas negras scopin

machete cocos open brown bodies surf

chill abuela chill

ganaste otra vez!

y tu abuela donde está mi abuela está enjaula

abuela lets blow this joint

throw blanket covers abuelas legs

push table out white corridor wheels

bust through double white doors bounce wheelchair off curb

mimi grabs one end me the other nursing home a blur

gravel bump roll laugh scream run car screech honk

music to ears of isolation carbon monoxide sweet to ivory fresh lungs

parked cars rainbow to white wall eyes

dodge cars to nearest mall free wheels aisles scan

chicle chocolate chancleta paleta peine peinilla menta mente vente viente

cash back

abuela eyes the clock cu ku wants u back

special bull e tin . . . 85 year old diabetic white looking his panic female black
hair 20

nails intact missing from white hall white wall tickukintockcuku wants u back
institution—

last seen wheelchair bound bustin through double white doors bounced off curb
racing

toward nearest mall hand under throw could be armed and dangerous . . .

accompanied by

two white looking his panic female . . . his panic is my panic . . . u should panic
too . . .

oh my god latest development . . .

three womyn spotted fitting description one wheelchair granny free wheeling
through

aisles of local bodega accompanied by two latina bombshells armed with time . . .
latina

bombshells timed . . . bombshells . . . two . . . timed . . . two bombs ready to go off
any

Working the Work

time . . . time will tell . . . tick cu ku tock . . . coro: repeat
race abuela back time had stood still madscapadesuccess
bendición abuela
qué dios te cuide te guarde la virgen te favoresca y te acompane
abuelas legs couldn't carry weight of sanity in a world gone mad
morir soñando gots ta mix the china and the milk just so pa que no se corte

Jaclyn Pryor

JACLYN PRYOR COLLABORATIVELY CREATES PERFORMANCES, HAPPENINGS, rituals, and events with and for communities. A conceptual artist with a background in physical theatre and community-based art, her intention is to create work that is physically, visually, and viscerally engaged as well as accessible, beautiful, and surprising. Often, her performance work is large in scale and/or site-specific, and frequently takes place in public places. Jaclyn received her MA in Performance as Public Practice from the University of Texas at Austin where she is currently a candidate for a PhD.

Sixteen hand gestures to be performed while standing still

1.
milk

2.
skinny body

3.
pulling things out of the trash

4.
heavy breathing

5.
oxygen mask

6.
cutting banana with one hand

7.
spilled milk

8.
OH GOD

9.
Joshua

10.
birthday boy

11.
photograph

12.
make a wish

13.
me, crying

14.
stolen ring

15.
last words

16.
help/eyes/no sound

Shia Shabazz

An inspired daughter, mother, activist, artist, Shia Shabazz is a creative writer for screen, page, and stage whose works have been widely produced. Her chapbook and most recent interdisciplinary performance, *Momentary*, produced by the John L. Warfield Center for African and African American Studies, explores epiphany. Her fourth screenplay, *Marmalade*, was designated a finalist in the Sundance Screenwriters Labs, the Tribeca All-Access Competition, and others. Shia is a Cave Canem Fellow, a VONA Voices master's suite participant, and a member of the Austin Project.

shrapnel

Although rape as a weapon of war has existed as long as war, in today's conflicts around the world it is taking a particularly heavy toll on women.

From the article "Rape Now Taking the Form of Genocide," *Japan Times*, August 14, 2004

I

this girl
eight the first time
she evaded her skin
retreated from her bed
to camouflage herself
in midnight corners
that harbor her fugitive
from her own innocence

this girl
unaware of what pieces of herself are lost
which limbs will grow back
what syndrome will thwart her growth
what it means anymore to not know

it is this girl

not the failing economy or fallen new york skyline
not the fatigued and fatherless households
not the flailing red white and blue ribbons on car antennas
or affixed to beds of pick-ups and minivans

but her
this girl
she reminds me
that we are at war.

II

war looks different these days

some trenches resemble tract homes
tree-lined drives
cul-de-sacs
½-acre lots with three treelings on each

others

single/multi/extended families
sectioned eight ways
between liquor stores and Baptist churches
shrapnel lining streets
where shoeless vagrants pine for pennies
will work for anything edible

soldiers are
preschoolers
prepubescent
premenstrual
preteen
pre anything adult
latchkey
casualties
who learn to live with a lack of

these soldiers
bury themselves nightly
craft foxholes of flannel and linens
prisoners of war
praying from morning to morning
submission   silence   amnesia
tactics for sub/urban warfare where
survival means more than memory

they plead for stays from sexual execution
for just one more day
to trust
before wounded and dying wolves
in sheep's clothing
feed on their need
brothers uncles fathers steps and grands
cousins once removed

sisters aunties mothers grands and steps
friends of the family
wolves, for whom real love is
as distant a memory
as a mother's womb
as distant as living

III

living names plaster newspapers and war memorials

this girl
this Eve, this Elizabeth, this nine-year-old girl in El Cajon, this Jessica,
   this fifteen-year-old boy in the school closet, this Ida, this Kimberly,
   this Adam, this eight-month-old baby in Africa, this Edward, this
   Ryan, this ten-year-old boy in Tampa, this Jane Doe, this six-year-
   old girl on a school bus in New Mexico, this JonBenet, this ten-year-
   old girl in Arizona, this Polly, this Samantha, this John Doe, this
   Jane Doe, this Jimmy, this Bonita,
   this Shia
this girl and
this girl and
this boy and
this eight-year-old girl

Tracey Boone Swan

Tracey Boone Swan's (a.k.a. Trace Sheridan) prose, poetry, and photography have been published in the United States, Germany, and the UK, and can be found in journals such as *55 Words*, *BluePrintReview*, *Nerve House*, *All Things Girl*, *apt: a literary journal*, *Mud Luscious*, *Cautionary Tale*, *Static Movement*, and *Libbon*, to name a few. She is a co-founding editor of *34th Parallel*, a quarterly magazine that features fiction, poetry, photography, and interviews with new and emerging writers and artists. Currently completing her MFA in creative writing, she lives in southern California with her husband and young son.

Excerpt from "my story begins with . . ."

4

Who are you? Where is my other mama?
I want her back—the strong one.
Not the one who can't get up some mornings because
she can't or won't.

You're supposed to be a soldier.
You're supposed to know how to survive
and take care of yourself, your fellow soldiers, and us.
At all times,
in every situation—prepared.
GIVE ME MY MAMA BACK!

I want the one who sent pictures
with sweet promises on the back like:
"To my darling Daughter from your mother with love.
Can't wait to see you in June"
or
"To my sweetheart—We'll be together soon!

Love, Mama"

I want the other mama . . .
the one who could run five miles
in the middle of the day with a fifty-pound
pack of gear on her back.
I want the one who could do
anything she wanted to, just because.
Not this one . . . not this one.
I didn't know it would be this hard
I didn't know it would be this hard.
I didn't know you'd need me to protect you . . .

6

    Poverty is paralyzing no matter where it is. But in the country it is
especially hard. In the town where we lived, there weren't any "projects"
or government housing until the late nineties—welfare housing
consisted of living at our Aunt Coreen's house. And when she got tired

                                                      Working the Work

of us, well, then we'd just swap houses, living with our ninety-year-old grandmother or living in the house right behind Aunt Coreen's or renting the house past the juke-joint across from Reds, splitting the rent with a cousin and her two kids. In the country, where we lived, there were no projects and the only welfare comes from the people across the street.

Cindy Bramblet has a bathroom suite in her bedroom. It's almost bigger than the room I share with my sister. I look around amazed but try to mask my surprise. It's incredible that she lives this way—and everyday.

Her parents have professional jobs. I wonder what they do. They look so rested in the photo next to Cindy's bed. They don't look as if they've worked a day in their lives. So I ask her and try to imagine them at work.

"What does your mama do?" She asks me after I ask her, brushing a long golden strand of hair from her face.

I try to fabricate an answer. "My mama doesn't have to work."

"Really?" the girl replies disbelief in her grass green eyes.

"Yeah, she gets help, disability from the VA."

"What's that?"

"She was in the army—she's a special veteran. So now they pay her every month."

The girl's eyes said everything she was too polite to say out loud—she mustn't be that special, considering where you live—she didn't need to say it, those eyes did.

It was the same reason Cindy and Lotta never came to my house after school or for sleepovers. Mama did work despite being a disabled vet. But I knew to Jenny it didn't matter that my mother had two jobs on the down low, one working at the EZ Mart during the night shift stocking shelves and the other sitting with Miss Baby-Doll on Thursday, Friday, and Saturday nights.

Cindy and Lotta stole their mother's Lancôme makeup to play grown-up. I had no use for lipstick and blush. I knew what it really meant to be a grown-up. Being a grown-up had to do with pawning the color TV your Granny gave you (saying, "Peety, the kids ought to at least be able to watch TV sometimes") so the lights won't get turned off; floating checks and praying that the disability check would make it before the other checks floated away; and going out with a man you couldn't stand because he promised to "help you out." Being a grown-up had nothing to do with 059 Ruby Red Wine, 003 Fresh Kissed Air, or 075 Pure Passion Peach lipstick, okay!

What did Cindy Bramblet know about anything, she lived way across town. She could afford to play grown-up because she could choose when to grow up. Next time I'll have to make up a better story.

7

"Why did you have to call them!" I say through the bathroom door.

"I didn't think you'd mind," my mother replies back through the door.

"I don't want them knowing all my private business," I say this time through tears and the door. I can hear them in the living room.

"We call them for everything else," mama retorts.

"But I don't want them knowing my personal medical business."

"Sweetheart, getting your period is a natural part of becoming a young woman."

"Why are you talking so loud!" I scream, "I don't want to become a young woman."

"I'm sorry, darling, but it's already happened."

"But why?" I cry into the hard wood face of the door.

My mother doesn't answer. I can hear her muffled voice from the living room. Then mama says, "Sweetie, come out of the bathroom, Aunt Coreen has to use it."

"That witch!" I whisper under my breath, ignoring my mother's request.

"Hey in there," this time it's Coreen, "Auntie has to use it, come on open up."

I ignore Coreen.

"Let me try," one of the other aunts, Aunt Lilly, says, "why won't you come out of the bathroom?"

I can hear them talking to each other now, right outside the bathroom door. My mother mumbles, "She's embarrassed."

An aunt replies too loudly, stretching out the syllables, "Em-barr-assed?"

"Shhh!" my mother says.

The aunt repeats softer this time, "Embarrassed?"

"Don't say anything about it," mama says close to the door.

Aunt Ida tries now, "Listen, honey, it's nothing to be embarrassed about."

The chorus interrupts her, "Nid! You weren't supposed to say anything!"

"Ida Fay!" Aunt Bettie says, "Good Lord, that one is sensitive."

"If you don't hurry up, Auntie is gonna pee on herself," Aunt Coreen says sweetly.

I mumble, "It wouldn't be the first time." Aunt Coreen loved to drink beer.

"What?" Coreen says.

"I could care less!" I reply.

"What did you say?" my mother questions.

"I'll come out when I'm finished!" I yell back.

"Now listen here, girl! Come out of that bathroom now! This is your mother speaking!" As if I could mix her voice up with any of the cackling hens beside her. Now the pièce de résistance, Granny comes to the door, "Listen, honey, come out. We all had to go through what you're going through. We understand." My eyes fill with water when I hear Granny's voice. I wipe my eyes and unlock the door with a loud click.

"There she is!" the aunts exclaim as if I've won a prize. At thirteen years old I am already taller than all six of them, including my mother.

"This calls for a celebration!" Aunt Coreen says simultaneously pulling a beer from her purse and popping the tab.

"I thought you had to use the bathroom," I say to her, confused.

"I do. Here, hold this," she hands me the beer, "close the door on your way out."

8

My sister leans over the iron-railed bed and kisses my mother on her cheek, "I love you, mama," she says.

"You sure you not hungry?" Aunt Coreen asks my mother.

"No, I'm fine," my mother says.

"What about you?" Aunt Coreen asks me.

"No, thank you."

"You don't want nothing from the cafeteria? I'm gonna walk your little sister down and get us something to eat. You don't want me to bring you something back up to eat?"

"No," I repeat.

"You don't want to come with us? Stretch your legs?"

"No, I'm fine, Aunt Coreen."

"Okay," she says, then turns to my mother, "Peety, we'll be right back. Listen, you decide you want to eat, just send that girl down and

I'll get it." The TV is bolted high in the corner of the room, where the walls and the ceiling meet. The angle seems uncomfortable to watch for anyone who isn't in the hospital bed.

"You doing okay at Aunt Coreen's house?"

"Yes, we're fine, mama."

"I know it's hard for you right now," she says.

"I'm not worried. I know we'll be all right," I say trying to reassure her. "Do you want some water?" I ask when I see her reaching for a plastic water cup. I jump up and grab the pitcher of water sitting on the bedside table, as my mother strains to reach for it. She adjusts the IV cord twisted around her arm.

"Here," I say, "let me get that for you." I pour the small glass of water and hold it to her mouth as she drinks it slowly.

"Thank you," mama says, and then she asks, "how was school this week?"

"Fine. I got an A on my math test."

"That's great. Baby, hand me that blanket. Will you throw it across my feet?" I grab the extra blanket and unfold it across the bottom of the bed.

"I'm glad you didn't go down to the cafeteria. I want to talk to you before your sister and Coreen come back." The room is silent for a moment. In the background, Richard Dawson says, *"For the next round of the Family Feud, the top ten things people do on their first date. You say, 'make whoopee,' and the survey says . . ."*

"I'm counting on you. You and your sister have to stick together now. Try not to fuss and fight. You're sisters."

"I know, mama, I know. We'll be good, everything's going to be just fine."

"I know these last few years have been really hard, with me being sick."

"We're okay, mama, really we're going to be just fine."

"I want to tell you thank you for helping me take care of your sister. She's younger than you—"" she begins and I interrupt her.

"You don't have to thank me, mama. That's what we're supposed to do—we take care of each other."

9

The lights dim, fade to black, until a spotlight reveals a girl standing in the middle of the stage. She is dressed in pseudo military garb, an army-green

sweater, dark green pants, a black beret on her head. She stands at attention,
arms to her side, head held high.
In a drill sergeant voice she says to herself,
but out loud so that we can hear, in loud commanding voice:

HOW WOULD YOU HANDLE THIS SITUATION SOLDIER?
YOUR LIFE DEPENDS ON IT . . . REMEMBER, THINK FAST,
BUT THINK WISE, THIS IS LIFE OR DEATH:
YOU'RE A SINGLE MOTHER WITH TWO CHILDREN, NO HUSBAND TO
    TAKE CARE OF YOU. CAN'T GO BACK TO THE MAN,
HE'S THE REASON YOU RAN OFF TO UNCLE SAM IN THE FIRST PLACE.

RECENTLY, HONORABLY DISCHARGED DUE TO MULTIPLE MEDICAL
    DIAGNOSES (MISDIAGNOSES THAT IS)

PARENTS DEAD, NO BROTHERS OR SISTERS, THE ONLY FAMILY YOU
    HAVE ARE YOUR MOTHER'S SISTERS. YOU'RE NOT STRANDED ON A
    DESERT ISLE, BUT CLOSE TO IT.

WHAT ARE YOU GOING TO DO, MISSY?
                Survive, ma'am!
I CAN'T HEAR YOU!
                Survive, ma'am!
DID YOU SAY SURVIVE?
                Ma'am, yes ma'am!
AGAIN, SOLDIER!
                Survive!
AGAIN!
                Survive!
LOUDER!

                SURVIVE!
                SURVIVE!
                SURVIVE!

She whispers: Survive . . .

CALL AND RESPONSE

Performance Pieces by Austin Project Guest Artists

The Austin Project invited nationally recognized artists, all of them important in the jazz aesthetic tradition, to mentor participants and to workshop new work of their own. Here, for the first time, we publish the work that the five Guest Artists—Laurie Carlos (Marion's Terrible Time of Joy), Daniel Alexander Jones (The Book of Daniel), Carl Hancock Rux (The No Black Male Show), Maiana Minahal (Worship/Singkil), and Robbie McCauley (Sugar)—created during their respective residencies. Each artist has prefaced his or her piece with a description of its connection to the communal, artistic, political, and spiritual principles of the Austin Project.

Laurie Carlos

L AURIE CARLOS IS ALWAYS CREATING A CENTER AT THE EDGES OF contemporary American theater practice. With a vision developed over forty years, she is excavating platforms for the development of emerging artistic voices. She is an Obie Award–winning actor who created the role of the lady in blue in Ntozake Shange's *for colored girls who have considered suicide/when the rainbow is enuf.* She is an inventive, two-time Bessie Award–winning director and choreographer for *White Chocolate* and *Heat.* Her work with Urban Bush Women and the performance collective Thought Music (with Robbie McCauley and Jessica Hagedorn) is legendary. Laurie has helmed the premieres of new work by now award-winning writers. Dedication and commitment to emerging voices is at the core of her mentorships with Sharon Bridgforth, Zell Miller III, Carl Hancock Rux, Grisha Coleman, Suzan-Lori Parks, Kim Thompson, Mankwe Ndosi, and Daniel Alexander Jones—all artists marking revelatory change in American theater. Laurie has received grants and awards from the New York Foundation for the Arts, the

New York State Council on the Arts, the Theater Communications Group, the National Endowment for the Arts, the McKnight Foundation, the Bush Foundation, and the Minnesota States Art Board, and she is a former board member with the Jerome Foundation. Currently, Laurie curates the late-night series "Non English Speaking Spoken Here" at Pillsbury House Theater in Minneapolis.

Syrup

Creating the whole voice of the artist is the work in which I have engaged for more than thirty-five years/ Using methods of improvisation based in the jazz aesthetic we incur language as tempo and melody as these lead us to gesture and character development/ Revealing a theatre practice steeped in an American vernacular based on the art of improvising through a core line of text/ Many voices lifting and falling into and on the sidelines of gesture/

The Austin Project offered me an opportunity to explore many techniques of performance in the voices of women writers/ In a workshop forum we created an environment for exploring together

Alternative ways of hearing language/ With exercises created for the particular artist participating in the workshops/ We developed unique performance pieces that showcased the sounding of the works of that group of artists/ Each of these four workshops included new and old participants/ Some artists returning for all four encounters and working through to a competence in the excavation of their creative process/ Many artists only in the process once were challenged to hear their work outside of a singular toning/ In configurations of lines layered in gestures, in movement, against emotional disclosures, alongside cultural assumptions, or imperatives of gender/ Personal, dream-evoked, spirit-tenured, these diverse female experiences are validated in a group dynamic/ Fraught with aesthetic distinction we create sets of agreements that allow each group to create a work for presentation/

We use writing assignments as well as dramaturgical techniques to compile a working text/ This collaborated text is set as a map for our work through movement, gesture, and landscapes of sound/ Many times the author of a text will have it reassigned to someone else in the workshop and become recipient to works of other participants/ No matter what the format of the text is, everyone is responsible for giving it absolute respect in the exploration/ Some bring lines of smudged color, pallets coarse with light, visual disclosures/ Exercises using breath, and eye contact, develop deepened physical awareness/ These assist in deconstructing assumed relationships and configurations of movement of gesture/ In our encounters with ourselves we keep these recipes open to our own measure/

Our own definition/

We are Sharon McCauley Hancock Rux Omi Latinanegra Jones

Marion's Terrible Time of Joy

The cooking pots hurl steam containing cumin, chiles, pepper, and pork/ The pots are in the rooms and on the table as well as the chairs and altars/ Veve are filled with the faces of all the world/ They are hung and light moves to reveal their particulars/ Long walks are given for remedy in songs remembered or created in the moment/ Clothes and props are formal and casual with specific colors for the women who arrive with their gestures/ The visions start with the smells while the story comes fused in oils, threads, lightly diced onions, marigolds, photos/ Voices glean their own pattern/ The women enter and tend to the pots/ They sit and stand and hum/ One of the three sets fires and turns thread in her hands/ Some come so close to each other as their faces look to the river/

ANANYA:
Behind us there are the temples and the deities are watching all of us/

MONKEY:
Is this your river?/

ANANYA:
This is the river I have wanted always/ Here it is now/

MONKEY:
You said black mustard seed?/ I've never used it/

ANANYA:
It's what makes it/ The black mustard seed and green chiles/

MONKEY:
I like a lot of lemon and yogurt with tomatoes/

ANANYA:
We have a name for that/

MONKEY:
Yes/ A name for every variation/ Green chiles!/

ANANYA:
This is where I have always wanted to be/

MONKEY:
Here? Are we in Calcutta or Manhattan or at the edges of Tunica?/

(*They move into the space and their faces turn out to the horizon as they watch the waves. In breath each retreats and the music tingles.*)

ANANYA:
You are standing here with our hands stirring pots/ Who are we feeding?/

MONKEY:
I can only smell this river/ The pots are filled with regret?/ When will the regrets get gone?/ Move into the foam?/ Become soot/

ANANYA:
Who are we going to give all this food to?/ Who is going to say thank you and clean the plates?/ Lick their fingers?/ Who will clean the nail with the tongue?/ Who are we feeding?/

MONKEY:
I've made salads of cresses with endive, olives, goat cheese, and chervil/ I don't eat them/ I serve them up to whoever wants them/ Who is gonna want them?/ That's how it is/ I don't clean the dishes or eat the leftovers or even serve/ Just let them spoon and pick/ What do you dream at the river/ Do the dances flow from this place?/

ANANYA:
I wade and remember/ The temples are behind us/

MONKEY:
The regrets are all I know now/ The inability to shake regret is all I know standing here at the river/ I want new clothes/ A disguise/ A revealing look that gives comfort/ New choices/

ANANYA:
Changing your clothes won't give you peace or bring you back time or cleanse regret/ (*ANANYA hums.*)

MONKEY:
I've known/ I know/ I have always known this/ Every day for hours at a time I dig into the wounds of it/ If when we hear the music we could know the emptiness of the melody at the first note/ So much regret/ He was dead all that time/ (*Oliver Lakes's horn blows, he sets it down, exits. ANANYA finds it and gestures.*) Which river is this?/

ANANYA:
My river/

MONKEY:
If the sea could take me home/

ANANYA:
If winds were blue in this dream/

MONKEY:
If all of it would just go up/

ANANYA:
If living forced some good/

MONKEY:
If goodness were all there is/

ANANYA:
My daughter makes this poem/ It's so beautiful filled with touching lines/ How does she know so much about love/ She knows her rage and does not keep it down/ I am always trying to keep it down/

MONKEY:
We all wrestle with the tides/ Don't drink the water/ Don't drink the water/ Don't drink it/

ANANYA:
My rage is out of all control/ These little people talking down at me/ I am a woman who comes from a deep well of prideful people/ My

father is the most moral, ingenious, and sacred person I've ever known/
He treats my mother with respect/ All of us were loved and we are
cherished in my family/ I really never knew I had rage til I met her
father/ Now everyday I battle myself for serenity/ Where do these little
people come from?/

MONKEY:
They come to assist you in your great challenge to yourself/

ANANYA:
They don't come to help me do anything/ How can you say that?/ Do
you really think they would do anything to assist me?/ You can't be
serious?/ Are you kidding?/

MONKEY:
In the days when I'm in battle I always know I will win/

ANANYA:
How/ How do you know?/

MONKEY:
Not how do I know/ But why fight/ It's always my battle with myself/

ANANYA:
No/ That's not what I am talking about/ It's these crazy small people
with their arrogance/

MONKEY:
Arrogance is the best battle cry/ It's what gets your feet up to dance/
You should thank the little people/

ANANYA:
Do you really think they deserve anything with their tiny minds?/

MONKEY:
With their short visions/

ANANYA:
I know you can't stand them either/

MONKEY:
I can't stand anything or anybody/ It all gets on my nerves/

ANANYA:
So what's all this about them being helpful?/

MONKEY:
I didn't say they were helpful/ They sure are not the reason for my personal battles/ I declare war/ Supply the troops/ Bomb residential areas and sign truces/ Rock in my rage I'm a good dancer/ The little people really couldn't ever play the music/ I got multiple rhythms with changing melody lines/ And I'm addicted to the Tango/ (*Oliver's horn clears space. They go to the river and look out. ANANYA takes to gestures.*)

ANANYA:
What is this?/

MONKEY:
Marion's love/

(*The pots are cooking as the aromas fly without restraint. The room is full with memory with spirit with prayer. The Veve opens into light. The pots need to be stirred. MARION moves through her belly to gesture in her delight.*)

ANANYA:
It's called what?/

MONKEY:
I've danced on St. Mark's Place with my shoes sinned in tides of blue/ Full to the end of Third Avenue awash with afternoon rush/ My heart so hungry for a voice/ I shaped wild days in a small untried noise/ No commitment to my own dreams/ The bones poking through skin held me up for blisters/ Gladys, Ketty, and the friends we made daily crashed in whispers through the night/ We walked sealed in hand dyes/ Tossed with second-hand care cross Eighth Street/ I've fallen in love on a daily basis in Eighth Street tangles/ The music is all I remember/ The baby and the music/ I remember the texture of orange as dream/

ANANYA:
With the sharp stick they would move your hands or tap your legs/ Tight/ My lips sugared in sweat/ When I chased away the air in my

face to make breezes tiny cuts laced my fingers/ My feet tripped to finish combinations ancient with serene misunderstanding/ Justice, I would note, was in the counts of rhythm slipped against fragile turns of rich tone/ I took my dance for the work of those women whose value was uncertain/ My father made it clear/ We were beyond any smudges/ The tinges of color on her fingers were completed schemes of patterns/ All change was of her own making/ Full with his love my mother stepped in the road a confident gentle movement of grace/ I would dance the woman from the bottom of the well/ This is what I knew about myself/ (*They hold open their mouths as they are fed foods from the pots.*)

MARION:
They was gonna come for my pots quick if they could smell me food/ When they smell it they just come up for it/ When I look up/ All dem cakes they done bring for my birthday/ Birthday ain't even come and already five cakes/ He sendin me flowers everyday/ Like I done dead/ I ain't dead/ So what he send me flowers for?/ I put all dem cakes on the table/ Whoever come to the door that one get a cake/ So much cake just keep comin into the house/ The chirren all of them could eat up what they want/ Just eat/ I ain't able with all of dis/ Then after me birthday he still sendin flowers/ The whole house lookin like a funeral parlor/

MONKEY:
He love you/

MARION:
You think so?/ What make him think to love me like dat?/

MONKEY:
We all love you Marion/

MARION:
Oh really?/ Cause it don't feel so ya know?/

ANANYA:
I know when my daughter starts to scream at me I just freeze/ Judgment and annoyance is what she gives me in her face/ Am I too lenient?/

MONKEY:
She has to live in a world where she will be responsible for her decisions/ Where her rage will protect her/

ANANYA & MONKEY:
Marion, she lived in the jungle it is said/ She made a tree her home/ The leaves feed so it is said dear Marion/ You saw the murders and the lies/ A vowel jammed inside the mouth/ As if the road could never end in the place of gray/ This is a color, the gray is/ It's just a tone against the blue/ The laugh you hear is someone's life getting recognition in the end/

ANANYA:
Cracked bracelets litter temple steps/ Everyone has so little/ Nothing to trade with/ Washing and mending the knots is an evil way to get from day to day/ The vast array of color and the interminable blue/ Great thick periwinkle left on broken cups/ Wailing as the end caressed empty mouths/ These rants of toothless poets laid along the roadside/ Every entrance to a small village marked in vomit/ Poison/ Retreat if you can stand and move in any direction/ Grab shale curbs to hold under the arms close/ Every door is marked indicating death/ The nonrefundable ticket purchased with trapped claws shedding skin/ The world breaks apart as war multiplies bone in piles/ Dust/

(*ANANYA marks this landscape in breaths and color.*)

MONKEY:
Ginger chocolate cake/

MARION:
Banana sour cream cake/

MONKEY:
Sugar glazed raspberry swirl cake/

MARION:
Butter peach schnapps cake/

MONKEY:
Black cake/

MARION:
Walnut cinnamon rum cake/

MONKEY:
You take the baby on your back and climb into a sunny day holding
your breath/

MARION:
Roof to be tarred/

MONKEY:
Balancing/

MARION:
I do balancing real good with the baby on my back/ Beautiful sun/

MONKEY:
You put in a bathroom too/

MARION:
Book/ Book tell you everything/

MONKEY:
The book don't tell you how strong the wind is gonna be in your life/
Book don't tell you that/

(*Horns and piano cross-cut into beats.*)

MARION:
Book don't know that/ Book know what it know/ You read the book
and maybe your pipes won't squeal/ Maybe you could keep the cold off
all your chirren's backs/ Could be that in the book maybe/ Cause I ain't
able with no cold froze up chirren/

MONKEY:
Sandals up from Mercer on to DeKalb snow/ All of these children to
warm with biscuits in their hands as they sleep/ Open a door as another
one with warm gloves, enters saffron, turnip, eggplant, laced tight/
Lunches of drum skins, beads, pleats and tucks/ Needled treasures
vortex of altars/ Shaped by the voice of her father dying in her arms/
Her hands empty for forgiveness/ Hands swollen weaving daily tiny

threads/ The children warmed with stories, stuffed with plantains, brown rice, fish cake and yam, glasses of sorrel rich in sweetness, delicate health as he was on the road/ The father of these children holds his horn as he tumbles through nights of hard rhythm-blown music/ The small hands open as she kisses the lines head to heart while they sleep/ Avocado walls in taupe trim/ Twenty-two drawings on the refrigerator door/ Nine loads of laundry every other day of the week/ Three dozen boiled eggs, salt and pepper/ Fifteen loaves wheat organic bread/

MARION:
The chirren was beautiful/ When they look at you I feel so/ Everyone has sweet inside they skin/ Six chirren was hard with they father on the road/ Six/ Oh my God did my papa see me into the world to take care of all them chirren/ So much time for to wait/ Wait for him to come home/ Just waitin for him to know/

MONKEY:
A woman can wait if she can wait/ A woman can wait if she can't/ Waiting on a man is never easy and almost always a waste of time/

MARION:
Black cake, huh?/ What you know about Black cake?/

MONKEY:
I know it takes a lot of work/

MARION:
Days and nights to mix up and get all of the ingredients/ It ain't the cha cha cha/

(*MARION dances in the quiet way.*)

ANANYA:
When did you find your river?/

MONKEY:
Marion came to take Amber in the end of the day while I worked/ My child was a true test of my own ability to keep living/ She knew me so little/ I had to try and make her staying with me better than it was/ The poems were clear to me and that I had no other capacity

was also clear/ Marion took her and watched her as she ate dinner and sometime lunch/ The child saw Marion and her face smiled from down in her eyes where she still lights/ Marion took her on the weekends while I worked/ She taught her how to weave cloth and cook brown rice and black-eyed peas/ They listened to horns of music while they danced and dined on oatmeal cookies made in Marion's kitchen/ The kitchen on Mercer Street where she placed her son in my arms/ "You the Godmother/ I make you the Godmother of the child"/ She bound us in that moment to raise children together/ Me awkward and fragile/ Marion always fearless/ Building houses from scratch/ Learning everyday anew while teaching her open way of trying/ We would grow tearful in the world as she learned her beauty/

MARION:
Sara give me a job at the store to work with her/ We did a lot of business there in SoHo/ Sara she know so much about buy and sell/ When she makes a deal it's a hard bargain/ Sara had me watch her and learn the store/ Sandalwoods, silver, patterns of indigo, cum cum, and hand-painted morrocan leather filled the corners/ You bought the striped rugs/

MONKEY & MARION:
Got them for the house on 110th Street that Olive gave me with medicine bags and pipes/ A long hall so cold Amber would tip and jump dance to the kitchen/ The three striped hand-dyed rugs warmed her/ Made her feel safe in that minefield of hard slaps and blows my sister dealt her while I worked/ I had two lovers there at the same time/ Made them dress up the same when we went to parties/ One of them was having an affair with two guys who lived together downstairs/ The other wrote love poems with his pretty penniless self/ He went to California while I had the Abortion/ He went with a friend of mine who wore red lipstick/ I understood/ With beauty like that you can do any damn thing you want and still be remembered fondly/ Patti LaBelle hollered in the long stretches of deep confusion/ Joni, Jagger, Nyro, Vivaldi, Saint Marie and Fats Waller turned the days over/ The baby was gone/ Some sweet tender child I could never take care of/ It was all right I told him/ Nothing had changed I told him/ I love you still/ Nothing had changed/ Next/ I continue even now swollen with love promised/ Next/ Swollen/ Moved nine times with those rugs/

ANANYA:

People see me here and think "exotic thing this girl/ This one/ Pretty fish/ You say she is a dancer?/ Let's see her move something/ That awful foot/ Let her move that awful dancer's foot/ Can you move like a liberated woman in your culture?/ In the culture of yours can you move like an American girl?"/ I am a dancer in the tradition of fire/ My mother works in color/ Her hands stained with her own intent/ In my country a woman has already been the head of state/ My daughter writes poems of love while her rage is in your face/ Brown world rage/ She will teach you what exotic has become/

(Oliver's horns blast through these last lines, calmly moving away for dancing.)

MARION:

While I am doing this I love/ *(She dances.)* The people who change me up flow from my hands/ All them that have give me love/ All them that cried with my name on their lips/ All what framed the world with my face in that picture/ Every skein of yarn I rolled into cloth touches someone I love/ Every thread/

MONKEY:
This river overflows/

MARION & ANANYA:
I don't know who you are but ain't that the trick of it/

MONKEY:
River running fast and away to the shore/

ANANYA:
We are going to eat this food/ Sit/ Take our time/ What do you want to discover?/

MARION & MONKEY:
How we find all these people in our lives who nourish and hold us close/ Like a mother but did not give birth to us/ I love you for always holding me close and being with me ever so long/ Olive Sara Aku Tamu Jo Ann Sharon Joni Susie Greta Teresa Annette Margie Tanya Kathy Soyini Lydia Diane Lourdes Jessica Robbie Donna Alissa/

Working the Work

MONKEY:
She could not go to the wedding/ She was not wanted/ A ceremony
reserved for the real mother/

MARION:
Cause I ain't the real mother of the six children whose father I waitin
for to return home/ All the days with dem chirren and I ain't nothing to
none of them/

MONKEY:
All the cooking, sewing, and sandwiches, soda, water, bread, hats,
blankets, homework, camping, trips, car rides, concerts, hands holdin,
singing, back rubs, clothes, washing, candle burning, cakes, wrapping
paper, soap, prayers, roti, curried chicken, hair combing, eye glasses/

MARION:
I ain't nothing to nobody/

ANANYA:
Rivers of tears/

MARION:
Every time my heart thinks I can get through to the other side I sink/
Sink/ How much tears is the world to hold?/

MONKEY:
The jukebox turned the song over again as she filled its belly with
change/ "Suzanne takes you down to the river"/ Hip Bagel The/ At four
in the morning after the date had gone so badly/ Pigs in the blanket
with jasmine tea and tears/ He left me without kisses or a word about
a next time or a maybe can I see you again/ This love for a summer
evening of forever had stepped onto McDougal/ I just shivered while
Odetta played Nina's Suzanne/ Weeping harder than me she returned
again and again as morning found us with dreams of love spent/ (*She
hums Suzanne and Nina's version clears the night.*)

MARION:
I love them both at first you know/ Both of them got my interest/ They
both can play a horn and are well respected for the music/ I wasn't sure
who it gonna be for me/ So I went out with each of dem/ And oh ma
God I am even more conflicted/ Both of these men treat me so nice/ I

am feelin really good in both they company/ Oh ma God/ So how am I gonna make up ma mind?/ And they both so sweet to me/ Oh God so sweet/ but then he sweetin me up so good/ I cannot stand to be away from this one/ So he is the one/ God he is the one/ (*ANANYA moves through into movement a memory.*)

MONKEY:
Can't help wanting to fight them/ Ananya her brows lifted/ Hand gesture dialogues in grace/ With her body in motion/ A warrior's teeth/ Open roar to the drum/ Ananya kicks 'em through the smoke into the strongest tones acrid/ She wages wounds from back when/ Grips the glass voice/ Smoothes it in the throat/ Ananya's war takes back the treasure/ Sucks the teeth/ holds on to the only breath/ Everyone is silent/ So much in the eyes/ Reruns of the rhythm cause fresh light and dangerous smoke/ A torn dress/ No shoes/ She is identified by gnarled kisses/ With this version of the battle she's gonna fight 'em and sing her weapon sharp/

MARION:
Aku is steppin out of the door/ She is steppin out just now/ She come back in to speak and tells her she remembers/ All the names she calls out with giggles for each/

MONKEY:
Australia is her voice while Joni's cuts cross the top of the past/ Now so full of Australia unlike then/ New York we laugh into the ears cross New Jersey and yesterday/ She repeats and lists all the names she remembers and birthdays and Zanzi's beauty/ And memory of Amber and Tamu/

MARION:
All three of them the same advanced intellect and choices/ All three doomed to define themselves with courage so clearly themselves/ All three with the same birthday/

MONKEY:
Tamu dead ten times would have been fifty/

MARION:
We, Aku, Us, our voices/

Daniel Alexander Jones

Daniel Alexander Jones is an integrator. His live art fuses writing, performance, design, and direction through dynamic collaboration. *American Theatre* magazine called him an artist whose work would "transform American stages for decades to come." His pieces include *The Book of Daniel*, *Bel Canto*, *Earthbirths*, *Blood:Shock:Boogie*, and *Cab and Lena*. Daniel's theater defies easy description and has been met with audience and critical acclaim for more than fifteen years. Daniel is a resident playwright at New Dramatists in New York City, is a national company member with Pillsbury House Theatre in Minneapolis, and was a core company member of both frontera@hyde park theatre in Austin, Texas, and Penumbra Theatre Company in St. Paul. Daniel's close collaborators include Walter Kitundu, Helga Davis, Barbara Duchow, Sharon Bridgforth, and Tea Alagíc, among others. Daniel is the twelfth recipient of the prestigious Alpert Award in the Arts in Theatre; was the recipient of the Playwrights' Center McKnight National Artist Commission and Residency Award in 2007 for his play *Hera Bright*; and has been lead artist on three Multi-Arts Production Fund grants. Daniel held a National Endowment for the Arts/Theatre Communications Group Playwriting Residency with the Theater Offensive in Boston, and was the recipient of a Howard Foundation Fellowship in 2002. Daniel's *Phoenix Fabrik* is a project of the Creative Capital Foundation, and has been presented in Minnesota and New York. Daniel is an assistant professor in the Department of Theatre and Visual Art at Fordham University. He previously taught at Goddard College, the University of Texas at Austin, and MIT. He frequently leads workshops on performance and writing in various communities. Daniel resides in Manhattan.

Eyes

The Austin Project (tAP) was familiar to me. Familiar in the archaic usage of the word: relating to or involving a family. The core impulse of the Project so closely resembled my own blood family's central ethos of embodied service that while performing my own duties as a guest artist I found myself quite literally visited by memories of my family's work. I also found myself reflecting upon the dictates of members of my chosen artistic family, truisms distilled from their copious experience of group work. This was work, in all cases, charged with the stated aims of empowerment, inspiration, and artistic exploration. I am in continuous conversation with the aforementioned family ethos, challenging my own and others' assumptions about the work and seeking out the most honest connection that I can have to it. I inherited

Arthur and Georgina Jones in front of Sacred Heart Church in Springfield, Massachusetts, on their wedding day, October 26, 1968.

similar urges toward community building, toward fostering generative civic discourse, and toward celebrating the dignity, grace, and beauty of people while honoring the ever-changing expression and ever-evolving nature of the free individual. But I also have the maverick streak in my makeup that urges me to cause a little trouble, to beware of pomposity and question authority. I have therefore been frustrated with the ego games, role-playing, political correctness, and emotional manipulation that far too often accompany these so-called "noble" pursuits. My experience as the child, grandchild, and apprentice of brilliant community workers has left me with a profound respect for those who do it well, but also a keen awareness of the drawbacks and dangers of the work. Familiar dynamics certainly played themselves out as I entered the fertile conversation set in motion by Sharon Bridgforth and Omi Osun Joni L. Jones. The Austin Project has, at various times, left me elated, frustrated, disappointed, or renewed. There is an inherently messy, even dangerous, quality about its experiment—thank goodness. It is nothing less than real. It is nothing more than human. It is sugar and salt. It is. Familiar.

I stand in the room of women. I move around. Take a hand. Walk hand in hand through the room with this person. Open the ears in my skin.

Another hand. Join the two together. You two are partners. Again and again until all the partners are matched, intuitively. I am the agent. Controlled disruption. There is always a why for the pairings. The why is never apparent at the top of the exercise. I regard the pairings for a moment. Sometimes a flicker of light in a set of eyes. Sometimes shallow breathing in another's torso. Not right. Break the pair, move around the room. Switch out. Listen again. Better. Better. Say hello. Giggles. What are we supposed to do? Take some space in the room. Sit across from one another. Cross-legged. Knees touching. Just breathe. Ah—no talking. No talking. We like to talk. What are we supposed to be doing? I recall the experiences of being seen, trusted, entrusted. I recall the women who developed these exercises, who taught them to me, carefully, who charged me with their proper execution. I recall the experiences of speaking from behind a mask hung on my face by others. The experiences of being rendered invisible. I recall the moment when, in the first workshop I taught for tAP, a woman stormed out of the room, enraged with me for my "patriarchal approach to the group, my obvious sexism, and inappropriate requests." The exercise asks the participants to observe one another, and to pay close attention to the details of a face, of a gaze, of a presence and to juxtapose, in quiet meditation through their durational experience of this person with the assumptions and conclusions they (consciously or not) projected onto them the moment they met. The moment we met. How to move beyond the initial moments of meeting? Moments of fear, shame, violence, curiosity, unexplained joy. (Man. Black. Lesbian. Ghetto. Uppity. Nice. Latina! Asian? Fine. Stank. Mean. Sweet. 40ish? Sexist. Certifiable?) Just breathe. Breathe. Your job, in the next five minutes, is to establish and maintain eye contact with your partner. That's really it. Giggles. Whispers. The rules are: no talking; whenever you find your eyes drifting away from contact with your partner's eyes (unless you are guided to do otherwise) gently return your gaze to them; and, pay attention to what you notice, what you feel. Breathe. Giggles. Shifting. Hands to faces. If you notice your body acting in a restless manner, gently remind it to give over to the exercise. Are your hands at your face. Are you crossing your arms. Just look. Maintain eye contact. Breathe. Move around the room. Tap one member of each pair on the shoulder. The person I'm indicating will be Person A. Just relax. Breathe. Observe. Fewer giggles. The click has happened. They are present. Person A, I'm going to ask you pay close attention to the eyes in front of you. Look at their shape. Are they close or wide set? Are they small, large, in between? How heavy are the lids? How long the lashes? What color are the irises? What colors, more accurately?

Dark brown. Wide pupils. Darker rings at the iris's edge. Heavy lids and long lashes. My father's eyes.

Marbled blue with hints of green. Sensitive as water. Piercing. My mother's eyes.

Sky blue. Streaks of teal. Glints of copper. Ocean at the iris's edge. My grandmother's eyes.

My grandmother, Bernice G. Leslie, ran the Springfield Girls' Club for many years. Born a Yankee farm girl in Shelburne Falls, Massachusetts, in 1908, her life spanned the twentieth century. Her birth family was as provincial as they come. The suspicion and judgment levied against anything and anyone different—often a clichéd characteristic about rural New England folks—were certainly in evidence with them. My grandmother, however, possessed a spark of curiosity and initiative; it led her past the boundaries of her known world. The oldest child, she took on much responsibility around the farm and in the home, helping her often-pregnant mother with the little children and the ceaseless chores. She loved school, and harnessed mule to carriage to drive to and from the one-room schoolhouse where she took her lessons. She became the first in her family to attend college, working her way through school as a waitress in a tearoom. She took a position as a teacher working with deaf students at the Clark School in Northampton during the Depression's early years. She met my grandfather, a musician, when paying for her sister's violin lessons with him. After marriage and the birth of her two children, she took a position teaching sewing at the Girls' Club, then a cornerstone institution in Springfield—a working-class, northeast town with notable black and immigrant populations. Her excellent work led to other opportunities at "the Club" including overseeing the summer residency camp for girls, Mishnoah, in Holland, Massachusetts. This camp became the site of her personal transformations and the medium of her agency as a teacher, a healer, and a leader. When she passed away in 2004, a memorial service was held at the Camp. Women from all over the country came. Many others, from within the country and without, sent remembrances. The attendees' easy sisterhood, across generation, race, class, and language was particularly notable.

Camp was also the site of many of my own formative developments. I spent significant portions of my earliest summers with her at Camp. I was the only boy in a world of women and girls. Now, looking back, I realize that the women's movement and feminism as an applied social and philosophical movement were nearing their apex. But I remember little overt politics at Camp. Rather, there was an easy embodiment. For me, it was a given that women were in charge, setting agendas, working through problems, and getting things done. Unfettered self-expression was a hallmark, as well; these white and black women represented a wide spectrum of representation, but shared a common natural beauty—full Afros, long wavy hair, almost

Working the Work

always unadorned by makeup. I have often remarked, when discussing my upbringing, that I was shaped, largely, by powerful women. The men in my life, including my father, were important presences, but were rarely at the center of the dialogue. The women represented different classes, ethnicities, language bases, and cultural realities. The men were almost always Black or Puerto Rican and sometimes working-class ethnic whites. Outside of the books on John F. or Robert Kennedy that were on the bookshelf, I had virtually no contact whatsoever with the so-called privileged white male patriarch. Indeed, no one in my world, at that time, seemed to regard white men as figures of authority any more than they would men of color, or women of any color. Even in my elementary school experience the vast majority of people "in charge" were women. These facts became important as I came to understand myself in the larger world because they helped to explain the powerful sense of disorientation I experienced when I realized that my upbringing was in many ways a radical departure from the societal norm. I had grown up experiencing my life mirrored in most everyone I met. I had to be taught apart. I realized that I looked at people, in great measure, through my Grandmother's eyes. I learned that this way of seeing was a transgression, was a taboo, was, ultimately, unacceptable.

There is a phrase that very often appears in group work between white people and people of color who are dealing in some way with concepts of race and culture. At some point during the workshop or discussion a white person will say: "I don't see color, I just see the person." Most often, the phrase is earnestly meant to say that "color," most often directly signifying "race," is not a determining factor in the speaker's judgment of another. They are focused on "the content of character." They are not racist. Equally often, one or more of the people of color will register their righteous fatigue with this persistent need for absolution from racism. Often the speaker will be challenged to recognize their need to deal with the palpable discomfort caused by discussion of a charged subject matter by brushing their hands of personal responsibility. Seeing color, acknowledging difference, understanding diverse cultural, historical, and personal experiences and paradigms . . . does this lead to further division or to a more complex understanding of a diverse social reality? This question buzzed at the heart of the oft-maligned multiculturalism movement out of which many of these race and culture workshops were born. The blanket dismissal of "color" and its significance carries with it, intentionally or not, a sweeping erasure of historical experience through an extension of the speaker's worldview. The insistence on acknowledgment of white culpability in the maintenance of racism carries with it, intentionally or not, a similar erasure of individual history and experience through a blanket indictment. These twin erasures strangely re-inscribe a familiar binary pattern that effectively collapses nuanced examination and further fixes a long intractable argument. They also, perhaps most importantly, offer us a way out of the crucible of change. What would it mean for us to stay in the fire a little while longer? To set down our armor and our weapons and meet each other's eyes?

Race is a fiction, culture is lived experience. America tends to confuse race with culture. Indeed, the fiction of race has been a chief mechanism by which the country has historically harvested the visions of people of color and utilized them to great success while condemning the people themselves, with rare exception, to marginal status in the society. The profound, transformative wave of resistance to this pattern coming from the civil rights, women's, workers' and gay rights movements did a great deal to make space for generative conversations. Indeed, my generation benefited directly from a sense of increased visibility and representation and increased agency. Yet, the radical violence of the Reagan revolution laid waste to much of the material progress made. Disorientation accompanied re-inscription— how could it be possible that progress could be so quickly and summarily eroded? It became a seemingly insurmountable fact that we would live marked by race, we would forever bear physical traces of this hungry ghost. Race is, for many of us, the most familiar of the many reductions used to attack and silence the human spirit in the service of a violent and greedy hegemonic urge. Radical acts of love and faithful leaps into the break are absolutely necessary if we are to undo the damage done by racism and its attendant reductions. tAP invested itself ideologically and practically in the maintenance of a true crucible. The women came to stay. Stay in the fire. Stay in the game. Stay the tide of assumption. Stay the easy answer. Stay opening. Stay beginning. Stay onstage.

Look. Look deeper. Imagine. Remember. Light travels faster than forgetting.

In the photograph, my mother, Georgina Leslie Jones, kisses her new husband, Arthur Leroy Jones, on the steps of Sacred Heart Church in Springfield, Massachusetts, on October 26, 1968. The hanging lamp . . . The carved stone of the building . . . My father's neat sideburns . . . The flowers . . . My mother's veil like a flag in the breeze . . . Of all the photograph's elements, it is the shadow that arrests me. The shadow speaks of time and timelessness. The shadow is a portent of challenges to come. The shadow makes the photograph real. They did not marry in the heat of the Summer of Love. No, their marriage occurred as a shadow stretched across the nation. King and Kennedy had been gunned down months before and the hours of daylight lessened on one of America's most volatile years. On the surface, the symbolism of their marriage seems clear, a black man, a white woman, a gesture of commitment to racial harmony in sympathy with the spirit of their age. But if I look deeper, as I have often, I see it as a pact between two people willing to take a plunge into the break. Willing to dance with uncertainty. As keenly aware of the encroaching shadow as they were of the fragile October light glancing off their hopeful faces.

When Omi Osun Joni L. Jones invited me to work with tAP and to present a new work, I accepted her invitation with one precondition. The precondition was for me, not her. I had to use this opportunity as a challenge to step into a new relationship with my performance work. I needed to walk my talk about a jazz aesthetic in the fullest possible way. Since my earliest engagement with the structural principles of the aesthetic under the tutelage of master playwright Aishah Rahman while at Brown University, I had consistently integrated ideas into my artwork. But there was one aspect that remained untested. With Omi's invitation, I chose to leap into the break and begin a project I had been considering for a while. *The Book of Daniel* would draw upon several sources. Autobiography. I loved reading people's life stories, and was particularly drawn to writers whose autobiographical explorations were also explicitly meditations on community, history, and culture. The solo. I had done solo work, but most always I got bored and wanted to play with others. I also just love the particular alchemy of the call and response between performers onstage. I knew that I could make moves to find this call and response with the audience itself. Improvised composition. I loved improvising in rehearsal. I loved departing from a known text in performance. But I had yet to take the risk of fully improvising an entire evening-length composition—to start "all the way out there" in space. Later recordings by John Coltrane and much of Alice Coltrane's body of work fed my courage.

I knew that this would be the first in a series of pieces that would function dramaturgically like a series of concerts functions for a bandleader or musician. Some of the components would be the same, like standards in a set list, some would change, new compositions, covers, spontaneously generated pieces—every time they would be played they would be different; and the listening/witnessing would be as important as the playing.

The first sharing of *The Book of Daniel* was an adrenaline-filled rush. I covered the floor with crumpled texts. I set up a flip chart with a sort of set list—an outline for a lecture on the foundational principles of jazz theory. I brought my favorite crazy hat. I hung large reproductions of my parents and grandparents around the space. I placed a bag of rice and a wedding veil next to a pair of chairs. I waited behind a curtain while the audience filled the space. When the time was right, I walked out and I played. My challenge was simple. To look at the faces in the room. To look at the objects, the crumpled text, the images . . . to keep looking . . . to stay in the heat of this risk . . . to greet fear and welcome the attendant information . . . to draw upon what I knew, my experience, what we knew, our experience, what they knew, all experience . . . to stay onstage . . . and play. And I did. And it was good. And I wanted to do it again. And again.

In the fall of 2007, I returned to the University of Texas at Austin for Omi's Performing Blackness Series. It was a homecoming for the work. I presented the seventh "chapter" of *The Book of Daniel*. It was created with my dear collaborative partner, Walter Kitundu, a genius in the truest sense of the word, who had worked with me on chapters five and six. We welcomed director Tea Alagíc, designers Leilah Stewart and Kevin Beltz, and performers Patrick McKelvey and Azure Osborne-Lee into the process to jam with us. Phrases from earlier work were referenced, including riffs from wonderful compositions gifted to *The Book of Daniel* project by Robbie McCauley, Erik Ehn, Rachel M. Harper, and Grisha Coleman. With chapter seven, subtitled "Immortality," we moved into a truly modal compositional and performance style.

In October 2008, my parents celebrated their fortieth wedding anniversary. A complex marker of time. Marked by fond memories, so many losses (including recently, the loss of my uncle, Gussie, whose stories about Malcolm X so deeply impacted me growing up), illness, betrayals, remakings, financial difficulties, hard-won achievements, change, change, change . . . Days after their anniversary, America elected Barack Obama as its forty-fourth president. The symbolic parallels or complements between Obama's narrative and my own family's experience had never been lost on me (the centrality of a photograph of a young white mother and her brown-skinned baby, was, for example, deeply resonant), and his victory had a significant impact on my psyche in ways that I'll probably be unpacking for a while. But I had been thinking of the shadow. The shadow in the photograph of my parents' wedding day. I called them shortly after the announcement of his victory. "How do you feel?" I asked. When they answered me, with their characteristic consideration and balance, I found myself listening beyond their words. I was listening to the sound of their voices. Deeper, careworn, tempered. Voices that had been through the fire. Voices of two people who forty years earlier had stood with open eyes on sunlit steps, beside a looming shadow, and leapt.

CHAPTER SEVEN: IMMORTALITY

DANIEL:
What happens when a star dies?

ALL:
Life shows through! Life shows through!

TEA:
What does it mean to be black?

DANIEL:
I don't know anymore.

TEA:
Aren't you black? I mean "black"—(*Power fist*)

DANIEL:
What it meant, what it means, what it means . . . what it meant . . . what it means . . .

TEA:
But your art comes from that experience. It says right here in your bio that you are a black artist—what gives?

DANIEL:
The *experience* is where I'm from. But where I *am*? *Who* I am? It's slippery, but it didn't used to be. I held Black in my fist. My palm. Not race, but place. Location. Where I'm from. Where am I from?

TEA:
Where you're from.

DANIEL:
Where are you from?

TEA:
It doesn't exist anymore.

DANIEL:
Come again?

TEA:
The country that I grew up in doesn't exist anymore. It's been disappeared. The name of the streets, our language, passports, identity as a people. They're gone. There is a whole generation missing. Maybe two.

DANIEL:
They did that here. Indian blood. The places keep shifting, keep being redefined.

TEA:
Reclaimed.

DANIEL:
Recolonized.

TEA:
Remembered.

DANIEL:
Refused.

TEA:
You are an artist.

DANIEL:
You are an artist. In your work you look for inner spaces. That don't belong to anybody. But where we can all travel together, and share.

TEA:
In your work you seek the possible. The yes where no has been said.

DANIEL:
Would you like tea?

TEA:
Cake.

LIBRARIAN 1:
Remind me . . . Race.

LIBRARIAN 2:
Yes, race. Always a race. Where were they going?

LIBRARIAN 1:
You mean racing.

LIBRARIAN 2:
Raisins? I only ever liked them covered in chocolate.

LIBRARIAN 1:
I meant race.

LIBRARIAN 2:
Race?

LIBRARIAN 1:
Race. Ruined my digestion.

LIBRARIAN 2:
Raisins?

LIBRARIAN 1:
Race.

DANIEL:
There is no force on this Earth like a Black LIBRARIAN.

LIBRARIAN 1:
Care must be taken where none was given. I know where each book is in the library. I know when they have been checked out. I know when they have been returned.

LIBRARIAN 2:
When they are overdue.

LIBRARIAN 1:
When they are missing.

LIBRARIAN 2:
Upon return you must run your eyes over them. Check.

LIBRARIAN 1:
Look.

LIBRARIAN 2:
Touch.

LIBRARIAN 1:
You wouldn't believe the things I've seen done to a book. The damage done. By people who have obviously lost their natural minds. Today I will show you the methods used to repair a book. *The Autobiography of Malcolm X.*

LIBRARIAN 2:
Gentle.

LIBRARIAN 1:
Josephine by Josephine Baker.

LIBRARIAN 2:
Gentle.

LIBRARIAN 1:
The book of . . .

DANIEL:
Gentle.

BROTHER MALCOLM:
Gentle. Gentle. Gentle. Hummingbirds go through an almost daily hibernation. Because if they used energy at the same rate they do during the day they would run out of gas and die in the night = so their rate of breathing, their heart systems slow way, way down. So that, in the morning, if you happen upon a hummingbird, you can lift it off its perch and it won't have the energy to go anywhere because they have to ramp themselves up. Gentle. Bet on gentle, what's beget.

ALL:
Life shows through!
Life shows through!

Working the Work

Green and bright mouth open to the Sun!
There is no force that can temper the expansion of the body of God.
(Spoken) 1975!

DANIEL:
They call the long yellow grenades = *buses.*
We go to school on the *buses* to integrate this place.

(Note: The following lines sung as anthem.)

Massachusetts.
        With your yellow buses shining.
Massa chews shit.
        Today we integrate thee.
Nasty flu shit.
Over your bridges.
Massachusetts.
        Down to our knees.
School is where we learn ourselves apart.

LIBRARIAN 2:
What are you?

DANIEL:
They raise their hands.

TEA:
I'm ¼ Irish, ¾ English.
I'm ½ Italian, ½ Irish.
I'm ¼ Irish and ¼ Scotch and ¼ French—I mean ½.

DANIEL:
She asks again, this teacher.

LIBRARIAN 2:
What are you?

LIBRARIAN 1:
I'm one hundred percent Black.
I'm Puerto Rican and proud.

DANIEL:
No one says American.

LIBRARIAN 2:
What are *you*?

DANIEL:
Her blue eye shadow glints ragefully.
I am a slippery square.
I do not come apart.
I do not dissolve.
I do not digest.
My father is Black . . . My mother is white . . . I offer.
She cocks her head.
Satisfied.

LIBRARIAN 2:
You are a mutant.

DANIEL:
As the weeks progress she will point out the differences to us all.
Who is smarter. Who is dumber. Who is quick. Who is slow.
She will hold her head in her hands and scream for . . .

LIBRARIAN 2:
QUIET!

DANIEL:
She will separate the troublemakers, pepper from salt.
She will stare at me, the quiet one, and twist her mouth.
By February she will have a nervous breakdown and be replaced.
Integration makes her anxious.
First grade leaves a lot to be desired.

BROTHER MALCOLM:
You chose us to come through. We knew who you were before you were
born. Y'all are our ancestors and our progeny. Ravens and crows and jays
are all corvids. Among the smartest of birds. They have been known to use
a stick to reach and irritate thick grubs in dead logs that they can't reach
with their bills—not to pierce them but to irritate them so they'll bite onto
the stick and they'll pull them out and eat them.

Working the Work

LIBRARIAN 2:
I was always partial to Martin Luther King, Jr., myself. Nonviolence and integration.

LIBRARIAN 1:
On whose terms. My question was, when could we just lose our foot in somebody's ass?

BROTHER MALCOLM:
What they'll tell you is that Martin Luther King, Jr., used nonviolence to advance the cause of the civil rights movement. The truth of the matter is, he used the civil rights movement to educate us all about the principles of nonviolence. Don't sleep. You are what you give away prior to the fire. I am, therefore, brotherhood.

TEA:
Lately I've been seeing my grandmother in dreams. She died when I was a kid. My grandmother was just incredible wisdom for me, and peace. I just see her, her face, really old. She was very, very skinny. And her eyes. Just her very peaceful look and her energy. I never see her body, I always just remember her face. Towards the end of her life, she was so sick, doctors told her not to fast . . . after that she died. She was Muslim. God for her was everything. If she were alive when the war started she would be so ashamed of what happened. She was a very, very peaceful woman.

LIBRARIAN 1:
(*Said while Daniel and Tea are eating cake so that they become the ancestral force observing them in the moment*)
The primary relationship is between the newborn child and the grandparent. The child has just come from the world they're about to go to. It's the grandparent's responsibility to let the child know why they came.

DANIEL:
My grandmother used to run an overnight camp for girls. When she died, we scattered her ashes in a circle all over the grounds of the camp. Around a fire, the fire she would build for the girls when they came to the camp year after year after year, and from every direction animals came: geese, deer, birds gathered overhead in the trees. All that life had come to honor her because she had honored it all of her life. She loved everyone. It's only now, looking back, that I see how unusual it was for her, a white Yankee

woman, born in 1908 to have fully supported my mother's choice to marry a Black man. My grandmother taught me how to bake cakes.

TEA:
In my father's family, for the last five hundred years, it has never happened that they would marry someone from another religion. When my mother said she would marry my father, people came to the house to see if things were okay with her—"is she okay"—"why would a Catholic woman do that." They lived in a small apartment for a long time, until both sides of the family accepted it, sort of.

DANIEL:
Who knows if they ever did?

TEA:
As children coming from these families, what do you do with that?

DANIEL:
Love us so well that we don't feel the absence of approval.

TEA:
But somewhere the idealist in me believes we are the future.

DANIEL:
It's not idealism, it's the truth. Josephine said:

"My children can pursue their brotherly education in peace without being influenced by bad spirits, for this is very important for the ideal that they represent. It must not be thought that I'm making little gods of them, but only normal beings—just, honest toward themselves and toward others, guided by purity and the conscience of sensible men. I know that we are ahead of our time."

What they did. What they did. They pulled the past into themselves and birthed the future into the present.

BROTHER MALCOLM:
You are placed for maximum visibility, flexibility, and agency.
Your placement will make navigation of their changing codes quite difficult.
There is, as you can see, a particularly steep shift in the frequencies accompanying your arrival.

Working the Work

The lot of you will be dispersed in order to achieve maximum coverage.
Trust that you will recognize one another as you walk.
Trust that you will be recognized. (*Daniel echoes.*)
This will place you in a precarious position.
You.
This place you are placed . . . it hurts the mouth to say . . . Massachusetts.

LIBRARIANS:
Are you a boy or a girl? Are you a boy or a girl? Are you a boy or a girl?
You headgear-wearing, greasy-hair-having, fat nerd sissified faggoty faggot
punk.

DANIEL:
Under siege in the hallways of Classical High. The only safe place today—
study class—where I draw. I look up and the study teacher is standing over
my desk. *I thought that you should know about this.* The study teacher is
also the drama teacher. Drama—you'd see them go through the classroom
sometimes. Dressed in togas carrying shields. Wearing wigs. Rehearsing
their "lines." Looking, and acting a bit more like me than I might like to
admit. The girl who walks like a longshoreman. The pretty boy, with the
bracelets and the Jheri curl, who wears lip gloss. *I thought that you should
know about this.*
We're having auditions, she says. I think you might be interested. My
heart is racing. What do I need to do? You need a monologue . . . pick
something that feels like you. Don't stray too far from home.
Do you remember libraries? The vault of shelves. The aggregate hum
of a hundred thousand books. For every book a spine. The pages of
tattooed flesh. Spread them and smell the spice of a new lover. Feel the
angle of light from a wider sky. Libraries were chock full of angels and
were, therefore, the most dangerous places. There, the angels come and
nestle themselves into the curve of your palm. Rub their names into your
lifelines. The plays are up the stairs, to the right behind the second pillar. I
hold out my palms. True story. The first book . . . *for colored girls who have
considered suicide/when the rainbow is enuf* by Ntozake Shange . . . the Lady
in Blue . . . *this* feels like me . . .

> "*One thing I don't need*
> *Is any more apologies*
> *I got sorry greetin me at my front door*
> *You can keep yrs*
> *I don't know what to do wit em*

They don't open doors
Or bring the sun back
They don't make me happy
Or get a morning paper
Didn't nobody stop usin my tears to wash cars
Cuz a sorry

I am simply tired
Of collectin
  I didn't know
  I was so important to you
I'm gonna haveta throw some away
I can't get to the clothes in my closet
For alla the sorries
I'm gonna tack a sign to my door
Leave a message by the phone
  If you called
  To say yr sorry
  Call somebody
  Else
  I don't use em anymore

I let sorry/didn't meanta/& how cd I know abt that
Take a walk down a dark & musty street in Brooklyn
I'm gonna do exactly what I want to
& I won't be sorry for none of it
letta sorry soothe yr soul/I'm gonna soothe mine

you were always inconsistent
doin something & then bein sorry
beatin my heart to death
talking bout you sorry
well
I will not call
I'm not going to be nice
I will raise my voice
& scream & holler
& break things & race the engine
& tell all yr secrets bout yrself to yr face
& I will list in detail everyone of my wonderful lovers
& their ways

Working the Work

I will play oliver lake
Loud
& I won't be sorry for none of it

I loved you on purpose
I was open on purpose
I still crave vulnerability & close talk
& I'm not even sorry bout you bein sorry
you can carry all the guilt & grim you wanna
just don't give it to me
I can't use another sorry
Next time you should admit
You're mean/low down/trifling & no count
Straight out
Steada bein sorry all the time
Enjoy bein yrself"[1]

When I look up, the room is silent. The drama teacher, the other auditioners, the longshoreman girl, their mouths are open. The pretty boy with the bracelets is all . . . (*Gesture*) In the middle of the book, there's a section of photographs from the original production. In the middle is a picture of the Lady in Blue . . . I commit a cardinal sin, and rip it out of the book and put it on my wall. Her name is Laurie Carlos. Awesome name.

BROTHER MALCOLM:
A note on appearance for intercession.

DANIEL:
If I'm not mistaken, intercession portends great danger.

BROTHER MALCOLM:
Or possibility.

DANIEL:
A change in plans.

BROTHER MALCOLM:
A choice.

DANIEL:
Intercession could be an interim session.
A session of sex?

BROTHER MALCOLM:
All of this should go on one of those long yellow pads of paper.

DANIEL:
You were saying?
You are anticipating intercession?

BROTHER MALCOLM:
You see those areas ahead, do you not?

DANIEL:
So, your note on appearance for intercession?

BROTHER MALCOLM:
Ravens.

DANIEL:
Ravens?

ALL:
Life shows through!
Life shows through!
Green and brightly veined and mouth open to the Sun!
There is no force.
That can temper.
The expansion.
Of the body of God.
All human disruption merely opens the possibilities for divine expression.
Cracks to let the light through.
Resurrection.
Embody the light!
Embody the healing!

DANIEL:
EAST—You, Daniel, will have few lovers. You will joke that you are celibate, a traveler in the desert. But there is more to the story. Your desire cuts through the glare with river twist. You will hear it before you see it.

You will see it before you feel the change in the air pressure. You will dip your fingers into the water before wetting your lips. And still you will hesitate before drinking. A mirage can lead to madness. Days without water blend into themselves. Better, you will say, to make a dream of water, than to bear a mouthful of sand.

. . . I love tea. It's proper. And it speaks to the *little* bit of WASP that still resides in me from my upbringing in Massachusetts.

TEA:
But tea can be a little bit bizarre, depending on the context. I work a lot in London and once I traveled to Egypt with a company of English actors and you'd expect in London that they would stop for tea every day the way they're used to doing. But we were in Egypt. I mean, you're here twenty days. Maybe you try something different. But no, they had to stop, and they were so frustrated . . .

LIBRARIANS:
Someone bring me a bloody cup of tea!

TEA:
No one brought them tea. They changed their flight to go home early. They were so unhappy but they have to have it their way.

DANIEL:
One of my favorite pictures is of a group of colonial English people in Egypt from the early 1900s. They've spread out a rug and a full tea service and the women are sitting in their hats, all corseted . . . right in the hot sand next to the Pyramids. They even broke for tea while colonizing . . . Brother Malcolm . . .

DANIEL and BROTHER MALCOLM:
Visited Egypt at the time when post-colonial African leaders were in the heart of articulating the pan African movement . . .

BROTHER MALCOLM:
Nkrumah . . . Selassie . . . Kenyatta . . . Nasser . . .

BROTHER MALCOLM:
The English and their Colonies.

LIBRARIANS:
The French and their Colonies. The Dutch and their Colonies. The Italians and their Colonies. The Portuguese and their Colonies . . .

DANIEL:
Pouring tea, I love London. But I couldn't live there.

TEA:
Spilling blood. I love London. But I couldn't live there.

DANIEL:
It was the first place I went outside the U.S. My friend Helga Davis and I were part of a singing group . . . we went there. My grandmother asked me to bring her back some yarn. Helga and I went to this yarn store. Amazing. Every color, every texture. But I won't lie. I walked up in there ready to rumble like I do when I go into pretty much any store here. And sure enough there were two proper English women behind the counter. And one of those women turned to look at me and Helga feeling her yarn and asked *may I help you, dear* and I looked her in her face and said *I'm here to buy some yarn for my grandmother!* They looked at each other. Then that English woman turned back to me and said *how lovely, I wish my grandson would be so considerate, come let us show you where we keep our best yarns.* When we left Helga and I cried on the step outside. We had to recognize how deep it had gotten in our bones. Only when we left could we look back and see where we are from, where we are, where we are going? Out of context, the inhumanity is revealed as a choice.

TEA:
Out of context, history is a choice revealed repeating. I'm better off being American.

DANIEL:
Malcolm had Mecca. Josephine had Paris. I have New York.

TEA:
We have New York.

DANIEL:
Do we really have New York?
(*"Reading" from Josephine's book*) Will you join me, Daniel? Me . . . the cross-eyed fool, the genius seductress, the shape-shifting adventurer. Will

you wander off-path, loose your hands from the moorings of self, of place, of space, of time? Perhaps you've been with me on one trip already . . . Is your appetite whet? Are you hungry for more? Can you close the door, now that it's been opened? If you walk away will you regret it? Now or never. What will it be? I'll have you back before you left.

My plan to be an actor has hit some bumps along the way. At college, I am told by the old, old, old, old, old theatre professors that while I was clearly talented, and hard working, and successful onstage, that a "drama major" really needs to be cast in a leading role during their time at Vassar, and that is highly unlikely to happen—so I may want to consider another major. After graduating with a degree in Africana studies, I go to a graduate program in theatre at Brown. Like a fish to water, I am off! One of my favorite professors is the brilliant playwright Aishah Rahman, the mother of jazz writers . . . I'm supposed to go to a workshop that a friend of hers from New York will be leading. My friend Shay and I are walking down Angell Street and we see Aishah in the bank, at the ATM machine. Now, y'all remember when ATMs are still new. And Aishah looks like she's having a time with the new-fangled contraption over there. We cross the street open the door and sure enough she says: "Dan, I'm so glad you're here, I'm having some trouble with this ATM." I get set to work when she gestures toward the corner . . . Shay, Dan, this is my friend who's leading the workshop. Let me introduce you to Laurie Carlos . . . Laurie looks at me and smiles. I know you . . . she says . . .

BROTHER MALCOLM:
The fate of things—the balance of which *you are not even aware*—depends upon your *conscious* participation in the stream of apparently *random* events, depends upon the sounding of your particular *human* vibration, your harmonic signature, confidently, in the face of adversity. *You are given the choice!*

DANIEL:
WEST—You will come upon one of the few lovers. You will have known each other before, in some simple way. As the night blooms, you will speak to one another. You will feel the awkward beauty of arousal. You will not be sure. Then the words will stop. The silence will embrace you both. You will kiss. Again. Longer and again longer. You will hear everything. His mouth will be sweet like melon. The night will caress all of you that his hands cannot cover. You will pull off his clothes and stare with joyful amazement at the possibilities. He will pull you down onto the bed and

you will drink more deeply than you ever thought possible. He will remark that your eyes seem to glow, silver brown. You bask in his glory. You will rock together, stretching, sliding through each other. You will both feel the same joy. Here you will lose all sense of direction. You will only feel the spin. You will only hear the spark of stars.

> *I want a lemon tree in my bedroom.*
> *I want to pluck a lemon from this tree.*
> *I want to give it to you to hold in your hands.*
> *I want you to pray it a prayer of trembling.*
> *I want you to hold it to my mouth.*
> *I want to bite the skin.*
> *I want to peel the skin together.*
> *I want to free the baby sun.*
> *Your lips are sugar.*
> *Your lips are sugar.*
> *Yellow like the sun.*
> *Sun in my bedroom.*
> *Sun in my eyes.*
> *Sun in our hands.*

ALL BUT DANIEL:

> *Life shows through!*
> *Life shows through!*
> *All of Negro history is like a ripe banana ready for pudding.*
> *What would you like to do now, love?*

DANIEL:

1993. I have graduated from graduate school and I have a JOB. A summer job doing BLACK THEATRE at the SMITHSONIAN INSTITUTION. We write and stage short, little, brief performances in the BLACK exhibit—FIELD TO FACTORY. For example, let's say you might come upon a Negro farmhouse in the wayback South and there we'd be inside it. SHO IS HARD WORKIN DOWN HERE IN THE SOUTH LAND. I KNOW THAT'S RIGHT, ELIAS! I SHO WISH WE COULD GO UP NORTH. NORTH? DON'T BE CRAZY!!! NORTH IS THE LAND OF OPPORTUNITY. OPPORTUNITIES FOR NEGRO PEOPLE AND A WHOLE LOT LESS LYNCHIN. I GOTS MY EYE FIX ON A CITY I HEARD ABOUT CALLED PHILADELPHIA. Then we'd run out the back of the little farmhouse and run on over to the other side of the exhibit to the Negro row house up North. ELIAS! WHY YOU SITTIN'

Working the Work

UP HERE IN PHILADELPHIA WITH YO HEAD HANGING LOW? WELL, I
SHO' THOT THE NORTH WAS GONNA BE A WHOLE HEAP BETTER THAN
THE SOUTH. SEEM TO ME THAT THE NEGRO MAN CAN'T HARDLY GET
AHEAD NOHOW. ELIAS, I HEARD OF A MAN CALLED MARCUS GARVEY—
HE GOT A BOAT GOIN' TO AFRICA. AFRICA—WOMAN IS YOU CRAZY? By
the end of the summer, my enthusiasm has waned significantly. This is
not the kind of theatre that I want to be doing. Plus, a lot of folks in the
program are giving me grief about my long hair, my colorful clothes, my
easy smile—too much like a faggot—familiar . . . We all pile into a van
and drive down to North Carolina for the National Black Theatre Festival,
a special treat I'd been looking forward to all summer but as we ride, the
reality of the scarcity of opportunity ahead begins to rear its head. I have
no plans. What's in my future. Panic attack. We pull up to the hotel and
conference center where the festival is housed. I step out of the van, eyes
glued to the sidewalk. I look up and who is standing there looking at me
but Laurie Carlos, and she says, "We've been waiting for you." She takes
me by the hand, and I walk away from the Smithsonian crowd before I
know it I am in a theatre, full of stars—I mean—stars.

LIBRARIANS:
Robbie McCauley
Rosalind Cash
Sekou Sundiata
Craig Harris
Rhodessa Jones
Carl Hancock Rux
Billie Allen
Keith Antar Mason and the Hittite Empire

TOGETHER:
Ntozake Shange

DANIEL:
I live in New York.

TEA:
I live in New York.

DANIEL:
New York shines on everybody from low to high, but never too much to
manage.

Call and Response

TEA:

New York has the most well kept damaged people.

DANIEL:

The prettiest ugly people.

TEA:

The most unfortunate lucky.

DANIEL:

Your voice? France? Italy? Japan? Turkey? Croatia? Serbia?

TEA:

Bosnia.

DANIEL:

America now.

TEA:

What is America today? I'm very confused! I'm very confused by this Bill of Rights that I just discovered. You know, "CITIZENSHIP." All men are created equally—but those people brought to this country from another continent by force—officially the end of slavery happened . . . I don't know when is it . . . '50s right?

DANIEL:

Close. By about a hundred years.

TEA:

But Freedom? Equality. Justice?

DANIEL:

. . .

TEA:

What was your inspiration?

DANIEL:

Brotherhood. Black people finding brotherhood.

LIBRARIAN 2:
Through reclamation of their full humanity.

DANIEL:
White people finding brotherhood,

LIBRARIAN 1:
Through a renunciation of their whiteness.

DANIEL:
Josephine Baker's Rainbow Tribe . . .

LIBRARIAN 2:
Children adopted from all over the world, raised together as an example of the possible.

DANIEL:
El-Hajj Malik al-Shabazz—Malcolm writing from Mecca—

LIBRARIAN 1:
Calling for brotherhood of all mankind.

DANIEL:
Sounding a *yes* when the world said no! Here's what he said in his letter. (*Malcolm echoes.*)
You may be shocked by these words coming from me. But on this pilgrimage, what I have seen, and experienced, has forced me to re-arrange much of my thought-patterns previously held, and to toss aside some of my previous conclusions. This was not too difficult for me. Despite my firm convictions, I have always been a man who tries to face facts, and to accept the reality of life as new experience and new knowledge unfolds it. I have always kept an open mind, which is necessary to the flexibility that must go hand in hand with every form of intelligent search for truth.

TEA:
Wait. (*Malcolm echoes.*)
But as racism leads America up the suicide path, I do believe, from the experiences that I have had with them, that the whites of the younger generation, in the colleges and universities, will see the handwriting on the walls and many of them will turn to the spiritual path of truth—the only way left to America to ward off the disaster that racism inevitably must lead to.

Call and Response

Malcolm X.
Mecca.
1964.[2]
I'm confused . . . What became of that potential?

DANIEL:
What became of your potential? What became of your humanity?

TEA:
It was violently taken away through the war.

DANIEL:
How did you get it back?

TEA:
I gain my humanity back by not believing in any country, patriotism, flag, language, or culture. So, Daniel. What is becoming of your humanity?

LIBRARIANS:
(*Softly*) Damn.

DANIEL:
ABOVE—When you wake, you are once again alone. You blush at the thought of his tongue, his hands, the ticklish spot below your navel. You welcome the sun as it spills upward. The light seems different from the heat; today, it nourishes you, it does not sap your energy. You move to run your hands through your hair and your fingers catch in the green and gold. Seeds fall from your eyes and you feel cool fingers of water weave their way through the core of you. You have flowered. At your feet, seven signs of gratitude from a weary traveler, who happened upon you, who drank fully, who basked in your glory. The caw of black birds above. The rustle of leaves in the sweeping wind. The sands gleam at the distant edges. You find that you have become the oasis for which you had searched.

BROTHER MALCOLM:
You drowned.

DANIEL:
Didn't we all?

BROTHER MALCOLM:
No. Some burned.

DANIEL:
But here? All.

BROTHER MALCOLM:
Some gone.

DANIEL:
For now? Gone? For now?

BROTHER MALCOLM:
Do you remember libraries?

DANIEL:
I believe I drowned.

BROTHER MALCOLM:
New York was persistent.
Persistence is a habit, there.

DANIEL:
Daniel.
It is still blue. Blue.
Daniel.
Yes. Most definitely. Yes, I do remember libraries
. . .
One question?

BROTHER MALCOLM:
Please.

ALL:
> *Life shows through!*
> *Life shows through!*
> *The fight is won without war.*
> *The fight is won through the generous gesture.*
> *The green cooked through to starlight.*
> *The starlight fed with a silver spoon to your open lips.*
> *Drink this sweetness!*

DANIEL:
Are we home?

BROTHER MALCOLM:
We never left.

DANIEL:
Is that you?

BROTHER MALCOLM:
Yes.

DANIEL:
I didn't recognize you for the feathers. For the leaves.

BROTHER MALCOLM:
It is me.

DANIEL:
You look so small.

BROTHER MALCOLM:
Don't we all.

DANIEL:
Is it far, remind me? Is it far?

BROTHER MALCOLM:
Spitting distance.

DANIEL:
You always were irreverent.

BROTHER MALCOLM:
Weren't we all?

DANIEL:
Will we be again? This time, I mean?

BROTHER MALCOLM:
Questions like that are like short-sheeting a bed, or tying a knot at the end of a sock.

DANIEL:
I haven't shaken it all off, forgive me. One question?

BROTHER MALCOLM:
Please.

DANIEL:
What happens when stars die?

BROTHER MALCOLM:
Good. You remember. Now we can begin in earnest.

DANIEL:
Growing up some children will dream of becoming an astronaut.

(*To TEA*) See? You will dream of a luminous work list, leading you around the globe, connecting cities like dots of light, weaving a web of extraordinary questions. You will spin many heads with your pretty feathers and blow many minds with your brilliant thoughts.

I will dream of shattering illusions of race and of queer theory, before there is such a thing. As you can tell, men will be attracted to me because I will smell like a dangerous combination of Bob Marley and James Dean, and for my mind. I will always be fascinated with those for whom the impossible is erotic. In fact, a substantial number of the men I will fuck will write me love letters . . . I will write them back . . .
"Angels exist between us. Between words. Between moments. Between breaths. Between day and night. Between death and life. Together, we are all the living fabric of infinity."

> (*Song*)
> *Cut my new life with a generous stroke of your knife*
> *Feathers draw blood under stars above over stars below*
> *Cut deep and wide*
> *Crossroad the heart with love and life*
> *Pray my gaze will drift from the road ahead*
> *To this map you score in the palm of my hand*

Carl Hancock Rux

CARL HANCOCK RUX IS AN AWARD-WINNING WRITER, RECORDING ARTIST, and performer. He is the author of the novel *Asphalt* (Simon & Schuster), the poetry collection *Pagan Operetta* (Autonomedia Press), and the Obie award–winning play *Talk* (Theatre Communications Group). Other plays include *The No Black Male Show, Geneva Cottrell Waiting for the Dog to Die, Yanga, Smoke, Lilies & Jade,* and the operas *The Blackamoor Angel* and *Makandal.* He is the recipient of numerous awards including the Alpert Award in the Arts. From 2006 to 2009 he was head of the MFA Writing for Performance Department at the California Institute of the Arts, and currently teaches writing at the University of Iowa. Carl lives in New York.

Writing Re/Search (for Live Performance)

We experienced it—and thought that was enough. We participated in the experience of it, were victims to and authors of it, and in the throes of our experience, we did not think to photograph it or jot it down or to videotape it. If we had thought to record it then, we would not remember it now. We would not have it if we had halted it for archival purposes. In so doing, we would have robbed ourselves of the event. The event, however, is not lost. It is stored, for better or worse, in the compression of our sciatic nerves, compressing us as we walk away. Though we may have spent too many years changing and exchanging our experiences for ones we could live with, though we clearly recall having left some of our experiences behind us on the cross-town bus, in the sea foam linens of a lover's sanctum, at a colloquium on the ostensible meaning of *significance* where we did finally learn the analysis of dissolve; though we were sure we'd wiped some of our experiences off on the tongues of bar-side strangers and on the clean white sheets of logic, or buried them in a hole under a baobab tree somewhere near the Danube; though we may have spent too many years testing too many supplications, visiting too many islets, eating so much food from the plate of the other—the unrecorded event we thought we had forgotten or effectively rid ourselves of, sits in us quietly like the well-poised usher standing before the great arched doorway of exits and entrances with one white-gloved hand positioned in the small of her back, waiting to make her presence known to us (again). Our experience, stored in the power of memory's continuum, is what we know. What we know now is not what we knew then, when it first *happened* to us, when so engaged we could not (not even if we wanted to) halt it to photograph it or jot it down. It is, however, filed away in the tips of our fingers, the calcification of soft tissue, and will stay there until we—having survived the matter—de-sanctify and dissect it, reenact its tragedy, and censure its narrative. This research is the process toward re-experience, is the process toward renewal toward knowing, is the process toward *being*, is the process toward death. A *pure* theater.

The No Black Male Show

PRODUCTION HISTORY

The No Black Male Show was initially written as a poem titled *Hell No Won't Be No Black Male Show Shown Today* (published in Rux's *Pagan Operetta*, and recorded on the CD *Rux Revue*) in response to the Whitney Museum's 1994 art exhibit *Black Male Show*. The performance version of that poem attempted to tragicomically address racist sociological studies and decades of overlapping riffs on the personal and political experience of the hypothetical Black Male figure. The performance was initially presented in New York City by The Kitchen in May of 1999 as *Pagan Operetta*, directed by Talvin Wilks, and further developed at the Penumbra Theatre in St. Paul, Minnesota, with additional staging by Carl Hancock Rux and dramaturgy by Laurie Carlos. In January 2001 the show was presented by the Foundry Theatre at Joe's Pub (the Joseph Papp Public Theater). The Foundry Theatre's world premiere presentation of *TNBMS* at the Edinburgh Festival, September 12, 2001, was canceled for obvious reasons, but the production toured nationally in the 2001–2002 season with lighting by James Overstreet; slide installation by Felicia Megginson; set, costume, and staging (based on initial staging by Talvin Wilks) by Carl Hancock Rux; and movement by Valerie Winbourne. For all *TNBMS* workshops and productions, original music was written by Jason Finkleman (except for "Don't Go to Strangers," written by Redd Evans, Arthur Kent, Dave Mann, 1954, EMI Music Publishing), and performed with the following cast.

THE BLACK MALE	Carl Hancock Rux
WOMAN IN GOWN	Helga Davis
WOMAN IN SLIP AND SHAWL	Valerie Winbourne
MUSE-ISHAN	Jason Finkleman

Cast of Characters

THE BLACK MALE	Victim
WOMAN IN GOWN	Classically-trained singer and pianist in the manner of Black Patti (Sissieretta Jones), sometimes lapses into blues or torch songs, inclined to sharp wailing. Game show hostess, concert pianist, ghost of Aunt Emma, West African prostitute, a walking tree
WOMAN IN SLIP AND SHAWL	Hyperintellectual academic, battered maternal figure possessed by the Holy Ghost (see *Mother*), West African prostitute, a walking tree
MUSE-ISHAN	Questionable white male figure with ethnic instruments

Prologue (Black Existencia)

(*When the dark comes, we are forced to remain in it . . . then the vibration of metal striking metal—resounding quietly until a pool of evening light expands itself onto the clearing of earned space—the MUSE-ISHAN stands before cymbals, sticks, drums, various objects of metal, bowls of grain, apothecary jars, etc. Makes somber sounds. Two faint spotlights fade up; WOMAN IN SLIP AND SHAWL leans against one wall, WOMAN IN GOWN leans against another. Both are expressionless. WOMAN IN GOWN sings "Don't Go to Strangers.")*

WOMAN IN SLIP AND SHAWL:
(*Reads the opening speech of the chorus of Aimé Césaire's* Et les chiens se taisaient *[published and broadcast in 1956, translated as* And the Dogs Were Silent*] with melancholy*)
For sure the Rebel is going to die
. . . no flags,
Not even black ones
No gun salutes,
No ceremony . . .

For sure the Rebel is going to die
The best reason being that
There is nothing more to do . . .

Working the Work

The season of burning stars
Is now at hand.

(Some poor light is cast onto some poor figure in formal attire and tightly knotted shoes. THE BLACK MALE sits upstage of the MUSE-ISHAN. Recorded DJ mix of questions is heard.)

VOICEOVER:
Tell me about your mother . . . please
Tell me about your father . . . please
Do you own a gun?
Tell me about hip-hop.

(The two women repeat these questions with the recorded voice until THE BLACK MALE speaks.)

THE BLACK MALE *(half-spoken, half-sung)*:
The call is tribal
The march is angry
The faces sharp
When my eyes
Opened this morning
I didn't see no sun
I looked out onto
The blinding dark
The night's fierce blade
What place is this?
And darkness cut deep into my sight
Split the canvas coat of my protection
Vision stabbed

I spilled my blood and water across the floor
Like rushing waves
Opened my mouth and screamed
Echo canyon high
Mountains cry
What place is this?
The abyss of nothing's happening-ness . . .
Wait to hear your soul drop to the bottom . . .
Falls for a lifetime

Call and Response

My silhouette is cut on the bias
Appliqué to an evil white night moon
Grin . . .
An evil white night moon—grins

Can you hear my sister praying?
How come the veil is draped across her looking glass?
Dare she ask why there's trouble in this land?
I can't stand to hear her tears no more
Valleys gash like tribal marks
Down her cobalt cheeks . . .

First Course of the Black Male Discourse

(*DJ mix of questions resumes. THE BLACK MALE stands with his back against
the wall, unaffected. New DJ mix of gospel, basketball, hip-hop, television
situation comedies, layered over each other, fills the air. WOMAN IN SLIP AND
SHAWL has taken a seat before THE BLACK MALE . . . plugs her ears with cotton,
waits for him to defend himself. WOMAN IN GOWN has taken her seat in front
of him, plugs her ears with cotton, waits for THE BLACK MALE to do something
she can applaud. They both cross their legs, fold their arms. MUSE-ISHAN stands
comfortably in the clearing of space he has earned and watches THE BLACK
MALE. They all do. Every now and then THE BLACK MALE adjusts his jacket,
pinches the crease of his trousers, unaware of the outline of his body scrawled in
chalk behind him. He looks to them for approval. Nothing. He eggs the MUSE-
ISHAN to play something. Nothing. The sounds build. THE BLACK MALE is
engulfed in layers of language, and does nothing about it even though the sounds
are deafening him. The women, impatient but prepared, reset their chairs facing
the audience, retrieve a tea service, and curl up in their chairs—a comfortable
morning talk show repose. Occasionally they will turn to the MUSE-ISHAN but
their conversation is with each other and the audience. They pour the tea. The
sounds fade as they blow into their cups.*)

WOMAN WITH SLIP AND SHAWL:
If we must discuss the so-called existential Black Male White Male
Thing—

WOMAN IN GOWN:
On the existential Black Male White Male Thing—

BLACK MALE (*from his seat upstage*):
On the Black Male White Male Thing with All Due Respect to the
Black Female White Female Thing—

WOMAN IN GOWN:
Frankly, I am not interested.

WOMAN WITH SLIP AND SHAWL:
If we must discuss THE BLACK MALE Thing—

WOMAN IN GOWN:
Which, of course, leaves no room to discuss the Black Female Thing—

WOMAN WITH SLIP AND SHAWL:
Operative word being thing—hers—female—

WOMAN IN GOWN:
Black. Which is much more interesting—

WOMAN IN SLIP AND SHAWL:
But if we cannot discuss—

BLACK MALE:
We are here to discuss—

WOMAN IN GOWN:
The so-called Black Male White Male Thing—

WOMAN IN SLIP AND SHAWL:
Then we must discuss—talk about how we see.

WOMAN IN GOWN:
Quite frankly, I am NOT interested.

BLACK MALE:
I am . . .

WOMAN IN GOWN:
No, I really mean it.

WOMAN IN SLIP AND SHAWL:
We must talk about how we see, and the linguistics of that discourse,
because—

WOMAN IN GOWN:
Because—in order to discuss how we see THE BLACK MALE Thing—

WOMAN IN SLIP AND SHAWL:
That discourse must employ a metaphoric vernacular—

WOMAN IN GOWN:
Regarding race.

WOMAN IN SLIP AND SHAWL:
Right, and we must concede that race in America (according to the pejorative perceptions of the relevant majority) has been fractured into only two relevant denominations of being—

WOMAN IN GOWN:
Black and White.

WOMAN IN SLIP AND SHAWL:
Right.

WOMAN IN GOWN:
Crude.

WOMAN IN SLIP AND SHAWL:
This inaccurate minimalist vernacular employed by the relevant majority regarding race identity primarily acknowledges only these two denominations of being.

WOMAN IN GOWN:
Inaccurate.

WOMAN IN SLIP AND SHAWL:
The populous American tongue gets tied when challenged to conceptualize or validate anything beyond conservative gender roles, sexual preference, political affiliation, or race reality.

(*THE BLACK MALE joins them. There are only two chairs. Politely, he squeezes onto the edge of one of the chairs already occupied. Attempts a comfortable pose for the audience. He tries to pour himself a cup of tea. The teapot is empty.*)

Working the Work

BLACK MALE:
This is not to say that identity and alternative definitions of identity have not inspired hip slang, slogans, expletives, catch phrases, and nicknames that have entered into the American polyglot.

WOMAN IN SLIP AND SHAWL:
But attempts at formalizing new linguistic practices for a preeminent mainstream tends only to employ inaccurate minimalist jargon acknowledging subdivisions of relevant identity.

WOMAN IN GOWN:
Shouldn't we ponder when and by whom Whiteness was purchased and assimilated into and when and by whom Blackness was imposed upon? Shouldn't we question the politics of who is, at present, White and who is, at present, Black, and shouldn't we identify those ethnic groups who, upon arrival in America, were recognized as and stigmatized as Black and remain Black without any possibility of ever attaining Whiteness?

WOMAN IN SLIP AND SHAWL:
Yes. There are, for example, people who appear to be of European descent or who are partially of European descent who consider themselves to be Black—

WOMAN IN GOWN:
And people who are of European descent who do not appear to be of European descent—

WOMAN IN SLIP AND SHAWL:
But who consider themselves to be White—

WOMAN IN GOWN:
But are not accepted as White, by a certain populace.

BLACK MALE:
And there are people who are of European descent—

WOMAN IN GOWN & WOMAN IN SLIP AND SHAWL:
White.

BLACK MALE:
Who actually appear to be of European descent—

WOMAN IN GOWN & WOMAN IN SLIP AND SHAWL:
White.

BLACK MALE:
But consider themselves to be—

WOMAN IN GOWN & WOMAN IN SLIP AND SHAWL:
Black.

(*All pause to consider what they have just said. WOMAN IN GOWN and WOMAN IN SLIP AND SHAWL slurp their tea.*)

BLACK MALE:
But I have not encountered the latter.

WOMAN IN SLIP AND SHAWL:
If we are to agree that identity formation—who we are—relies heavily upon the role of the other—who we are not—then we are forced to think about how we see ourselves . . . perception.

WOMAN IN GOWN:
And, quite frankly, we are all too preoccupied.

WOMAN WITH SHAWL:
Race is an invention (for purposes of colonization) used to make a distinction between how the humane figure sees the inhumane figure.

WOMAN IN GOWN:
Too preoccupied to continue to pay attention to marginalized identities.

WOMAN IN SLIP AND SHAWL:
The perceived image of race is based on individual (or collective) sight.

WOMAN IN GOWN:
America's too preoccupied with Manolo Blahnik shoes.

WOMAN IN SLIP AND SHAWL:
Race boils down to what you see and how you see yourself—appearance,

WOMAN IN GOWN:
I'm too preoccupied, what with the decline of American theater . . .

BLACK MALE:
Or how you are seen—

WOMAN IN SLIP AND SHAWL:
A set of appearances—

BLACK MALE:
Detached from the place and time in which it first made its appearance.

WOMAN IN GOWN:
Not to mention the decline of American opera and Broadway musicals, and with that, I ask you—what's left?

WOMAN IN SLIP AND SHAWL:
Your failure to perform as a Black male is our failure to detach ourselves from our inherited perception of you.

BLACK MALE:
Thus I may have been unable to perform simply because at that moment I was unable to perceive myself . . . in this room.

WOMAN IN GOWN:
The truly dying breed, the truly dying species is the classically trained diva of yore—

WOMAN IN SLIP AND SHAWL:
You may have been unable to perceive yourself in this room because you were being witnessed . . .

WOMAN IN GOWN:
Who finds herself in twenty-first-century America standing outside in the cold, waiting on line, warming up her five octave mezzo-soprano just to audition for background vocal work for some hip-hop star!

WOMAN IN SLIP AND SHAWL:
Therefore in this room you have no relationship with yourself, you have only a relationship with those of us who witness you.

BLACK MALE:
And those of you who see me.

WOMAN IN SLIP AND SHAWL:
A different relationship.

BLACK MALE:
Because?

WOMAN IN GOWN:
Because we're all TOO PREOCCUPIED TO CARE!

WOMAN IN SLIP AND SHAWL:
No, because those of us who witness you may not see you at all.

WOMAN IN GOWN:
I have my own preoccupations. I'm still learning to pronounce words
like Pashtun, Tajik, and Al-Qaeda.

WOMAN IN GOWN:
But, nonetheless, as far as the Black Male Thing goes, you have been
given a stage on which to perform your identity.

BLACK MALE:
I'm not sure . . .

WOMAN IN GOWN:
My husband is too preoccupied with next year's property taxes, up or
down, will they or won't they?

BLACK MALE:
I'm not sure what stages are for—lights, curtains . . .

WOMAN IN GOWN:
On finding a decent contractor.

WOMAN IN SLIP AND SHAWL:
To perpetuate illusions . . .

WOMAN IN GOWN:
Buying some decent air space—

WOMAN IN SLIP AND SHAWL:
To compel us all toward false air, false light, false language . . . all chief components of the race concept. Well . . .

WOMAN IN GOWN:
Too pre-occupied with our annual international travel plans—I MEAN, WHERE DO YOU GO?

BLACK MALE:
What I would have liked to have done is a dance, or a poem, or maybe taken some questions from the audience but all of a sudden . . . there was this terror . . . this fear that time was spinning on its axis and the earth was retreating into some ether, or ephemeral region of disbelief . . . and suddenly, all that I had prepared to do, all the stories I was prepared to tell at that moment . . .

WOMAN IN GOWN:
Because you were just too preoccupied . . . me too.

BLACK MALE:
With what?

WOMAN IN GOWN:
With what? With . . . with . . . which country is terrorizing which. With . . . you know . . . the holidays—I'm going absolutely NUTS trying to sort out greetings cards, making three separate piles for Ramadan, Chanukah, and Christmas—god forbid you should get them confused—especially these days.

WOMAN IN SLIP AND SHAWL:
Which is to say?

WOMAN IN GOWN:
Which is to say, it's all TOO MUCH. I came all this way, ball gown, primitive musician and authentic black male figure in tow—to do WHAT?

(*Their words fall out of their mouths, into silence. The* MUSE-ISHAN *plays his gongs, they cover their faces with cardboard minstrel masks stapled to flat sticks. A DJ mix of their prior conversation swells as they assume several positions throughout the space, remaining in a calm pose for a period of time*

Call and Response

before assuming another. They do this for a time, their words now swinging on particles of dust, then remove their masks and sing from the encroaching darkness.)

ALL SINGING:
If I could be Black like Eminem
Oh Lord, maybe then . . .
If I could be Black like Britney Spears
Oh Lord, no more tears . . .
If I could be Black like that
Like that . . . Oh Lord . . .

(They fan themselves beneath the weight of heat . . . a hot plantation walk. The WOMAN IN SLIP AND SHAWL exits and returns, wheeling a lectern on stage. The WOMAN IN GOWN retreats to the grand piano, adjusts her gown at the bench, and flips through sheet music. THE BLACK MALE is unsure of where he is supposed to go or what he is supposed to do at this moment so he stands there, looking stupid. The WOMAN IN SLIP AND SHAWL struggles to lift an enormous leather-bound book covered in dust onto the podium. She flips through its crumbling pages, settles on a passage, dons a pair of reading glasses, and looks to the WOMAN IN GOWN who strikes a violent chord from the first theme of a concerto, then proceeds with a delicate tinkling of keys.)

Primitive or Savage Music: An Illustration in Retrafro-futurism

WOMAN IN SLIP AND SHAWL (*reading*):
"Although most savage music is crude and to us disagreeable, its interest for the student is considerable. By noting how it arises, how it is used, and with what it is associated, we gain insight into the essence and relations of the musical impulse. It has been thought that ideas of harmony or part-singing are impossible for the savage mind. But it appears some tribes of Africa and Australia do sing in parts and even attempt concerted effects between voices and instruments. Such combinations, however, are RARE and do not show any REAL SYSTEM. The widespread combination of song with dancing, mimicry, and poetry, as well as with religious exercises, CHALLENGES attention. The painstaking care in fashioning instruments is impressive and instructive. The NAIVE experiments in scale-making suggest the probable sources of modern theory. The analogies between the musical efforts of primitive adults and those of civilized children have a bearing upon

　　　　　　　　　　　Working the Work

current pedagogy. For the critical student of either history or aesthetics, therefore, the facts of savage music are valuable."[3]

(*THE BLACK MALE exits, returns wheeling a second lectern out on stage, dons reading glasses, hurls a big dusty book onto it, flips through its crumbling pages, settles on a passage, gestures toward the MUSE-ISHAN as he speaks. The MUSE-ISHAN demonstrates the following text with his instruments.*)

BLACK MALE (*reading*):
"Clappers of bone or wood are frequent, and various hollowed tubes and the like that can be beaten. Castanets of shell or metal are often found. Everywhere rattles and jingles abound, made of bunches of pebbles, fruit stones, or shells (occasionally of a human skull filled with loose objects). All sorts of gongs or tam-tams occur, made of wood, stone, brass, copper, iron; these sometimes appear in sets, so that rude melodies or harmonies are possible. The varieties of drum and tambourine are endless, all characterized by a stretched head of skin over a hollow bowl or box, the latter being usually a gourd, a hollowed piece of wood (as the trunk of a tree), or a metallic vessel. They are sounded either by the hand or by sticks. Much ingenuity is sometimes shown in devising signals and intricate tattoos, and drums are OFTEN used in combination."

WOMAN IN SLIP AND SHAWL (*vehemently disagreeing with him*):
Excuse me! In PRIMITIVE conditions, music is FIRST OF ALL a social diversion or PLAY, affording an outlet for surplus animal spirit, stimulating emotional excitement, and helping to maintain muscular and nervous energy—

BLACK MALE (*abruptly correcting her*):
While it is TRUE that external nature supplies SUGGESTIONS of primitive music, such as the sighing and whistling of the wind, the rippling and roar of falling water, the cries of beasts, the buzzing or calls of insects, and the songs of birds—the influence of these on PRIMITIVE SONG is APPARENTLY slight.

(*They proceed to talk over each other as the WOMAN IN GOWN races through her sheet music. In response, the MUSE-ISHAN builds his primitive percussion to a reverberating rage.*)

WOMAN IN SLIP AND SHAWL:
Singing and dancing are ALWAYS conspicuously social—a center of interest for perhaps a whole village or TRIBE. The craving for popular activity in these ways often leads to stated gatherings of a festal character, the ceremonies usually being specifically associated with an occupation or event, as with HUNTING, agriculture, worship or WAR, or with birth, sickness, or death.

BLACK MALE:
Herbert Spencer argued that song is primarily a form of SPEECH, arising from the reflex action of the vocal organs under stress of emotion (as a cry follows the sensation of pain). More likely is the hypothesis that music is derived from some attempt to work off SURPLUS ENERGY through BODILY motions, to coordinate and decorate which rhythmic sounds, vocal or mechanical, are employed, and that what was at first only an accessory to dancing was finally differentiated from it.

(*The MUSE-ISHAN and the WOMAN IN GOWN have long stopped playing. She removes her glasses and stands next to THE BLACK MALE and the WOMAN IN SLIP AND SHAWL, who continue to argue as they present their thesis.*)

BLACK MALE:
First of all Beee-atch, the traditions—

WOMAN IN SLIP AND SHAWL:
Bitch?

BLACK MALE:
The traditions of many races recount the importation of instruments or musical ideas to men by the gods!

WOMAN IN SLIP AND SHAWL:
Did he just call me a—

(*The WOMAN IN GOWN proceeds to stand between THE BLACK MALE and the WOMAN IN SLIP AND SHAWL, sways and hums a steady dirge.*)

BLACK MALE:
These myths are significant, not as historic statements of fact, but—

WOMAN IN SLIP AND SHAWL:
You don't KNOW me!

BLACK MALE:
But as an idea of music as—

(*The MUSE-ISHAN tries to restrain her; a Jerry Springer moment.*)

WOMAN IN SLIP AND SHAWL:
He don't KNOW me to be callin' me no BITCH!

BLACK MALE:
Maybe some form of music is found in every part of the uncivilized
world, from the islands of the southern Pacific round to the Americas—

WOMAN IN SLIP AND SHAWL:
Don't you eeeeeeeever call me out my name!

BLACK MALE:
And from the equatorial zone far toward the poles—

WOMAN IN SLIP AND SHAWL:
I got your pole right here! He don't know me!

BLACK MALE:
As testimonies to the strange potency and charm residing in musical
tones, these speculations are not especially fruitful. It is true that some
form of music is found in every part of the uncivilized world—

WOMAN IN SLIP AND SHAWL:
You ain't seeeeeeen uncivilized. You must not know 'bout me! You don't
be callin' me no—

(*WOMAN IN SLIP AND SHAWL falls under the spell of swaying and humming.
The MUSE-ISHAN returns to his table. THE BLACK MALE is still talking when
he realizes the two women are standing on either side of him, swaying and
humming a steady dirge. He removes his reading glasses, does the same. They
hum in unison, then break into harmony; first a somber moan, then a classic
aria, then a hip-hop flow, then handclaps and field hollers, repeating the same
lyrics.*)

WOMAN IN GOWN, BLACK MALE, WOMAN IN SLIP AND SHAWL
(*singing*):
Hell No
Won't Be No
Black Male Show
Shown Today

(*They hold the final note until all breath leaves their bodies, and collapse into one final chain gang exhalation. They bow to the audience, gracefully. Lights transition to moody blues. WOMAN IN GOWN sits on top of the grand piano and crosses her legs. BLACK MALE moves to the other side of the stage. WOMAN IN SLIP AND SHAWL takes a seat upstage in a circle of light. WOMAN IN GOWN breaks into a jazz scat. WOMAN IN SLIP AND SHAWL appears to be enjoying the jazz scat, quietly. Closes her eyes, basks in it. THE BLACK MALE returns to his space at the wall. He speaks slightly above the scat.*)

BLACK MALE:
I think Archie Shepp played "Hambone, Hambone, Where You Been" in our living room the night faces and fists melded mellifluous melancholy madness onto red river carpeting—spurt, splash, torrent falls, gushing reds, primeval screams crashing through vodka spittle, sharp tenor sax and subjective alto, trumpet, trombone, hambone bass, and Roger Blank drums . . . blank . . . drums . . . blank . . . Shepp's lyricism lurking behind fichus and forlorn fruit and rhythm patterns lined in gold fringe, clutched, clutched in, in our living room, in "Where You Been?" arrangements scattered from kidney-shaped cherry wood coffee table and Camels sleeping in red-river-woven carpeting, caravans of Camels and Kools and vodka and blood and Shepp and rhythm . . . I think *Garvey's Ghost* came to play with me between Charlie Brown's sheets to the percussion of belt buckle slaps and cracked wall mirrors and ripped Chinese watercolors, or was it *Mendacity?*

WOMAN IN GOWN (*singing*):
Mendacity . . .

WOMAN IN SLIP AND SHAWL (*whispering to herself*):
Mendacity . . .

(*Uncomfortable beat for all.*)

Working the Work

BLACK MALE:
Either way, the party was in my pillow, where cut-outs held court
with *Right On!* magazine centerfolds, conversation was had freely, and
maybe Junior Walker interrupted for a moment, or might have been,
then again, I think, it was . . . no, yes, it was Mendacity, it was Abbey
Lincoln who sent herself into my restlessness and jazz frenzy and comic
book high, and quivering and quake and not sure now what the silences
mean after Johnnie Walker Black Black Black came crashing down
to the harmonic freedom and improvisation of Roach and Mingus
and Hawkins and Dizzy . . . Dizzy . . . Dizziness . . . I know Jimmy
Garrison summoned a nature boy to come my way, we entertained
battering and long fingernails broke against leather strap, against cheek
and ass and eye, I played to Jimmy Garrison's plucking, sucking my
thumb in corner circle rhythm patterns, Brilliant Corners, creative
post-bop, Monk's *Brilliant Corners* a hiding place, while ass whoopins
are taking place, like what seven-year-olds like me supposed to get for
stealing or lying or the kind maybe you hear women who can sing—

WOMAN IN GOWN (*singing*):
I fall in love too easily—

WOMAN IN SLIP AND SHAWL (*lighting a cigarette, a private lament*):
Too easily . . .

(*Another uncomfortable beat for all.*)

BLACK MALE:
Women who can hang tough with *Willow Weep for Me*, and take a
swing, take a swing, a swing and a hard-hitting fast blow down crashing
fruit and floral patterns and primeval screams through vodka spittle,
the kinda ass whoopin maybe women who sing supposed to get after
they done tried to do *Afro Blue* but you don't hear about broken nails
and Jimmy Garrison and split lip and Eric Dolphy and swollen cheeks
against red river roads where Camels and Kools caravan away from
cherry wooded areas, spilling themselves away, like the long and vibrant
notes of "Yardbird Suite," with the sweet repose of "Holiday" on.

WOMAN IN GOWN (*singing*):
There is no greater love, . . .

Call and Response

BLACK MALE & WOMAN IN SLIP AND SHAWL:
. . . not in your living room.

(*Percussion builds softly. Scat resumes. WOMAN IN SLIP AND SHAWL closes her eyes, tries to stay within the safety of music.*)

BLACK MALE (*loosening his tie, air boxing*):
Jamming . . . jamming . . . jamming . . . they don't tell you about this in record jackets, what to expect when Booker Little sings on that trumpet, when Carlos Valdez gets to cong, cong, congaing, the beat, to beat, to beat, the beat, the beating taking place in the circle of frenzy, in your living room, and there are no sequins for the diva, no boas, no rhinestone tiaras, no pencil-black eyebrows arched in pride across her forehead, or gentle shadows softly sleeping above the lid of her falling eye, her falling eye in sweet repose, no straightened hair illuminating lights and gels and gobos, not in your living room, just Charles Tolliver's *Plight* to her modern dance ballet, rond de jambe of the knee, to the fall, to the fist, straight back, and lip split side turn, ever so gracefully, ever so soft, and hard, and swing, and bop, and bam, and pow, and Dizzy . . . Dizzy . . . swelling cheeks, weak alto sax, strong bass. (*Bob and weave, beat. Scat halts.*) I think it was Etta James screaming—

(*WOMAN IN SLIP AND SHAWL repeats with him, hands across her face.*)

BLACK MALE & WOMAN IN SLIP AND SHAWL:
JAMES . . . JAMES! JAMES! JAMES!

(*Beat. Scat resumes carelessly.*)

BLACK MALE:
Or maybe not . . . or maybe it was just the rustling of the knees and elbows, and the matchstick struck across the board, and embers, and smoke rising, and flames, lifting broken body beaten like how, beaten the way seven-year-olds like me supposed to be beat, or maybe if you Abby Lincoln and sing that good, maybe if you can do primeval screams to Max's drums, and then there was nothing there . . . and then nothing . . . no voice . . . somebody hollered one last time and I can't recall if it was Grachan Moncur with Sonny Rollins, and Joe Henderson, but I think maybe it was the silences, and Moncur's "Intellect" that came up next, in our living room, with nothing there . . .

no voice . . . I think it was the silences . . . finger turning rotary dial . . . door shut . . . locked . . . running water . . . or was it? . . . no, I'm sure it was Moncur . . . who played with me . . . unveiled trombone taking me up in gentle long notes and tickling vibes, texture and shape, and safe brilliant corners to suck my thumb . . . I think it was the silences . . . next . . . I think it was the silences.

Social and Mental Traits of the Negro, or Aunt Emma's Zuni Recipe for Soul Transition

(*WOMAN IN SLIP AND SHAWL recovers from her stool, takes a moment. BLACK MALE recovers, takes a moment. WOMAN IN GOWN proceeds to the lectern, dons her eyeglasses.*)

WOMAN IN GOWN:
From "Social and Mental Traits of The Negro" by Waldo Selden Pratt. (*Reading*) "The Negro woman is not infrequently the head of the Negro family. Negro men who are regularly employed are at home little of the time, and those who do not work regularly are more of a hindrance than an assistance. Many Negro men loaf about the home, depending upon their wives and children to support them, while they work a little here and there and abuse the family. Will thus be seen that there is little orderly home life among Negroes. Sometimes an entire family consisting of father, mother, large and small children occupy the same rooms. Nor do they ventilate, and especially when any of the inmates are sick they loath to let in fresh air. Many superstitions constrain them to endanger their health by foolish practices. Consequently there is less hope of recovery in case of serious sickness, and more opportunities for sickness to grow. In the day, at night, when sick or when well, the Negroes have no conditions for inspiring love of home or for health of mind and body."

(*Projections; rural landscapes. Shadows of a woman reflecting on the walls of wood shacks. A boy. His mother. A ghost. Downstage, three old sturdy chairs. THE BLACK MALE sits between the two women. Listens. They all do. DJ mix: boiling water, pots and pans. THE BLACK MALE now has the subtle countenance of a twelve-year-old boy. The WOMAN IN SLIP AND SHAWL has removed her shawl, places it in her lap. Folds it, unfolds it, drapes her head with it, repeats. Pauses. Mumbles to herself, giggles. The WOMAN IN GOWN is stoic and centuries old, leads the boy and his mother in recalling recipes for soul survival.*)

Call and Response   219

WOMAN IN GOWN (*husky whisper*):
Yes?

BLACK MALE:
August. Sunday. 9 a.m.

WOMAN IN GOWN (*husky whisper*):
Celery . . .

BLACK MALE & WOMAN IN SLIP AND SHAWL:
Seven sticks.

WOMAN IN GOWN:
Garlic?

BLACK MALE & WOMAN IN SLIP AND SHAWL:
Seven cloves—save some for altar space.

WOMAN IN GOWN:
Pork sausage . . .

BLACK MALE:
Made immediately after—

WOMAN IN SLIP AND SHAWL:
. . . the death of the beast.

WOMAN IN GOWN:
Cayenne pepper.

WOMAN IN SLIP AND SHAWL:
Seven dashes.

WOMAN IN GOWN:
Bell pepper.

BLACK MALE & WOMAN IN SLIP AND SHAWL:
. . . from someone else's garden.

WOMAN IN GOWN:
Fresh tomatoes.

BLACK MALE:
. . . from your own garden—

WOMAN IN SLIP AND SHAWL:
. . . crushed to the consistency of blood and pulp.

WOMAN IN GOWN:
Fresh chicken livers?

BLACK MALE & WOMAN IN SLIP AND SHAWL:
Store the body of the bird for later consumption.

WOMAN IN GOWN:
Onions . . .

WOMAN IN SLIP AND SHAWL:
Sliced in seven rings—

WOMAN IN GOWN:
Then chopped.

WOMAN IN SLIP AND SHAWL:
Three tablespoons of all-purpose flour . . .

BLACK MALE:
Bay leaf—

WOMAN IN GOWN:
Save some for altar space.

BLACK MALE:
Salt from your tears . . .

WOMAN IN SLIP AND SHAWL:
Seasoned with the blood of your last flow.

WOMAN IN GOWN:
Sweat?

BLACK MALE & WOMAN IN SLIP AND SHAWL:
Seven dashes.

WOMAN IN GOWN:
From?

WOMAN IN SLIP AND SHAWL:
From the last breast to give last offspring suck.

WOMAN IN GOWN, BLACK MALE, & WOMAN IN SLIP AND SHAWL:
Gather ingredients into the tips of your fingers . . .

WOMAN IN SLIP AND SHAWL:
On the day of the death of your first son.

WOMAN IN GOWN:
Store in a cool place.

BLACK MALE:
On the morning of his interment . . .

WOMAN IN SLIP AND SHAWL:
In the presence of your son who still breathes . . .

BLACK MALE:
Combine ingredients in one-gallon cast-iron pot.

WOMAN IN GOWN, BLACK MALE, & WOMAN IN SLIP AND SHAWL:
Simmer.

BLACK MALE:
Pour into an unwashed bowl last used for the last meal served before—
before . . .

WOMAN IN SLIP AND SHAWL:
The day of death.

WOMAN IN GOWN:
Wait.

BLACK MALE:
Return to cast-iron pot.

WOMAN IN GOWN, BLACK MALE, & WOMAN IN SLIP AND SHAWL:
Stew. (*Beat*)

(*WOMAN IN GOWN makes the slightest noise every so often with her breathing,
WOMAN IN SLIP AND SHAWL continues to fidget with the shawl, alternates
between crying, laughing, acknowledging an unseen presence making
conversation in her ear. The boy speaks.*)

BLACK MALE:
Brother lay dead in a box. We sit living in a box. Inherited house. Zuni,
Virginia. A southern box, facing northern light, with one window.
One soulless chair. A bed for quaking. A stove. No music. Bland
food. Ghosts give recipes for soul. I be nothing, unrecognizable child;
watching television. Waiting for the hour when Father and Mother take
my hand to kiss the cold face of Brother. I be without my self today.
Brother, he be fixed, hushed. Waiting for the hour when the spirit
divorces itself from the flesh. Hebetudinous young man in slumber.
Hands crossed, palms face down. White suit.
    Flower. Quiet. Asleep in Apostolic Holiness . . . across the ditch . . .
just outside the window. Waiting for roar of tears and thunder of clap
and stomp and "Save me, Lawd! Hep me, Jeezus!" Father be drinking
Wild Turkey too early this morning, staring out of window—impatient
with Mother's disjointed scurry. He be drinking Johnnie Walker Black
when Wild Turkey finished, and cursing her nonsense to himself, and
cursing her cooking. Father likes to believe he can control his emotions.
"This is the northern way," he has informed us all. He and me, we wear
identical suits and shoes, and parted hair. We wait, like the apostles
on the Mount of Olive. Mother, she be skittish, jumpy, tremulous
woman in fear. Mother be dressed early this morning; hair controlled
and arrested in pins and net, perfectly pressed black suit trying not to
fall from thinning frame. Legs want to move. Want to shout. Throw
themselves up and out again, like they did in the days of birth pains.
Stockings say *no*. Say *quiet*. Say *still*. No soul. Don't lose it. Feet try to
move, try to pound heel into wood floor, try to grieve like other women.
Women who can't care about how their panties show when they fall
over pews and drape themselves over caskets. Patent leather pumps
rationally ask *why?* Request sensible steps. Careful walk. From here
to there. No throwing out of voice or flinging up of hands. No Holy
Ghosts. Ignore the quake and quiver and tremble of hand. Mother likes
to believe she can control her emotions.

BLACK MALE & WOMAN IN SLIP AND SHAWL:
"This is the better way"—

BLACK MALE:
She says to Father in agreement. (*Beat*) "Wife?" Father asks in perfect pitch through drunken slur, "Are you do-doing all right?"

BLACK MALE & WOMAN IN SLIP AND SHAWL:
"Yes."

BLACK MALE:
Mother replies in normal octave—

BLACK MALE & WOMAN IN SLIP AND SHAWL:
"Yes, I am. Thank you."

BLACK MALE:
"Have you f-finished?" Father asks, poised and sure with unsteady stance, "Have you finished pr-preparing?"

BLACK MALE & WOMAN IN SLIP AND SHAWL:
"Not yet."

BLACK MALE
Mother replies in soft tone and broken heart . . .

BLACK MALE & WOMAN IN GOWN:
"Not yet."

BLACK MALE:
Mary outlived Jesus. Sometimes mothers outlive their sons.

WOMAN IN GOWN:
Yes.

WOMAN IN SLIP AND SHAWL:
Sometimes mothers do.

BLACK MALE:
Aunt Emma outlived four. Lost—

BLACK MALE & WOMAN IN GOWN:
One to fever, one—

BLACK MALE:
—to a woman's tumultuous husband. One to—

WOMAN IN GOWN:
—homemade whiskey.

BLACK MALE:
One to an angry union of men. Aunt Emma outlived four and called on Jesus 'til she heard from—

BLACK MALE & WOMAN IN GOWN:
Mary.

BLACK MALE:
Mother says Aunt Emma closed her eyes one morning and died in this house. In the chair where Father sits on the day of the interment of his eldest son. Father says the dead are dead for good. Mother says Emma's six-foot frame rushed out into the fields of Zuni, Virginia—barefoot— with her machete in her fists, and slaughtered hogs and picked her vegetables from around the yard, and massaged the necks of sleeping chickens so she could slit their throats. Mother says Aunt Emma prepared a stew for revival and changed her garments. Let God change her name. Aunt Emma's been dead now some twenty-five years. She left this house in Mother's name. Father calls it his. Father, Mother, and Brother migrated south bringing with them boxes of northern ways. I was not yet. That was before now. I have met Aunt Emma before. Years after her death. She is here today. Even now. Ignorant and uneducated sister of Mother's grandmother, born to former slaves and Sha'lako Shamans. Aunt Emma stands in doorways and looks at Mother from mirrors. Looks over her shoulder as Mother prepares the stew. Says—

BLACK MALE & WOMAN IN GOWN (husky whispers):
"Dis' whut be yo' transition now. Ah pray tuh Jesus, hear from Mary. Make da stew. Dip yo fanger in da pot—you be speakin' in tongues aftah while. Tarry some, you be speakin' in tongues aftah while. Ah outlive fo'—you got one in da basket—but ya still got one waitin' tuh be a man. No soul wiffout dis kine sacrifice/ dis' kine rituah."

BLACK MALE:
Aunt Emma, in bloody linen and sweat-soaked head rag, six-foot frame, with the hands of a man, looks at Mother and listens to her careful speech, and northern ways.

BLACK MALE & WOMAN IN GOWN:
"Heh . . . ya need tuh dance tuh da coon shouters! Delta Blues . . . Niggah Blues . . . Leroy Lasses White can hep ya—call on 'em! Call on 'em! Albert King, Mamie Smith, Charlie Patton, Son House—CALL ON 'EM! Did ya add da innards o' da hog to da stew? Ya 'member to stir whif ya las' flow? Transitional. Change ya gawments, girl. Dat'll be all right. Yep . . . Dat'll be all right . . . Change y' gawments. Transitional . . . yep."

(*WOMAN IN GOWN, fighting back tears, hums softly to herself.*)

BLACK MALE:
Mother hums a gospel song for the first time in years, listening to Ghosts for instructions, stirring all the while. Father drinks gin and tonics now and stares out of one window. Brother lay silent. Still. Brother left this house some four years ago. I was eight. Mother says he could not contain himself here. His spirit restricted by bloodstained walls and shattered glass spittle spewed from fraternal throat. Danced out the door and up the hill, with busted eye and broken hip. He died somewhere in the hills . . . free. He died for our sins. We all smell of chicken livers and tears and garlic and blood. Father curses Mother's foolishness through tight lips, and Mother sings spirituals louder from tight lips, and Brother sleeps quietly, face drawn back with tight lips, and I say nothing of the smell in this house. I say nothing. Aunt Emma finds the records, piled away some many years. She spins 78s and guides Mother's hands as she stirs the stew. Mother laughs to herself a little. Makes the stew for the day of interment. Hopes for transition. Resists lack of control. About these things Mother knows nothing. The music plays. Emma says—

BLACK MALE & WOMAN IN GOWN:
"Big Bill Broonzy curse Ray Charles for gospel voice and blues rhythm. Heh . . . I say combine de two!"

(*WOMAN IN GOWN begins to clap her hands and hum to a steady beat. A conjuring.*)

BLACK MALE:
Mother serves the stew. Aunt Emma blesses the table from behind
Mother's eyes.

(*WOMAN IN SLIP AND SHAWL hums pleasantly to herself, a hint of laughter
sometimes, masking deep wounds.*)

BLACK MALE:
Aunt Emma, she hovers over us like some great warrior bird from the
Southern Mesas flying at dusk, singing tribal chants and summoning
Ma Rainey to bless us all. We eat in silence, except for Emma's blues
wail. It is small and private. The stew is thick and smells. We eat in
mourning, except for Mother's laughter.

(*WOMAN IN GOWN gains in volume, increases the intensity of her claps and
rocking. Change of spirit. Slow build.*)

BLACK MALE:
When the cedar bowls are empty, with no trace of flesh or soup or spit,
the table is cleared and the cloth is cleaned with water bile.

(*WOMAN IN SLIP AND SHAWL gives herself over to the hum and clap. Resists,
pulls back.*)

BLACK MALE:
Retiring to the chair facing the window that looks out over the hill,
Father drinks and grumbles and curses. He walks toward the kitchen
as Mother places the clean white sheet carefully over the dining room
table. Mother is naked—has discarded the suit and shoes.

WOMAN IN SLIP AND SHAWL:
Let's go, pours out. Intense build.

BLACK MALE:
She rends the tablecloth in two. Emma lays out the pattern for new
garments. Instructs her hands to cut and rip. To sew and fold. Garments
of white, ragged and free. Flowing cottons and head rags. Long skirts
and ruffled blouse. Mother drapes herself in grandiloquent silence.
Emma's hands pick through Mother's hair. Hair unbound. Hair singing
and stomping in percussive wails. Chorus of braid and bush. Clapping.
Intense voice of his father over the noise.

Call and Response

Father wants to get to the church where Brother sleeps. To—to say things to the corpse he never said to living flesh. To grieve and hurt and break and bend, without a flinch or winking eye. To dance and scream and blame himself without a sound or stir or failing gait. But his wife—his wife takes her time and wastes the hours. Changes her garments and laughs too much on the day of their son's interment! His wife has not asked him—she has NOT asked HIM about HIS GRIEF! About HIS apathy toward this thing called life and death. She has not asked why he could not touch or look upon the thing that was once his son. The boy integral and elegant in all his manner. She has never inquired ONCE why he must sometimes break his holy vow! The loss of control, the beating away of beauty when it is present all around him! NO! She does not CARE about him, the living! She spends these hours with NO concern for the economics of time! Stands in silly attire—and now the waiting and too much drink will surely challenge the steady calm he has worked SO HARD to maintain today. Father says—

Standing, fist raised; a roar bouncing off the walls.

"WHAT THE FUCK YOU WEARIN'?"

Silence. Reverb.

"YOU DONE LOST YO' MIND?"

Silence. Reverb.

Mother says nothing. Hair singing and stomping. His tone familiar. Her feet, still and quiet. Father says, "People comin' from outta town, you gon' shame me? You gone EMBARRASS ME by wearin' RAGS?"

Silence. Reverb.

Mother says nothing from tight lips. Does not make a sound—only percussive wails come from scalp and root. Nigger blues. Leroy Lasses White. Coon shouters singing from her tangled bush. Father says, "Get holdta yourself! COMB your hair! Turn OFF dis music, early in da morning! You tryin' to make me act a fool! I know what you up to! You gonna TELL people it's MY fault the boy left—huh? MY fault he died young—huh? MY FAULT!"

Silence. Reverb.

Mother says nothing. Tight lips loosen. Mother sings. Just sings and moves. Mother's hair is dancing. Her feet are bare. Ingredients for the post-funeral collation meal are placed on the table. Father curses and father yells, "MY fault I lost my job! MY fault we had to move back down here, in YOUR aunt's house! My fault the boy never listened to me! Can only be ONE MAN IN A HOUSE!"

Silence. Reverb.

I say nothing . . . I see nothing . . .

A boy again.

Aunt Emma's palms veil my mouth and eyes . . . Aunt Emma folds me into an unmade bed . . . my head resides on the pillowcase and I am fully dressed in black suit and black shoes and tie . . . on my back . . . like Brother . . . asleep . . . aware . . . deaf ears to slaps and crashing glass . . .

Sitting back, eyes closed.

Brother dances for me from the dark of Aunt Emma's palms, integral, in all his elegance . . . and fragile ways.

(Sudden darkness. Light on faces. DJ mix: boiling water, pots and pans.)

WOMAN IN GOWN (*husky whisper*):
For sores inflicted by someone who wants to take your power?

BLACK MALE & WOMAN IN SLIP AND SHAWL:
The lard of male hogs, one pound
Spignut, one half-pound
The extract of dandelion, 1 ounce
The seed of lobelia, one ounce
Turpentine, one ounce
Beeswax, two ounces

WOMAN IN GOWN
Make into a salve . . .

BLACK MALE & WOMAN IN SLIP AND SHAWL:
. . . and apply until the pain subsides.

WOMAN IN GOWN:
For bleeding at the nose?

(Uncomfortable beat for all)

WOMAN IN GOWN:
For bleeding at the nose?

BLACK MALE & WOMAN IN SLIP AND SHAWL:
Take birthroot and cranesbill—pulverize and snuff into nostrils.

WOMAN IN GOWN:
For hysterics?

BLACK MALE & WOMAN IN SLIP AND SHAWL:
Take a portion of mountain tea, white root, and unkum root, pound them, and make into pills with Canada balsam and yellow poplar. Take two with water.

WOMAN IN GOWN:
For spitting blood?

WOMAN IN SLIP AND SHAWL:
Two spoonfuls of nettles.

WOMAN IN GOWN:
For dizziness?

BLACK MALE:
Peel garlic—

WOMAN IN SLIP AND SHAWL:
Dip it in honey . . .

BLACK MALE:
Put into ear . . .

WOMAN IN SLIP AND SHAWL:
With a little black wool.

WOMAN IN GOWN:
For the trembling of hands?

BLACK MALE & WOMAN IN SLIP AND SHAWL:
Mugwort soaked in water.

BLACK MALE:
Wash hands—

WOMAN IN SLIP AND SHAWL:
While singing to Morgana King.

(Transition; Jesus and light coming through wood slats and stained glass.)

BLACK MALE:
Still a boy
One corpse
One red velvet room
One lithograph of Jesus and sheep
Seven mourners wailing
One ancient woman on the organ
One thousand songs
  Mix and stir, and shake hands and heads. View the body, speak well of the soul.
(Beat)
  White night. Milky glare. To the left of me, women in straw and plastic fruit holding pocketbooks and clean white handkerchiefs. This brownstone has been abandoned by the spirit of rhythm. Brick and damp wood exposed. Walls strong and flat, brass candleholders and red velvet things draped over platforms and stands. To the right of me, Mother is blackened and bruised and smiling. Father does not share the front row. He waits in the back, by the door—just in case the walls cave in. Men in shiny polyester shake strong hands and speak in loud whispers while the organ plays itself a dirge. Brother is the fairest of them all. Reminding me of a pigeon, dead just outside the door—where the hard white pavement meets the foundation of gray mortar. A gravesite for broken neck and severed wing. Still, beautiful gray and beautiful white feathers are guided by evening gale forces, moving even though the twisted body is still. There is movement in stillness. Movement, still. Brother looks like that to me. All words come from folded hands across the chest. All holy songs come from his painted lips. Can anyone else see the body moving? Aunt Emma leans into me.

WOMAN IN GOWN:
You speak. Gon' on.

BLACK MALE:
I have nothing.

WOMAN IN GOWN:
Gon' on. Make it right. Reach. Resurrect. Sow up the pieces. Make it right. Cup the fragments. Make 'em one thing.

WOMAN IN GOWN & BLACK MALE:
Whole.

(*WOMAN IN GOWN rocks and claps in four/four, summoning spirits*)

BLACK MALE:
Brother's face sings, Canaan, I'm on my way, and I am well able to
possess the land!

WOMAN IN GOWN:
Gon' on!

BLACK MALE:
It is finished. The word made flesh. The eulogy was performed by me,
from my seat.
    Preacher's cadence coming through.
    Brownstone walls echo a jazz fusion. Classical violins are played by
spirits like fiddles. Feet pounding into hard wood floor.

(*WOMAN IN SLIP AND SHAWL is caught up. Ghosts march up and down the
aisle chewing tobacco and dancing with their thighs and stomachs. The room
is fragrant with cayenne and pork, and Mother's hands throw themselves up
and out again, like they did in the days of birth pains. Legs move up and down.
Shout precious memories into the carpet. She drapes herself over pew and casket
while women in fruit and flower lay white sheets across her legs and fan her face.
Quake and quiver and tremble of hand.*
    Beat.
    *The lid of the casket is closed. Father stands in the back, by the door, calling
out.*
    "Wife! Wife! You doing all right? Wife? . . . You . . . doing . . . all . . . ?"
*WOMAN IN SLIP AND SHAWL, still caught up. Quake and quiver and tremble of
hand. Lights change. The kitchen.*)

BLACK MALE:
Mackerel fish, cut open and cleaned
One tablespoon of olive oil, save for anointing every member of
household
Medium leeks, seven
Spit three times
Let cool, then serve. Be cool, then serve. Warm hands in the steam.
Rub together until you feel the friction. Until you feel the spirit. Until

                                                 Working the Work

you feel the soul return to your body. Serve yourself first . . .

WOMAN IN SLIP AND SHAWL:
Let the guests serve themselves.

BLACK MALE:
I be waiting for people to come to the house after they leave the burial ground. Father removes his coat and sits quietly, his foot tapping to rhythm. Brother sleeps in a box underground. This house changes. Aunt Emma dances in her blood-soaked smock. Mother holds her hands up in the air, feet stomping into hard wood floors, lips loose and rolling words—unintelligible. Intellectual language between her and the ghosts. The fish is waiting for invited mourners. She speaks in tongues. Father waits for the walls to cave in around us. Brother's body ascends. Carried off in the arms of Eddie Kendricks. Garments, new and flowing—garlic and olive oil and cayenne on our faces. We sit, living in a box with one window—walls turning. Changed. There will always be music, and seasonings, and free-flowing garments. No shoes. From now on. Mother's steady rhythm and rapid dance dent parquet floors. The walls cave *out*. Open air. We sit, living in open air. Changed. Father drinks and smokes with trembling eyes to Otis Redding and waits for redemption. Mother holds onto a doorknob to sustain herself, and dances. Bopping head tilted toward rapid feet. There will always be music and free-flowing garments in this house. Open air. Aunt Emma bustles up a path toward Zuni dirt roads. A bird's secret dance through ancient mesa-top ruins, amid song and prayer and sacred recipe. Ending this offering. Native Negro woman with man's hands, bestowing blessings on us all, moving . . . up the hill . . . bloody linen skirts traversing to a six/eight pulse.
(*Lights fade to black*)

Projection: Common Contemporary Preoccupations of the African American with Africa

(*WOMAN IN SLIP AND SHAWL proceeds to podium. WOMAN IN GOWN exhibits cards. BLACK MALE makes maps across the outline of his body.*)

WOMAN IN SLIP AND SHAWL:
Common Contemporary Preoccupations of the African American with Africa:
1. The Ankh—An Egyptian symbol of life and prosperity.

2. The Pyramid—An Egyptian architectural structure.

3. The Dreadlock—A process of matting, coiling, or twisting the hair into cylinderlike locked positions. Most effective with Negroid hair, but occasionally appropriated by other cultures and races. Most often this style of matting dead hair follicles with living hair follicles is fashioned with the assistance of numerous Negro hair products, also a preoccupation of the Negro; the most popular products being beeswax, African Hair Pride Pomade, Dax, or any hair product containing shea butter.

4. The African Mask—Self-explanatory.

5. Mud Cloth or Kinte Cloth Textiles—Patterns thought to come from West Africa, printed onto woolen or cotton fabrics.

6. The Eye of Osirus—Also an Egyptian symbol of prosperity

7. Africa—The continent.

8. African heritage, origin, and a return thereof.

(*WOMAN IN GOWN proceeds to podium, reads from index card.*)

WOMAN IN GOWN:
According to "Blacked Out Through Whitewash" by Suzar, 1999, "Based on the evidence of recent findings, modern white science has officially declared that ALL of present humanity came from one race . . . the Black race—the oldest race. Scientists have unearthed the ancient bones of a Black African pygmy woman who is indisputably the mother of humanity . . . a woman who lived 20,000 years ago and left resilient genes that are carried by all of mankind. This overwhelming evidence shows that Africa was the cradle of modern humans. The story the molecular biology seems to be telling is that modern humans evolved in Africa 200,000 years ago . . . therefore white skin is a form of albinism. Frances Kress Welsing, author of "The Isis Papers," argues that the albino Caucasian "came into being from Blacks; Born of coal black parents. This albino gorilla named 'Snowflake' has platinum blonde hair, white or pink skin, and blue eyes." Similarly, according to Suzar, "other scholars theorize that Africans who migrated to Europe and were caught in the Ice Age, gradually lightened until their genes mutated to adapt to the scant sunlight, thus producing a race of whites."

(*Lights change. Dirt roads of Ghana, West Africa. The women vanish behind a scrim, THE BLACK MALE proceeds to the podium.*)

BLACK MALE:
Himself
Jesus
Is changing winding sheets
In New York,
A final kiss on
Unleavened head.
The flesh embarrasses.

One: The sun, a puissant flame circumnavigating; the sky: magenta acquiescence surrounding; the ground: terracotta water color omnipresence; Kwabina: cool cobalt skins pulling through azure shadows and smiling, holding my hand up hills and over ditches, over the cool calm of the ocean waves and sugar waters, little girls with licorice hands yelling sankara from the side of the road, load of fresh fruit balanced on top of their heads. The dead are calling from Suruwi waters where daughters dance to the drum. Kwabina and me, we hitchhike to Ashiemen, in the car of men and red leopard upholstery moving too fast down dirt roads. Kwabina's girlfriend lives in the marketplace of Ashiemen, near a kerosene lamp, in tin and cardboard condominiums, spilled oil and roosters screaming. We weave, he and me, through alleyways and over sewer ditches to find her. Florence: sorrel blush dappled with citrine hues. I think she is asking him for money, and he is asking her for touches. Ashieman is an old woman in vapid dress and platitudinous mask. Ashieman is perfumed in goat meat, and hickory and yellow yams tonight. Florence is happy for two hundred cedes and the touch of cobalt pulling through azure blue shadows. Ashieman is asking why I come to this earth with glamorous ideologies and mystic expectations. He and me, we move too fast down upward hills. In Legon, I trade poems with A-level students, and Kwabina is happy to receive a music box from a Milwaukee woman who once played Desdemona to his Noble Savage. She has sent him a couple of dollars and a photograph of herself. She is plain, I think. She is old, in drab jeans and shirt and wide flat ass and damaged hair. Damaged skin stretched across sticks of bone to dry. She has sent him a letter reminding him of her visit last year, her first time on this terracotta earth, her first time having this earth in her, and she has sent him an application to Milwaukee Technical College, and money, and pictures of her hueless face smiling in front of a daisy yellow porch. She has enclosed an opaline mirrored jewelry box from Woolworth's or Pathmark or someone's garbage can, and it is ugly, very ugly, like her, and I am angry for the memory she holds of red clay soil, cobalt, and azure between her pointed knees. Ugly angry. Kwabina tells me he'll fill out the application to Milwaukee Technical College and send it to her, not this year, maybe next year, not now, maybe then. And he'll bring drums with him to Milwaukee, from Kumasi's wood-carving village, and he will sell them for at least one hundred Milwaukee dollars each, and he will be rich, he says, because there are no drums from Africa in America anywhere, and it means nothing that his father's blood covers the floor Kumasi, and it means nothing that Kwabina cannot read and he cannot write and he has no mother except for the apathetic hands of Ashieman and cast-iron fingers scraping Elmina's ocean floor, he will move to Milwaukee, not this year, maybe next year, not now, maybe then, and he will bring drums with him to Milwaukee, drums from Kumasi's wood-carving village, and he'll sell them for a lot of money, because there are no drums from Africa in America, and he will be very rich and very famous, for bringing these drums, and then he will retire in Freetown and become a chief and I will, if I want to, also become a chief, in a neighboring village, and we will be Christian, and we will always race down upward hills holding hands, and by then Florence will be out of his mind, because she only wants money. There are no drums from Africa in America. Anywhere. He will forget about Florence: citrine dappled blush . . . she only wants money. There are no drums in America from Africa anywhere. None. No drums. There will be three children, one boy, two girls, not now, maybe then, and when men come to his home to ask to marry his daughters, they will offer gifts and good wine . . . Ashieman walks slowly away from me, spitting up blood carrying seven suckling corpses from her tit, and I am ugly angry very ugly and I am: a thick asphalt gray, and he is: looming blues washing up poppy orange and there is: no sky right now, and no drums . . . from Africa . . . in America . . . anywhere . . .

(*Interacting with the MUSE-ISHAN*)

Two: He and me, we play tricks on white faces in Nkrumah circle. We hold hands and walk up to white faces and I speak gibberish and Kwabina tries to interpret and the white faces are confused and upset because they can only understand French, German, the King's English, and they are white faces turning red, opaline masks bleeding, and I speak gibberish and Kwabina tries to interpret, his hand in mine, and they demand French, German, the King's English, and syllables strung haphazardly roll from my tongue, tongues as ancient as Hittite dances, rapid and loud, and clear, like storefront basement sonatas, eclectic dialect, ecclesiastical phraseology, anti-ecumenical phonetics, talk, talk, talk, loud, to shouting opaline masks, and they scream, speak French,

German, the King's English, and I break, I break inside, break my jumbled dialect, break up my fallowed ground, disrupt my holy tongues, and I scream back, Ga Twi Fanti Ga Twi Fanti Ga Twi Fanti . . . their language, not your language, not my language?, their land, not your land, once my land . . . not my land . . . not my . . . land.

(*The women, visible behind the scrim, have become silhouettes of nude bodies walking through trees. Endless walking. Girlish laughter and whispers amplified over drums. THE BLACK MALE speaks with trembling recollection.*)

BLACK MALE:
Three: Her carrion, damp shiny, bulbous-black, dusky dirt, painted earth of eyes and dead of night, hill of iridescence, lips and lid of colors, dun, dark, darken. Impervious face of mirrored earth, thick, black as coal, Kohl-black, wash of pink and red and baby blue pale across the terrain of obscurity. Smooth face, inviting earth, quake and quiver of cheek and sucking lips, eclipse of lash and rising brow. White hands marauding her dusky earth, nipples wedged between fingers, white faint fingers touching crevice of land, wet, black as coal, Kohl-black inviting earth. Milwaukee white hands, King's English hands, milky white fingers, fingers pallid, cold, bleached hands traveling, frost moving across sable penumbra, sooty dark, resplendent earth. She leans in with knees crossed and toes crammed in heels. Fake ore of gold, foreign and fashioned into something of nothing, lynched and hanging from her lobes. Imitation stone of paste catching no light, dead, buried above the ground of her hands, no light, dead on third finger. German Rastafari leans in, touches ass and sips gin from her bottom lip. Blonde roots meshed into sickly turds of apple green. Tresses falling over shoulder, caught in bulbous constellation. Red, Black, Green thread entwined and roped around his waist, pale, sickly blue eyes and blonde lashes, marauding her neck and thighs and shiny ass, then leaving change, consuming last of beer, and taking hand—and taking her, away from Nkrumah circle, through crowd of vendors and kerosene light, from the sound of yelling voices and open call, up the road, on foot, foot on terracotta soil, to tiny field, not far away, out of the circle, just left of here, on foot, foot on earth, earth in his hands, and finger in, then lay it down, and pull it up, and bend it down, and rend the veil, the veil twain, pallid stake pushed into dusky earth, and steady motion and rock and roll, and Mother Land is on her knees, frosty fingers in, fake gold swinging off, corpses dangling from ancient ears, and nothing like this, dark and wet and smelly too, on Mein Stein Strasse, or cobbled

hill. Blonde snakes fall over face and now stand up, saliva mouth, and scrotum breath, now on two feet, feet on the ground, terracotta soil, and open hand receives the bills, and folds them into a shoe and she smoothes back her plastered locks, fried and sheened, and spits out the taste of pubic hair, then returns to the circle, where we wait . . . we wait our turn, to reclaim this land.

Four: He and me we share the fish and share the beer and Mother Land, who sells herself and the fruit thereof, and I am holding a breast in my mouth and fingering the ass and he is inside her and we are sweating. Azure shadows. Crimson lipstick spread across a blaze mouth. Calloused hands kneading big thighs fragrant with cum and spit. He and me we share the motion and rhythm and money for her willingness and she is impatient with the stabbing and the spanking and the biting and she does not dance to our percussion. We have not paid enough for two. To cum a second time and I am on my back feeling yearnings and she is on my stomach feeling nothing, and Kwabina is behind her feeling impervious, and the moon is a voyeur masturbating beneath a sheath of sky, and he and me, we share perversions. Fried hair. Cherry fire broken nails, digging into terracotta earth, and I say I want, I want the, I want the, give me the, my turn, to have, the, yes, I want, I say I want it now, speak it now, I want—

French, German, the King's English!

I have not cum yet and I demand, give me my turn, to have the, I want it now, I have come to be baptized, I have not cum, and I have come to be baptized, and she says pay first and lights a cigarette and says pay again first and Kwabina grabs a fistful of grass to wipe himself off. Her dress hiked up still, fried hair escaping from behind her ears and neck, the blues jazz whistle of early day and the hum of sleepy-eyed skies, land where my father's must have died, over a bed of nails. Here. And I am not enough inside. I want to push in and be and call it a place and make my bed and stay but it she has no place inside herself for me, has not made room for me or him, or the white mask threaded with blonde locks, or any of us, who want a home inside her self. She laughs at my teary eye and heaving breast and erection spilling from zippered pants, and she has not made a place inside her self for me or him, or any of us.

He and me we share the cigarette and the hands and she finds another face in Nkrumah circle and he and me we share our hands and the hills and the sky and moon, and Ashieman is an old woman over us in vapid attire, laughing at the sun, a flame circumnavigating through a magenta sky. The ground: terracotta soil omnipresent. Kwabina: cool cobalt skins through azure shadows. I am a thick asphalt gray. There are no drums from Africa in America anywhere. No drums . . . Not anywhere.

(*Show lights up—back to the beginning. VOICEOVER of questions. WOMAN IN SLIP AND SHAWL takes her camera and snaps photos of BLACK MALE. WOMAN IN GOWN plays the piano and sings her aria.*)

Projection: Hell No Won't Be No Black Male Show Today (Due to Technical Difficulties)

(*BLACK MALE looks out over the audience. Backs away.*)

BLACK MALE (*to himself*):
Huckabuckin' . . . The ghosts are huckabuckin' round your bed at night masturbating you empty, demanding rent and laughter and food-stamp tithes . . . each morning no mercy, each noonday no cool to calm your village fear . . . you be marginalized on Fulton Street, vomiting upwind into the face of your Latino buddies who welcome you back from your European tour with beer and blow . . . you all be composing broken bilingual dramatic and lyric verse 'bout Bakongo slaves singing ancient freedom and resistance songs from the silver mines of Zacatecas and the sugar plantations of Veracruz building themselves a new land—cuz you and your Latino buddies know we the same nigger . . .

(*A chant, back against the wall*)

We
speaking one same nigger
language in the
same nigger
neighborhood

we the
same descendants
of the same souls
from across the water
brought back
together
in urban nigger realities
and the niggers

who don't know we
all the same nigger
are the niggers
who can't speak nigger
bilingually
and that's a damn shame cuz if all of us
who the same nigger
spoke the same nigger language
we wouldn't have to be the nigger
somebody made us
we could be our own nigger
a new nigger
who's one nigger
living the same nigger urban reality
and then and only then
can niggers who think they ain't
niggers at all and don't want nuthin' at all to do
with nigger music
nigger poetry or niggers period,
well until they learn bilingual nigger
they can't even have
conversations with niggers
about no longer being niggers or
perpetuating that word
nigger . . .

(*BLACK MALE writes frantically on the blackboard.*)

WARNING: Li'l Kim iz not at home waiting for you in thong and lip gloss with Foxy Brown, who is also not at home waiting for you—they do not call you to discuss their reinvented ideas of black blue-collar contemporary feminism in Popular Culture and its influence on Versace and Prada
WARNING: The slam judges don't know the difference 'tween a sestina and a simile
WARNING: This may be hazardous to your health
WARNING: Broadway is only interested in you posthumously
WARNING: Publishers aren't buying books about nuthin but your tragedy
WARNING: The record companies want to buy you and your publishing rights with free Hilfiger gear (for the poem your father died for), want

to mix it to machine drum samples that drown out the verse—want uninformed theory about revolution. Want to edit all terse language that may offend the money people. They want to dress you in spandex, put a glock and a blunt in your hand, and stand you under a Phillip Morris sign on stage at a bar mitzvah bash. They want your *black* ass, not your *black* art . . .

(*To himself again*)

And you be dreaming' of dying naked in Andy Warhol's arms . . .
Huckabuckin'. The ghosts are
Huckabuckin' round. Huckabuckin'.
The ghosts are huckabuckin' round your bed at night.

(*A final prayer in final fetal position*)

E'li, E'li, la'ma sabach'thani?
No show. Not today. No show.
Please, turn off the lights.
I'm sorry.
I had intended to . . .
Please.
Lights out.
Please.
I'm sorry.
No show.
Please.

(*Lights fade to black. End of show.*)

Maiana Minahal

Maiana Minahal is a poet and educator. She is the author of the poetry collection *Legend Sondayo* (Civil Defense Poetry), and of the chapbooks *closer* and *Sitting Inside Wonder* (Monkey Press). She received her MFA from Antioch University, and was formerly director of the Poetry for the People program at the University of California, Berkeley. As an interdisciplinary artist, she created a collaborative multimedia performance called *before their words* that combined poetic narrative with precolonial cultural traditions of the Philippines. She has performed and taught poetry workshops throughout the United States and in the Philippines. Minahal was born in Manila; she currently lives in Oakland, where she teaches writing.

Untitled

"What is your style of facilitation? What is your history of facilitation?" Sharon Bridgforth asked the group of us around the table. "What is the tradition that your tools of facilitation come from?" Her questions made my blood pump faster. I was one of a small number who had been invited into this diverse group of women teachers and facilitators-in-training, and we were sitting around a table in a small room in Austin, Texas, one weekend in April. When I came to the facilitator training for the Austin Project and for Sharon's Finding Voice method, I had come swimming in all my many selves, my carefully constructed identities. Much of how I valued myself and my work had recently suffered a crushing disappointment—I was wounded by a badly broken heart, a gravely demoralized spirit. I had been working with students (the majority of whom were of color) at UC Berkeley, trying to help improve their writing and teaching them pedagogical methods for creative writing. As the year progressed, I discovered that a small but influential group of provocateurs had gained a stronghold over the class; they were not at all interested in learning new pedagogy, but continued to remain in the class to use it as a forum for acting out their rage on other people. They banded together during class to attack other students and to wear me down with power struggles, claiming they were only acting to maintain the radical politics of the program. They tried their best to bully me, as instructor, into officially rubber-stamping their punishment of anyone in the program that they deemed politically inferior. I was disgusted and dumbfounded by their mastery at manipulating the rhetoric of militancy to justify their abusive behavior; and more damaging yet, their constant attacks and grandstanding in class succeeded in making me feel more insecure as a teacher as the year progressed, and I could not find a way to stop feeling powerless and change the situation. I became so emotionally triggered that I was unable to name their attacks for what they were. Much later, and too late, I would recognize that, in a program whose goal was to empower marginalized young people through writing, these students were manipulating the safe space in order to lash out at the people around them. More than the institutional oppression they had suffered in their lives, what most poisoned these young people was their refusal to honestly recognize the places where they held privilege alongside their oppression; and so they continued to justify the ways in which they perpetrated violence on others in response to being oppressed

Working the Work

themselves. That refusal stunted their ability to transform their rage into anything more illuminating; they were trapped in the limits of their own personal pain and never achieved a greater level of insight nor activated their potential to respond constructively to oppression. My unsuccessful attempts to challenge the ways they engaged with their suffering in the world would raise deep questions for me about how my own internalized oppression kept me locked into destructive dynamics with them, and how that ultimately destroyed my visionary leadership and potential to transform the situation.

Don't tell. You'll only get in trouble. You'll get us in trouble.

When Sharon asked us about our facilitation styles and about our history of facilitation, I found that I had to take a deep breath. She may as well have asked, "How did you facilitate the fights your harried parents had every week after your family immigrated to this new country? How did you facilitate your parents' inability to explain in English, to the judge sitting on your parents' case, that the landlord had never fixed the shower in your basement apartment and sued your parents instead so that he wouldn't have to pay to fix it?" These incidents forged my first understandings of my own power and powerlessness, as a young child desperate to facilitate a just and humane resolution to situations where my family was systematically isolated, socially and economically, and thus made vulnerable to others who knew how to take advantage of the system better than we. Because I was suddenly cut off from access to my family history at a young age when we moved from the Philippines, I had no stories or firsthand experience of positive role models in my family for proactive and successful facilitation skills. The most I learned of facilitation would come decades later in college from my professor, the Black poet June Jordan, who hired me as her teaching assistant. But her style of facilitation carried the aura of celebrity: she told students what to do, and they did it. If they created problems, she kicked them out of her class. Her style worked for her, but it would not work for me. My path to leadership looked very different from hers; I had a particularly different set of oppressions to dismantle, and I was still trying to figure out my own relationship to authority and authenticity as I moved forward in my teaching work.

Why should anyone trust me to be a leader?

And how did I end up at a workshop on improving facilitation skills? Specifically, how did I, a queer woman of color—as well as a silenced immigrant Filipina child adjusting to U.S. elementary schools who later became a withdrawn teenager and honors student that never spoke in her high school classes—how did it happen that I would be called to the path of facilitation? How did it become possible for me, through art and writing, to become a teacher and leader within my community? That road began in 1994, when I signed up for June Jordan's Poetry for the People class and program at UC Berkeley. Little did I know then that what I would learn in this program would not only transform my relationship to my own creativity and writing, it would also empower me with the courage to name and dismantle long-standing secrets in my family and community. My own emerging leadership qualities were slowly unfolding; what I learned as a student in the program would transform my very sense of self. From that first class, I began to believe in my capacity to be creative as a writer and thinker, and unexpected areas of growth cracked open for me. Challenged by the rigor of an artistic practice and supported by the camaraderie I cultivated with other student artists, I began to feel empowered to make changes that I had previously thought were not possible. I was able to start naming myself on my own terms, both as an artist and as a person. I began to believe it was possible for me to dedicate my life's work to the creation of transformative art grounded in a model of social justice. I was able to accept my queer sexuality, and I came out to my family and friends. The decision to accept myself as an artist liberated me to accept myself in every other aspect of my life, and the community of writers I had found in Poetry for the People was integral in making my journey to self an empowering and successful one. After I left college, I continued the same work for many years and delved further into teaching for writing programs in the local community. And then, three years after June Jordan passed away and twelve years after I sat in my first class with her in Dwinelle Hall at UC Berkeley, I applied for and was hired as the new director of the program. I was elated; I had come full circle. I had been given the opportunity to instruct a new generation of poets coming through the same program that had helped me to grow in ways far beyond my wildest imaginings. It was with this faith, this idealism that had inspired me for the past twelve years, that I entered into my new position. And so, in my first year of directing the program, I was tragically under-prepared for the blow when students in the program that had irrevocably changed my view of myself, college-age students of color whose experiences I could relate to—when they perpetrated the most abusive and vicious behavior in the classroom that I had ever seen in all my years of teaching. I was devastated, and completely unable to reconcile these students' actions with my expectations for the program.

June, please give me the strength to name this truth.

Poetry for the People was founded on the principle of democratic education, the aspiration of shared power inside the classroom. Yet students deliberately manipulated that collective ideal to create power struggles and to tear down my vision and leadership. In class after class, one disruptive student would verbally attack me, and then another or more students would join in. Because I had been trained as a facilitator and writing instructor to believe that my most important job was to create "safe space" for students, I chose not to exercise my power and not to kick them out of the program when I should have. I also knew that kicking them out would provoke a bigger fight than what I, a woman of color and first-year adjunct instructor on a limited contract, had departmental support for at the time. So my response to their attacks was restrained; I responded even-handedly to their outrageous behavior because I did not want to shame young people of color in yet another classroom. I naïvely trusted that this tactic would call forth their personal integrity, that they would modify their behavior without me having to resort to disciplining them. I was wrong. The attacks only intensified, as the rest of the class watched, fearfully and silently. The end result was that I lost the authority I needed to lead the group through the difficult work set before us. To my detriment, they had successfully used the fuel of rage to position themselves as those most authentic and best suited to dictate the dialogue of the classroom and thus, to steer the goals of the program. As a woman of color teacher who was already contending with stereotypes that predisposed students to disregard my leadership, once I lost my authority inside the classroom (when I never had any outside of it), I was at a loss for where to look for role models or resources on how to get it back. The disruptive students were then emboldened to act out their rage unchecked. Their abusiveness peaked when they banded together to attack one (white, female) student during class, reducing her to cowering in a corner, before they dramatically walked out of the classroom, only to then yell from the open doorway at those of us who remained, threatening that she must be removed from the class. I was numb with shock. Not only had I never experienced hostility in the classroom to that degree before, I had never expected that kind of behavior from students of color who claimed to be politically radical. Their actions devastated me to the core; they had betrayed my hard-earned faith in working within a framework of community and collectivity.

What were the reasons, the *wrong* reasons, that I allowed the students to define the terms of authenticity? In my community work, I had been trained to believe that students were not only my community, but also my constituency, and that I had to win them over to my vision. I see now how this was inaccurate. Their roles were as students, and my role was that of their instructor. If I had listened to my intuition, I would have seen that my recognition of their refusal to face the ways in which they themselves perpetrated oppression in the classroom threatened the culture of blame that they had created in order to leverage their own power in the class, and I would have seen the real reasons why they needed to constantly attack me. I believed that I could redirect them towards my vision for the program, but again I was wrong. I let my trust in myself be sabotaged by my own conflict over the privileges that I have had, in spite of immigration; although my siblings and I grew up working class immigrants in the United States, our solidly middle-class family history in the Philippines helped us overcome many of the economic barriers that face other immigrants. In my community work, there was no conversation about how activists grappled with their own contradictions in identity, which reinforced my continued conflict and the loss of confidence in my own authenticity.

How do I find a way to stand up to them?

I was demoralized in a fundamental way, and it killed my dearly held idealism that revolutionary artistic practice could create transformative social change. When I lost that faith, I lost touch with an important part of my identity as an artist and catalyst for social change. I was heartbroken through and through. I felt isolated in all the intersections of oppression that I had always been told that I was subject to as a queer woman of color, the same areas of oppression that I had been working my entire career to fight. And yet, it seemed to me that these same oppressions were still able to ensure that I would not be able to succeed in a leadership position at that university. It was even more personally painful because the attacks I suffered took place within circles that I had grown to believe were safe spaces within my own community, by people whose experiences of oppression I could relate to. Rather than acknowledge to myself that these students were manipulative, all I could do was feel shame that I was not able to stop them and protect the students in the class who were sincerely trying to learn. I was taken in by my own internalized oppression that told me that the way for me, as a woman, to get through conflict and to become a leader, whether outside or within my own community, was by "being nice," by "thinking of other people first." Indeed, I consistently got this message from my family, and many times even witnessed close friends respond similarly in their own families and in our shared communities. In that classroom, I was isolated as a woman of color who was grappling with the contradiction of working within an institution while at the same time trying to resist institutional hierarchies. When I felt like I had failed my students, I also believed that it was my own fault; the most malicious and misguided students even told me that it was. Caught as they were within the institution, it was easier for them to blame me, just as it had been easier all year for them to perpetuate a culture of blame than to consider alternatives that expanded their perspectives.

How far back does the shame go?

All weekend, I had been plagued by the ghosts of my family history, by how much I had lost in moving to the U.S. from the Philippines decades ago when I was six years old. That all started to break open when Sharon started talking about history and ancestry. A few years ago, after my father's death, a cousin told me that one of our uncles had been a jazz musician in the Philippines. His father, my *lolo*, had disapproved because he believed that his eldest son's jazz playing made him look bad. As an esteemed judge in the Philippines, my *lolo* valued his appearance more than my uncle's dreams, and so he forced my uncle to give up playing a kind of music that was, to him, completely unacceptable—African American music. Perhaps my grandfather believed that my uncle would change his taste to something more acceptable, like classical European music. It was one of the many disagreements with his father that, years later, would lead to my uncle's suicide. So when Sharon Bridgforth described her teaching method as one based in the jazz aesthetic, the moment resonated with me: my ancestor had been culturally enriched and informed by his exposure to African American music (whether my grandfather wanted to admit it or not). And here I was now, having traversed many oceans and numerous time zones, in order to learn about the jazz aesthetic from a queer African American woman. The recognition that these global connections have crossed the boundaries of time and geography has helped me to have a more informed understanding of multiculturalism in the United States, one that includes ancestral history as a site of possible connection and healing.

How can I claim authenticity?

Sharon asked us: "What are you feeling? What is that about? How does it affect your writing?" Since I stopped working with those students, I have had to ask myself, how was I able to and not able to deal with the situation? I see now that my inability to articulate my pain and their abusiveness was directly related to my grief over my father's death, combined with my high level of tolerance for dysfunctional family dynamics. That kept me locked inside a cycle of silence, remaining complicit with abuse that was reinforced by lack of institutional support. At the time, I did not know how, nor was I encouraged, to get the support that would have helped me to change the situation—not from my family, not from my community, not from my then-partner, and not from the rhetoric of activism. I felt completely abandoned by all the sources of community I had come to count on. I had been trained to not ask for help when I most needed it, and to accept the blame if I didn't know how to figure it out on my own.

"What are the things that you know that you tell yourself you don't know? What is that about? And how does that affect facilitation?" I did not believe in myself or in my intuition. I did not want to recognize that my students had entrenched themselves in a culture that was poisonous, and worse, I did not know how to stop them. The group was not working towards libratory practice; instead, they hid behind a twisted militant rhetoric that justified punishing other students as they wished.

I had failed to name my students' rage for what it was: inappropriate and self-concerned, and they were unwilling to acknowledge their own privilege alongside their oppression. I had failed to change the culture of those students that had degenerated into bullying the students and teachers around them. I had failed to redirect their energies towards the true sources of their rage: their disconnect from their own ancestral connections, and their deep suffering as a result of their lost histories. I had failed to step outside of my own fears and internalized oppressions in order to ask for support from my community in dismantling the vicious and poisoned energies of those students. I had tried to create a safe space, but failed to make it contingent upon accountability; the students failed to honor their commitment to share safe space.

How can I claim authority?

As a member of overlapping communities, it was difficult for me to negotiate my boundaries with my students. Because they had many experiences of oppression that I could relate to, I failed to see that relating to their painful experiences did not then mean they should be allowed to viciously act out towards others in response to their pain. By indulging them, I was trying to heal my own unresolved pain and pretending that I could fix it through them. I was triggered by their abusiveness, and responded with the same misguided coping strategies that I had internalized from my family. In the same way that I would have responded to family dysfunction, I applied an internalized strategy to an abusive situation in the community with similarly unsuccessful results. While those students and I may have had similar past experiences with oppression, we disagreed on a fundamental issue, which was how to respond to oppression: I wanted to focus on channeling my energy towards making creative responses, and they wanted to focus on punishing those that they mistakenly equated with their oppressors. In our difference of opinion and strategy, the students saw fit to become bullies in my classroom, while I found myself taking on the familiar (and familial) role of peacemaker who tried to placate their rage.

How can healing begin?

After my aspirations for my work with the program that had laid the foundation for all my creative and political ideals were crushed, I was overwhelmed by feelings of pain and failure. On the heels of my grief from the loss of my father, I questioned everything I believed about art and social justice; I questioned whether I was adequately equipped to undertake the healing work that being a teacher or artist required. I see now that I was completely demoralized to discover that the harshest betrayal I would suffer in my work would come from within the circles of my own communities. I struggled with writing this essay for fear of revealing the "dirty laundry" in marginalized communities of color, but I believe that it is more important to lift the veil on the isolation that continues to gravely damage the leadership of women of color. Isolated as I was within the institution of the university, I had felt disempowered by the need to keep up the appearance of the program as a successful venue for the voices of young people of color, as well as my own appearance as an able and professional queer woman of color, for the sake of my future teaching and financial stability. On top of the difficulties I already faced as a first-year instructor, I had little training in the self-sabotaging group dynamics that can plague communities of color, and was ill equipped to cope with becoming the scapegoat instructor in the culture of blame that the class had constructed. I can only hope that one day, those students can reflect on their actions and come to greater insight on a new way to respond to the same situation.

As for myself, with more distance and healing from this experience, I have learned a great deal about myself as a teacher and facilitator. As a teacher, I refuse to continue to reinforce my own (or my community's) notions of internalized oppression that prevent us from developing better models of empowerment. I learned that rhetoric is never more important than behavior, and that I expect people in my community to act with respect towards one another, even in the most vehement of political disagreements. I learned that I sorely need more role models of the kind of facilitation that taps into students' energies while holding them accountable for their actions. I have grown to see the importance, in this work, of becoming a spiritual warrior who names the truth fearlessly, and that it is also vitally important to become a healer who reestablishes the connections with our true histories and ancestries that have been lost.

In spite of this experience that damaged my idealism at the time, I try

---

Call and Response

to remember that I was able to make positive strides in that class with the students that I was able to reach. I have now come to a clearer understanding of how internalized oppression can harm our communities and sabotage our collective empowerment. Especially for women of color, the difficulties of working within the institution while resisting institutional oppressions can be quite treacherous and painful at both a personal and professional level. Years later, I have returned to teaching with a renewed commitment to models of empowerment that both recognize the contradictions within our communities and also resist the fundamentalism (no matter how radical) that exists within them. I hope that this renewed faith honors the legacy of the spiritual warriors and healers who have come before me.

There is much work to do.

Worship/Singkil

Note: This piece is performed in conjunction with the music and dance of Singkil, an indigenous Muslim dance of the southern Philippines. This dance of varying rhythms revolves around a central female dancer, a Muslim princess. She is accompanied by a female attendant and a Muslim prince. They dance to the music of traditional Philippine kulintang gongs, the stamping of bells on their feet, and the quickening and rhythmical clapping of bamboo poles.

I

before their words built boxes to bind me
before their schools crushed my crayons to dust
before their god banished woman from the garden
before they could whittle my bones down too sharp

I discovered my love, a wide-open door
I discovered my love, a genderless sex
I discovered my love in summer on my arms,
the luminous moon, the rain-singing sky

I discovered my love in the fragrant rain falling
the leaves on the sidewalk, dewy and crisp
I discovered my love in the noisy gray cities,
the streets and the alleys, scoured with wind

I discovered my love, I discovered my love
my sweet precious love, for
you

2

I always wanted to be the one
to take away your pain,
to keep the glass of milk
from spoiling on the table.
I imagined you'd curl into me, untroubled
in the night's long sleep.
I could see myself, the hero
in the story.
And you,
so worth saving.
So handsome and hurt.
So pretty and pert.
I'd give up my best friends for you,
forget my appointments,
let the cat go hungry.
Make my mother leave voicemails.
All in the name of love.
The gauzy dream
of lesbian utopia.
I was running and running
down a long drowning tunnel
that would spit me out
onto the rough terrain
of learning, finally,
how to love myself.

3

I will worship you even if they tear us down
I will worship you
even if they tear
us
down

I will worship you worship you

struggle for love
worship you fight for you
struggle for love

walk with love in my footsteps
love in my breath
love living in us
luminous breath

worship you fight for you
struggle for love
worship you worship you

4

oh
daddy
handsome little
cherry pie / so
gruff / my
man-girl
tender worship
heat / your
hands on my
hips slip a
rose in
blooming

oh
baby
sweet sweet
pretty thing
 / so
tough / my
girl-boy
honey-suckle
lemon drop / your
tongue / a
sun in my
mouth on
fire

---

oh
daddy
sugar baby
suckling sweet
/ so
rough / my
girl-man
diamond starry
sparkle kiss / my
skin / the
fruit juicy
ripe with
bursting!

Robbie McCauley

ROBBIE McCAULEY IS AN OBIE AWARD–WINNING PLAYWRIGHT FOR *Sally's Rape*, and a nationally recognized performance artist and director. Her directing credits include the premiere of Daniel Alexander Jones's *Bel Canto*, co-produced with the Theater Offensive in Boston, which she also directed at the 2000 Sundance Theater Lab. Her recent acting credits include *Circles of Time* by Shirley Timmerck at the Lyric Theater, and her performance work in progress, *Sugar*, at the University of Minnesota and the University of Texas at Austin. She is anthologized in several books including *Extreme Exposure, Moon Marked and Touched by Sun*, and *Out of Character*. She is currently professor of performing arts at Emerson College.

Dear Omi

Dear Omi:

Like most people I love food and sex. There is nothing remarkable about that.

My angst around those two passions has a scream in it due to my having diabetes. Like most pieces I make, *Sugar* was started to articulate and transmit stuff from the energy of the scream. I see, think about, and feel oppression in my life that I know as connected to oppression in the world. I knew and performed from this sensibility when I told my daughter the stories of her grandfathers she'd never meet in this life. Those stories were about them having to go to war to get me to where I could holler against war. My life as a black woman is the lens through which I gaze. Theater is the process through which I focus. This intelligence about what I do is my jazz, gives me permission to play for people. I am also a professor of theater, always from the stage and often in the classroom. Without my theater work I could not possibly teach.

Because the angst and passion about the subject of sugar, the memory of some moments of performing it on another stage, and the materials I had decided to bring (including food), were all I had of the piece by the time I got to Austin for the residency you invited me to do, I knew that I had to trust the jazz. I remember you asking me over and over what I needed, and I kept saying, "I need a piano." You seemed puzzled, but trusting my need, you found me a room with a piano in it, and I started hitting notes. You came in after a few moments to announce that I had about a half hour, and I may not have said it but I clearly knew that I needed to go to the space where the audience was and step into my fear. I hit notes thinking about the range of feelings all the notes depicted until it was time to go to perform. The whole time I faced fear. The whole time I trusted my need to scream and felt the notes play through me instead. I learned in the performance that talking about diabetes to black people, which is always the audience I imagine, no matter who is in the room, has to be beyond truth, has to push people beyond accepting disproportionate dying, that home is earth. I wasn't thinking about Augusto Boal, but later, thinking about Austin, I remembered his stunning statement on page 13 of *Rainbow of Desire*, "Theater is the first human invention."

I have not yet understood what that means to me, but I find it profound. He is now someone I take with me whenever I work. I always bring Laurie Carlos and Jessica Hagedorn for real jazz, and all the rest of the interdisciplinary theater posse. So I came to Austin with *Sugar*, the work in progress—you know, the phrase I've been using forever to say artists have to work in progress, not backwardness, as well as that I'm studying while I work all the time. The other thing I found was that the information for women about how diabetes hurts having sex, and learning to eat right can help is funny enough to say.

Here is a passage I knew from the time I was in Austin had to go in *Sugar*.

Love,
Robbie

Working the Work

Excerpt from Sugar

II

(*Light change down center. She pulls out needles, prepares insulin, shoots up, and begins to eat banana and almond butter sandwich and nonfat yogurt in this passage. Whole wheat sandwich with avocado and lettuce and cheese and tomato and orange juice.*)

When Nikos first met me, he thought I was a junkie. He didn't tell me until years later. It was about 1987 and we were on a bus to march to Washington against the war in Nicaragua. It was my last march until the one last week in Boston against the war in Iraq.

I'd just met him, flirted with him. Like he found out I wasn't a junkie, I found out he wasn't straight. Now he's one of my best friends; I couldn't get through this war without him. Anyway, back then, he told me later, I pulled out my needle on the bus. I don't remember this because it was always such a no-no, but he said the bus was dark, and another friend I was with was helping me, 'cause I had to hold the needle up to the light to see the numbers, like I'm doing now, but when I think about it, now I do it every now and then, especially on buses because trying to get up to go to the bathroom is dangerous. I think people should just do it discreetly when they have to, and it should be accepted, like nursing babies.

(*Moves about down center, exercising*)

Ever since I can remember, I wanted to eat just salad. I wanted raw green things to clean out my body, which was slimy dark green and red mud inside. Instead I ate hot brown food, even the greens were too wet and full of fat white meat. Chocolate cake, chocolate ice cream, peaches and figs, dark bird legs. Wet bitter red drippings later in New York seemed to be the be-all, but I was looking for greens, dry and clean.

The first diets said I could have a drink a day, said I could have a scoop of vanilla ice cream, said I could have a slice of angel food cake. The thing about diabetes is that you're addicted to sugar, like alcoholics are addicted to liquor, so you can't have none. America wants to keep people addicted.

(*Yoga stretches in all three spaces, lights follow*)

Way back a doctor could suspect men had diabetes by seeing the remnants of sugar on their shoes from their pee. Nobody back then cared about women. I was a child with it in Georgia. You know I supposed to be dead. Used to have to pee all the time. Didn't nobody know nothing, and we were halfway-educated folks, never did no particular research, except Aunt Jessie was a closet Black Nationalist even way back then, even though all she worried about was "wonder what the white folks think about anything." Anyhow there ain't nothing about women and girls. When I was real little and had to scratch between my legs and pee all the time, even back then, they kept asking me if I'd been doing anything with the boys across the street. I hadn't really, but any chance I had I'd go rub up against boys, it helped the itch as well as got me turned on to having sex real early, but from the first, if it wasn't for the old ladies wondering if I didn't have sugar, 'cause my sores healed so slow, I'da never suspected. Didn't nobody want to hear nothing 'bout no chronic conditions for children. I'm so glad I ain't get diagnosed til I paid for it outta college. Them Negro folks that brought me up, and I 'ont mean no harm, I'da been dead if them Negroes hadda tried to do anything about it. The ignorance and despair woulda cut me up. They just as well nota handled it, because by the time I did get outta college, I could begin to take charge myself, but a whole lot of shit had to happen first.

III

(Lies down down center, facing audience)

During the transfusion I dreamed I was in a
village of rapists. No one could be trusted.
The women were silent and the men accomplices.
I remembered to look defiant. I was more furious
than scared. Fear disables me. On the falling airplane
first I scream, then instruct the others how to breathe.

I learn from my heart, no longer just a beating thing. It hurts
and heaves and breath gets caught in my chest.
No one can describe the facing of death with
the crappy dimmer dickheads. Still scared o' anything communist.
My father's heart broke for America, mine for the world.
Hot for capital everybody going backwards. California, Canada,
China . . .

(Sits rocking down center)

I wanted, like my mother, to be stronger in old age, but then came my father's heart and the sugar and the war, all my fault. Had I been stronger, I'da stood stronger inside the contradictions of it, and let everybody know what need not happen. I'da looked whatchamacallum, can't say his name, the president who ain't, woulda looked him in the face and tol' him to shut up a long time ago, looked at 'em like the mythical ol' colored women I woulda been by now used to do, woulda said we can change the world, look at us, still here, still clear, all the rhetoric would have served me, if it hadna been for Daddy's heart and the sugar and the war, but myth is myth, and old-time religion, the right thing to do, holding on, and keeping it real, losing the urban wars so that police brutality has been renamed racial profiling which is now against the law even on the New Jersey Turnpike, if alla that hadna failed miserably inside the harsh contradictions of brutal truth, real politics and dead children havin' me wake up weeping like my mother did that Wednesday September morning in 2001, not remembering the day before, both of us older colored women feeling like noncomplicit German grandmothers in 1938, ignoring trains, like any old women weeping in the middle of war.

(Light change over right)

Is there a relationship between health . . . and politics? The authorities, who own the future, now admit it's over. They know both China's capitalism and its medicine. My body is a city. I have stalked sidewalks with long white lovers, with panic and li'l deaths. Late in the last century the United States admitted why my heart was broken. Printed in New England, from all over the land. I am an aberration, it said. Black people were ignored, even by Black doctors. Black cops harassed us just as well. I keep surviving sugar and a breaking heart. If the future is over, maybe we can finally learn from the past. I 'ont believe I can say no more til I fall down a minute.

(Light change, all over off and on)

Once, in Canada, drunk at Stratford on the Avon . . . people there stood in lines to buy large amounts of liquor once a week. It was a semidry town with many drunks. Trying to kill myself, I rode my bike into a tree. When I woke up in the hospital, a soft hand was rubbing vitamin

E oil on my face, all broken. It will heal soon, she said. Afterwards I asked how much I owed. At the desk the people looked puzzled. Pay? Someone spoke to another. I'm working here I said, I'm from the U.S. She wants to pay, someone said. So they wrote down some figures and said twelve dollars, and smiled at me as if they were doing me a favor. They were.

Chapter Five

AFFIRMING CONNECTION

Pre-Show Artists' Performance Texts

A central goal of the Austin Project is to connect national, regional, and emerging artistic voices in the jazz aesthetic tradition. In this chapter, Austin-area artists who presented work as "opening acts" for the Austin Project Showcase in 2002 and 2003 publish those pieces for the first time. Brief biographies of each are included. The artists are Martha Perez (dancer and choreographer), Darla Johnson (dancer and choreographer), Zell Miller III (interdisciplinary theater artist), Jeffery "Da'Shade" Johnson (poet and performer), and Daniel Davis Clayton (performance poet).

Martha Perez

In this lifetime, Martha is native to Mexico City. She has a PhD in cultural geography with a focus on the phenomenology of earth-based lifeways and the Haitian cultural landscape. She has researched ancient ways of knowing from an academic and an experiential perspective, and directs her efforts to shift our human relationship to the earth with the wisdom left to us by our ancestors. Martha's life has brought many opportunities to be amazed at various traditional healing systems in non-traditional settings. Growing up in Mexico, she was fascinated by local *curandero* culture, which fueled her excitement toward ethnographic work. Martha loves to dance. She sees dance traditions as spiritual wisdom carriers. She taught Afro-Haitian dance from 1990 to 2006. In 1999, Martha wrote and choreographed *White Darkness: the body as offering*, a spellbound fusion of poetry, storytelling, and traditional Haitian drumming, dance, song, and religious symbolism. Martha's ability to share the healing power of dance has touched the lives of many movers and shakers.

Roots-dance-jazz: Ayizan Velekete in ink and paper

Ayizan means "Sacred Earth," and her name comes from the Fon people of Benin where "ayi" is earth and "zan" is sacred; Velekete means the same for the Mina of Benin, where "vele" is earth and "kete" is sacred. The Fon and Mina ancestors seed in us the sacred path of Vodoun through this lwa (spirit). In the womb of Ayizan Velekete the child-seed is nurtured to serve the great road of Vodoun— Mother Earth purifies the vodouisant as s/he enters into the healing community. Her emblem is the tallest frond of the royal palm tree; during initiation rites, the Vodoun child is cleansed with this frond, a leaf never opened or soiled, ritually being purified through Ayizan Velekete. She is the highest frond of the royal palm; she is Vodoun—purity, integrity, force, and rectitude. She is married to Legba Atibon, the crossroads' spirit and, along with Loko, she is protector and guardian of the priests who serve this tradition.[1]

Dancing Ayizan in a postindustrial setting is in many ways an extraordinary notion. It is an experiment in time that can only be brought forth by connecting to each other in a sacred way. The drums in many cultures have the explicit purpose to create a fold in time and space to bring forth who we are as a sacred being. The time that we spend sharing the richness of our being is virtually sacred time. Dancing for the deity and embodying her starts by connecting to the earth in love. Our bodies begin tuning to each other with her chant, centering, rooting the voice in the nakedness of being. There is no separation between you and me.

Kreyol sonde miwa oh Legba eh, Kreyol sonde miwa oh Legba eh,
Ayizan viye viye, Kreyol sonde miwa oh Legba an' ye oh [2]

Life experience is rooted in the humus of time. The Vodouisant life reaches to be the highest frond, like her royal palm tree, rooted on earth reaching to the sky, a vehicle between heaven and earth. Human life is lived on the surface of the mirror, the crossroads between dimensions of the world of separation and the spirit-world of oneness. To travel through the mirror, the sacred arts support the body in time and space to bring forth the energies of the spirits. Vodoun unfolds in sacred rhythms—music brings wholeness to the fore of our consciousness. When we experience coming together with the intention of tasting the sacred, we are together in real time as full human beings. The drummed healing arts of Haitian Vodoun transform space in this way. The drums attune us to our primordial being-ness. Dance establishes a connection opening our conscience to the possibilities of exchanging time in the presence of the divine.

Djo miwa sa eh Ayizan do le Vodoun la su do dose miwa[3]

I have asked myself and tried to understand why the drums reach me so. Rhythms seem to be like acoustic codes intended to transform time and space. Dance is attunement to the language of the ancient preserved in the rhythms of the drums—a vibrational field connecting living bodies and the invisibles, the mysteries. The sound of the drums calls the spirit forces to enter into our realm and live in us. Rapture comes at the beat of the drum. Everyone and everything is vibration. All things, whether alive or inert, are fields of movement on this earth. As we dance deeper and deeper into the drummed fields of fundamental particles and electromagnetic waves, our bodies transform into fields of resonance and as one collective body, harmonized, larger fields are created. The ancient ones gave us a path to open these dimensions through a sense of oneness, enraptured. These rhythmic fields are pools of knowledge passed on through aural, oral, spiritual, and kinesthetic language.

It was a dream of the deity of the drums, ounto, which made me "see" the power of the invisible coming through us—vibration and resonance.

As dancers attune to each other, synchronized by the drum waves, the bodies' electromagnetic fields increase in magnitude. The dancer as a vibratory membrane resounds impulses up and down neural networks. When these fields coalesce, dancers are able to carry the force of the *lwa* as a divine horse (*cheval*) mounted by their force.

Ritual space is a crossroads, an opening in time into timelessness where, as humans, we encounter our divinity, our passion, and our need to be healed in a community of those who dance to serve the *lwa*. The vodouisant dances to open up to his/her true self as a path to the divine.

Art brings forth sacredness in each other. The soundscape of Vodoun is a pool of ritual knowledge thousands of years old. Immerse your body in the dance and taste the ancient ways.

Today for us, Creole people, Jazz reconstructs the path to reclaim and remember the ancient ones who knew that the artist is like an alchemist who can transform our inner life by inspiring us in a timeless moment.

Darla Johnson

DARLA JOHNSON IS AN INDEPENDENT CHOREOGRAPHER AND A TEACHER living in Austin, Texas. She was the co-artistic director of Johnson/Long Dance Company for fifteen years. JL/DC performed nationally and internationally in such cities as Los Angeles, Honolulu, Little Rock, Albuquerque, and Hamburg, Germany. She founded the dance department at Austin Community College and has twice received the Teachers Excellence Award. Since 2007, she has worked with the Spelman College Dance Theater, through which her choreography has been performed in Atlanta and in Austin at the Black Arts Movement festival. In 2008, Darla's work was performed at the Edinburgh Fringe Festival in Scotland. She was invited, in 2009, by Northumbria University to the Dissolving Borders symposium, which focused on collaboration and pedagogy in dance. There she created a collaborative dance/theater piece with Nicole Wesley that was performed in Newcastle-upon-Tyne, England, and Dundee, Scotland. Darla received the NISOD Excellence Award in 2009 for excellence in teaching and leadership. Future projects include the publication of a choreography book and continuing collaborative dance performances.

A Woman Scatters

> A woman scatters rose petals in a semicircle
> between herself and the others
>
> "I am half my mother's age."
>
> She folds herself over behind the branch of a tree,
> holding on to the trunk
> head down
> listening
> to chanting.
>
> Her head begins to sway
> and she looks up
> hands climb the tree
> walking up the branches
> navigating the terrain of the bark.
>
> She reaches higher,
> still,

opens her hand
up
watching, head tilted lifted
is it a bird, her mother, her self?
that flies away.

Arms embrace the branches
pelvis glued to trunk
hugging supporting rocking
rustling rattling death rattle
dry leaves falling
shaking
limbs breaking
the tree, the woman
collapses onto the floor
her head touching the fallen petals.

Zell Miller III

ZELL MILLER III IS AN INTERDISCIPLINARY THEATER ARTIST RESIDING
in Manor, Texas, with his wife Marcia and their children Zell IV and
Blaise Marley. Zell is a co-artistic director of Uprise! Productions. His
one-man show, *The Evidence of Silence Broken*, was awarded "Best Out of
Town Production" by the *Minneapolis Star Tribune*. Other honors include
"Best Original Play" from the Austin Critics' Choice Awards for *My Child,
My Child, My Alien Child*, and "Best Original Script" from the Austin
Circle of Theaters for *Radio Silence: a word opera*. Zell is also an award-
winning performance poet, voted "Best Poet/Author of 2004" by the *Austin
Chronicle*.

Eyes of Fallen Genius

Eyes of Fallen Genius
         3:00 a.m. under a full moon
this is where the poets dwell
there are these secret conversations that are happening that no one hears
but God
consciousness is an extension or the pure unfiltered translation of God
and I find myself

looking behind at a long night and thinking ahead to an even longer day
but the seduction of silence
the 4bidden ness of it all
shit
nigga can't help but be intrigued youknow seduced to the
sexiness
yaknow the idea of spirit speaking just for you to translate
3:00 a.m. under a full moon
and I wouldn't know sleep even it kissed me deep and wet
tongue tight and offered herself to me completely
I long for the noise busyness of a home where a 4-year-old rules
but this right here this quiet

                                    brings visions of dreams

I never knew they were not the same
                            visions and dreams

until then
and I remember to be surprised by their entrance
I catch a moving one by the front of its breath and I am moving
light speed
                            wishing for the ability

                        to hear with
Miguel Pinero's ears
Rican and junkie
                    genius and madness
                                                        I
wanna hear them talking
hear them in a muffled conversation until I can't take no more
until I need to put a needle filled with death in every vein until the veins
become 2 small and I find myself in a mirror drawn out
strung out
                        out
                            out there on the edge of reality
floating in o gravity
unshaved and unbathed in some junkie hold up hanging out
etching my manuscript in the ears of the fallen too brave to be heroes

---

I wanna hear children speaking
in broken English and Spanglish clapping out beats with feet and smiling in
the heat that burns like the center of my palm hot from the ideas that brew
and stew in me shit I wanna hear Hollywood calling Broadway begging
then I wanna hear the sound of broken dreams as they splash against the
window of my reality and when death comes knocking I will escort them
cats in 'cause the wind will whisper my name and the sand will hold and
move me through time and space and shit every now and then give me the
opportunity to blow across the bosom and cheek of some whore who whores
for reasons that could be fixed with government programs but she caught
in the bam and boom won't let her groove and body rocking mocking drum
machines won't let us soothe have to keep that body popping baby
yeah
it's 3:00 a.m. under a watchful eye of a full moon I consume the
space
like she

       we hover long shifting focus

Marcia sleeps strong and long
        in dreams that I have missed out
on

it's 3:00 a.m. under a full moon
                    I pray to
see strong with the eyes of Jean-Michel Basquiat
it's the winter of my descent
cold blazed in blue I gather unlike the hunter
boxed in cardboard
            middle class upbringing but the

world never looks quite like I see it
crafting the graffiti in street terms
the words of modern time critics stirs and burns
I bask in every area code but no one hears me
the trustees are blocking my path
they won't let me leave
              I am my own oppression

white powder burned to liquid gold
goal being

straight to
the soul of my sole lingers
and I see
see strong and long
see
all this against the N.Y. skyline
like Jean-Michel
a target for the pen who never wanted the black hand in
I see the daggers in the faces and places
I leave the traces of my pain tattooed to the skin
my skin
again
and
   again
             I am
                    akin
"graffiti will never B art" in the eyes of a vast minority parts
they come

                  they come
                        and I came
all over their daughters' sheets
how is it that I'm not supposed to weep
my mother's voice bounces off the bells
I hear them 2 well

                    see too many of her in these N.Y.

streets
that's all I have I tried to do was speak
                          for
those who can't speak
get it in sync but the timing always falters
then fails
the trustees
            are bothering me
                    they won't let me

sleep
won't let me sleep
        the trustees

are at my door
again
it's 3:00 a.m. and this is where poets live to die

again
and again
        and again.

Jeffery "Da'Shade" Johnson

JEFFERY "DA'SHADE" JOHNSON IS AN ARTISTIC EXPRESSIONIST WHO
blends spoken-word poetry and rap with the disciplines of martial arts,
dance, and stage combat. He believes expression is a way of life and a
path to which all things are connected. Da'Shade has been active in the
National Poetry Slam community since 2000 and was a member of the
Austin slam team, which he helped take third place in 2003 and 2008.
Da'Shade was also ranked twelfth in the world and awed the audience at
the 2008 International World Poetry Slam Finals. He was the 2004, 2007,
and 2008 slam champion of Austin, Texas, and is one of the stars of the
upcoming documentary *Slam Planet: War of the Words*. Outside of poetry,
Da'Shade works on film, maintains an action choreography group called
Cry Havoc Action Choreography, and tours the country with his hip-hop
group Blacklisted Individuals.

For My Aunt

The syringe sent a turbulent lullaby screaming
throughout her body forcing legions of succulent
sirens down already manic hallways
To fondle her heartbeats and seduce the pain of living to slumber.
Her arms are road mapped, taboo tattoos of torment,
From tracks laid into, one too many times.
This song is like a cancer, coursing courageously through her,
Dancing with her blood flow, and touching her in places.
That textbook angels no longer trek
She wants to taste salvation in her skin.
Those mangled memories claw at her sanity,
Begging her to send something to ease their sorrow.
This song feels like love in her throat.
Filthy and forbidden, running rampant under her skin.

Touching those blurry unloved places
Where silhouettes are soaked with regrets.
It's regulating the rhythm within, and until she returns,
Those long blackened tracks feel like hellfire in her arms.
That injection is heaven's doors pried open and
If you look into her eyes, those windows will
Tell you of how angels took flight.
Of how silver-tipped lips, sipped iniquity from over cooked spoons.
And how she continues to push chaos further into herself
In order to function.
This is how she fights the battle within,
How she combats the struggle surrounding her.
She'll tell you what's real, without speaking.
Her gaze can carve its way past the bullshit and expose the blinding
    truth . . .
And the truth is:
Sometimes gain doesn't eliminate the pain of
Being experienced. Sometimes aspirin won't cure
Your headache.
And sometimes salvation can be as vile and
Corrupt as the foulest of sins. I wish that I
Could give her the peace that she suffers for.
I wish that my breath alone could be the song that carries her through.
But as long as she has some shred of hope,
I pray that there is a song out there that can help her change her
    tune . . .

Daniel Davis Clayton

Daniel Davis Clayton is a native-born northeast rural Texas town negro stream of cultural consciousness creative. His recordkeeping preserves green moments unprepared for the picking and stews them with the blues. There is particular instability in verb-visual communication and he admits to constantly constructing confusing colors. This attempt at liquidating language allows snapshots of life to be strung along like the filmmaker's manipulation of multiple moments which can become one when pooling into low places. Clayton has suffered certain bittersweetness in retelling secrets unshared for he's found truth: family roots are sometimes no longer stronger than their fruit.

Working the Work

The History of Jazz

jazz is the kink in my grandmother's hair

I brush
        I brush
     I brush
              and that jazz is still there

jazz is her high yella golden saxophone song
         not quite as dark as the Blues
            long since gone

Dancing
         Dancing
      Dancing

When we walk she hears a tune unknown to me
                Perhaps I am just too young to hear it
     She leads me in our jazz dance
     After three rounds we rest

Jazz is her soft skin
     its notes written in the wrinkles
When I kiss Jazz's forehead she shows off her jazz

twinkling
         twinkling
       twinkling

                 she is my child now
         and when I bend to cheek and kiss
leaves scent of Jazzmine on my lips
              she is my fragrance

My love of the Jazz leads me to feed her soul's food
          She enjoys and does the same
        hints of Coltrane in her name

        That's some damn good jazz, Miss Davis
         don't you

know that?

Then she say to me,
Then why you keep brushing my hair in the morning child?

        so perhaps I should compound my own
        an organic recording locked into tight configuration

Have you ever woke Jazz up in the morning with sunlight and fresh air

Bathed the Jazz   Clothed the Jazz

Kissed Jazz on the cheek with your masculine lips

Walked with Jazz   Talked with Jazz

 Let Jazz lead you in its own dance to a tune you couldn't even fathom
I even washed Jazz's dirty draws

    that's   that's   that's
Loving the Jazz   Loving the Jazz   Loving the Jazz

Hugging the Jazz   Hugging the Jazz   Hugging the Jazz

Needing the Jazz   Needing the Jazz   Needing the Jazz

Feeding the Jazz   Feeding the Jazz   Feeding the Jazz

        oatmeal and bananas for breakfast

Good morning sugah   you are my child now

You see
    blue black Blues gave birth with its yella Jazz gene pool
        (my grandfather's croon and my grandmother's womb)

I return to you when
        ever I'm weary
                   haven't you noticed that Jazz
I came home when I was weary
        couldn't you see the blues in me

your Big Band did she even cooked me rice

You once said I favored the Blues that caught your eye
with whom you harmonized nightly
Gave birth to two Swing Dancers
and a Big Band
being my
mother
the second of three
children
Three rounds then rest
a tradition indeed
Jazz, Blues, Bands, then me.

We are a generational peoples

Some of the other musical forms
Even the Swing Dancers
have forgotten that without you . . .
as if their own creations were immaculate

Baby, everybody ain't got Jesus
everybody ain't got jazz

and so they honor the Jazz in Passover
passing over responsibilities

Birthdays and Christmas are great times to play the Jazz
dust off that wax and
Spin
spin
spin   but those are scratches on our records

As your record
skips and repeats
skips and repeats
skips and repeats

You see, Jazz don't recognize the blues quite so often
Nor Big Bands or the Swing Dancers which prance around the Jazz

As if Jazz owes them something
    jazz is so cool it doesn't even know when it's being played
        nor should it
Nowadays Jazz comes in small increments
I pieced together its partial songs
    and sometimes brush its hair

I cherish the Jazz
Put the Jazz to bed
Wake it up in the morning
Play it and play it and play it and play
    until I knew the Jazz
Gave Big Bands short rests when I formulated my own song
        spending time learning the saxophone
the bass in the Blues is long since gone
                long since gone
I guess I'll be the new bass of my own bit of blues

    I be   Hugging the Jazz   Loving the Jazz
Ensuring my nephews respected the Jazz
        taking its fragrance on my masculine lips

As I pass Jazz along to those pregnant hips
      telling my incubating ovarian child within you, my wife
        the history of her music

                Everything feminine is jazz baby
                     didn't you
                  know that?

There's even Jazz

There's even Jazz

There's even Jazz   in me.

SPOKEN-WORD ORCHESTRA

A Full Script from the Austin Project Jam Session,
December 2005

DIRECTED BY LAURIE CARLOS

*This full-length script is an attempt to do the impossible: to document the
ephemeral, improvised, imperfectly remembered, in-the-moment experience of
one evening of performance by the Austin Project. In 2005, Omi Osun Joni L.
Jones changed the format of the performances at the end of a session of the Austin
Project. Instead of a showcase of local guest artists and individual readings by
participants, Jones asked Laurie Carlos to do a two-week residency and create a
full evening of ensemble performance using the women's writing. The experience
was electrifying for performers and audiences alike and remains the signature
style of performances by the Austin Project. In the script published here,
reconstructed from video footage and performers' notes, we have attempted to
indicate some of the most elusive aspects of live performance in the jazz aesthetic:
simultaneity, presence, breath, improvisation. Our hope is that this form of
documentation is legible enough to be read as well as performed.*

*Written and performed by Florinda Bryant, Bianca Flores, Kristen Gerhard,
Erika Gonzalez, Virginia (a.k.a. Vicki) Grise, Omi Osun Joni L. Jones, Krissy
Mahan, Rosalee Martin, Carole Metellus, Lisa Moore, Courtney Morris, Shia
Shabazz*

THE AUSTIN PROJECT JAM SESSION WAS ORIGINALLY PRODUCED BY OMI
Osun Joni L. Jones with support from the John L. Warfield Center for
African and African American Studies at the University of Texas at Austin
and allgo, a statewide queer people of color organization in Austin, Texas.
The jam session documented here was performed on April 1, 2005, at allgo,
and on April 2, 2005, at the Lab Theatre at the UT Austin Department of
Theatre and Dance.

A Note on the Austin Project Performance and Writing Style

It is important to note that individuals who come to work with the Austin Project are at different stages in the development of their craft and artistic identity; they range from emerging writers, to first-time performers, to highly trained artists. In addition, while these stories come from the performers' own experience, the primary speaker of a piece is seldom its author.

This text is best experienced when read across the page, as one would read a musical score. This clarifies the simultaneity of the words being spoken. Vertical space on the page indicates a group or individual pause, typically accompanied by an energetic discharge or shift. When text columns are placed next to each other, this indicates the words are spoken simultaneously. When text is spread out on the page, the words are spoken at a languid, expanded pace. When text is condensed, it is spoken at a faster, tighter pace. Italicized text in parentheses indicates unspoken stage directions from the original production. Bolded text, especially of the same word spoken by different performers, indicates a moment of choral speaking, usually for emphasis or to increase its resonance. Underlined text should be echoed by other people on the stage. Text with a dotted underline indicates that everyone on stage should speak the word or phrase in unison.

This script is an amalgam of writing by tAP ensemble members, and we have retained their unique spelling and punctuation.

(*Lights up on a stage empty except for eleven chairs arranged in an arc. Each actor was asked to bring a piece of fabric and a pair of shoes or boots. Shawls and cloths belonging to the actors are draped across the backs of the chairs. Freshly cut flowers [also brought in by the actors] are placed in shoes and boots, turning them into vases. These are scattered across the stage.*)

(*Performers enter the space, some from the house, some from upstage right and upstage left wings. A call-and-response begins amongst the performers, as if they are saying to each other, "I'm here, are you?"*)

SHIA:
Na na na na.

CAROLE (*crossing through audience*):
Na na na na.

UPSTAGE RIGHT PERFORMER (*responds*):
Na na na na.

PERFORMER (*crossing through audience to stage*):
Na na na na.

PERFORMER (*responds on a lower pitch and with punctuating hand gesture*):
Na na.

SHIA:
Na na na na.

CAROLE (*crossing through audience*):
Na na na na.

UPSTAGE RIGHT PERFORMER (*responds*):
Na na na na.

PERFORMER (*crossing through audience to stage*):
Na na na na.

PERFORMER (*responds on a lower pitch and with punctuating hand gesture*):
Na na.

(*As each performer crosses to the stage, she joins the voices. The voices build in urgency and begin to overlap each other, gaining in rhythm and momentum. Performers are now crossing the stage and settling into their chairs. Upon seeing each other, the performers smile and greet one another with "na na" and rhythmic hand gestures.*)
(*All performers settle into their chairs, scripts in hand.*)

FLORINDA (*stands*):
I write this hungry
Chewing words like (*sits*)

ALL:
glass.

LISA:
I crushed you, Grandpa.
You didn't break

ALL:
me.

LISA:
I took my first steps

LISA *and* THREE OTHERS (*as echo*):
listening

LISA:
as you

ALL:
died.

KRISSY:
Later, I felt my heart swell, crack, bleed.
I blamed a

ALL:
lover.

SHIA:
Maybe I was mourning you
all you'd never be to

ALL:
me.

LISA:
Your heart broke
long before your chest collapsed.

Your son escaped to the woods
with little brother and a gun.

Your daughters stayed behind,

washing blood from panties.

You hit the calf with a two-by-four.
Your son hit me with an open hand.

CAROLE:
Your wife's tears hissed
on the old coal

ALL:
stove.

ERIKA:
My mother braced herself
at the electric

ALL:
range.

VICKI:
Such a lovable girl
you whispered in your daughter's ear.

LISA:
Don't make me so mad
your son hissed at me.

SHIA:
I stared at yellow farmhouse curtains,
upside down. Bedsprings squeaked.

LISA:
Later, so sad I couldn't eat,
I forgot the day you died.

BIANCA:
I was thirteen months old.
The car I rode in

CAROLE:
jacked up, you under it,

crashed to the ground.

LISA:
Grandma left for the neighbor's.
Did you know I was still there?

OMI:
There?
Is that when I lost my appetite, gained
the knot in the chest, the hollow

OMI (*and* THREE OTHERS *as echo*):
belly?

LISA:
You eye your food
like it's your enemy, she joked.

VICKI:
Love closed my throat.
I lived giddy, on air.

CAROLE:
When she left
I couldn't

CAROLE (*and* THREE OTHERS *as echo*):
swallow.

LISA:
This is the worst thing, I told my friend,
that has ever happened to me.

OMI:
This is the worst thing:
a pain so deep

KRISSY:
it lives before memory, wordless
in the belly, heart, throat.

ALL:
You had been dead by then
twenty-three years, Grandpa.
(*Looking at each other and panting*) Huh, hah, huh, huh, hah. (*Rising in emphasis while making a pumping hand gesture, building in momentum*)

(*Carole stands. She is the primary speaker while other performers echo and loop text underneath her words.*)

CAROLE:
metal tacks on knuckles
rocks
fists
bleach
boots
held in place with scotch tape
leather belts   with silver studs
leather belts
with silver studs
they call it
10 seconds
it's a game
10 seconds

MULTIPLE VOICES (*starting low and sparse, building in intensity and rhythm*):
KRISTIN: rocks

SHIA: metal
tacks on
knuckles
metal tacks on
knuckles

fists

bleach

fists
boots
metal tacks on
knuckles
they call it
10 seconds
it's a game
10 seconds
in the bathroom
a group of boys
shove a kid into the bathroom
so no one sees

they call it
10 seconds

it's a game
10 seconds

in the bathroom
a group of boys
shove a kid into the
bathroom
so no one sees

they make a circle					they make a circle
beat him with belts					beat him with belts
for no reason					for no reason
leather belts with silver studs					metal tacks on
leather belts					knuckles
with silver studs					rocks
					fists
					bleach
					boots
					held in place with
					scotch tape
					they call it
					10 seconds
					it's a game

KRISSY: 1   2   3   4   5

KRISTEN: 6   7   8

KRISSY: 9   10

My biggest fear is getting put in juvie. I wouldn't know what to do cuz there are plenty o' boys in there bigger and stronger than me.

VICKI: My biggest fear is getting put in juvie. I wouldn't know what to do cuz there are plenty o' boys in there bigger and stronger than me.

KRISTEN: so im sittin in my seventh period math class and the cop and vice principal come to get me and i think oh shit what i do? you see last week i got caught taggin in the second wing bathroom / i wrote my name in a stall with a black permanent marker /

KRISSY: you see last week i got caught taggin in the second wing bathroom / i wrote my name in a stall with a black permanent marker / well before that i tagged my girl's name in the third wing and they didn't catch me doing that

VICKI (*stands*): so im sittin in my seventh period math class and the cop and vice principal come to get me and i think oh shit what i do? you see last week i got caught taggin in the second wing bathroom / i wrote my name in a stall with a black permanent marker / well before that i tagged my girl's name in the third wing and they didn't catch me doing that   (*VICKI sits*)

KRISSY: so i thought maybe that's what they wanted to talk to me about so they call me to the front of the room and ask me to empty my pockets so i do and i got a blue marker in my pocket right?
(*CAROLE stands*)

           Working the Work

FLORINDA: **so they call me to the front of the room and ask me to empty my** pockets
so i do and i got a blue marker in my pocket **right?**

so the cop looks at me and says this is
contraband
cuz we cant have markers at **school**
but i just keep my mouth shut right
so then he tells me to turn
around
he puts his handcuffs on me right in front of everyone
in front of my entire math class
and then he takes me away
and the vice principal thanks my
math **teacher**
and then walks me out just like
that and i think **they**
doin all this for a marker? but i
dont say shit you **know?**

KRISSY: in front of my entire math class and then he takes me away and the vice principal thanks my math teacher and then walks me out just like that and i think they doin all this for a marker? but i dont say shit you know?

(The following numbers interrupt the text.)

CAROLE *(speaks as others say "pockets")*: 1

CAROLE *(speaks as others say "right?")*: 2

CAROLE *(speaks as others say "contraband")*: 3
CAROLE *(speaks as others say "school")*: 4

CAROLE *(speaks as others say "around")*: 5

CAROLE *(speaks as others say "everyone")*: 6

CAROLE *(speaks as others say "away")*: 7

CAROLE *(speaks as others say "teacher")*: 8

CAROLE *(speaks as others say "they")*: 9

CAROLE *(speaks as others say "know")*: 10

KRISTEN: i aint ever been arrested before and i aint gonna lie im scared shitless / every time i move the cuffs get tighter round my wrists / they pinchin my skin and my legs are right up against the backseat and its like i cant move and i still cant believe this is happenin

KRISSY: keep my mouth shut /
so then they take me into the
office and the cop tells me
hes arresting me for assault
and im thinkin what? but i
still don't say nuthin just
keep my mouth shut you see i
know better.

FLORINDA: they call my mom and
the cop he takes me and puts me
in the backseat of his car / i
aint ever been arrested before

ERIKA (*stands, speaks at slower tempo*): in front   of
my   entire   math class
and   then   he   takes
me   away   and   the
vice principal   thanks
my math   teacher
and   then   walks   me
out   just   like   that
and   i think   they
doin   all   this
for   a   marker? (*Sits.*)

FLORINDA: / i aint ever been arrested before and i aint gonna lie im scared
shitless / every time i move the cuffs get tighter

VICKI: the cuffs get tighter round my wrists / they pinchin my skin and
my legs are right up against the backseat and its like i cant move and i still
cant believe this is happenin / i was in the lunch line when this kid came
up to me and started messin with me you know pinchin my titties and
shit just jokin around and i told 'em to step off and he just won't quit /
keeps up his mess so i told him wait till we get outside cuz you know i aint
gonna play inside shit i wanna eat right

OMI (*with echoes on <u>underlined</u> words and (inserts) by MULTIPLE
PERFORMERS*): so after we eat we go outside into the yard and we start
messin with each other / you know he's grabbin me (**what?**) and im slappin
at him he pushes me (**oops!**) and <u>i</u> push him back right (**right!**) and then
well im done playin but he just wont quit the little boy is necio i swear
(**held in place with scotch tape**) so <u>i</u> grab him from behind / <u>i</u> put my
hands round his chest and shoulders and threw him to the floor (**metal
tacks on knuckles**) you know to make him stop and he did

Working the Work

KRISSY: you see thats what happened / thats what they arrested me for and they call it assault put a pair of handcuffs on me in front of everyone / i cant move i cant talk im just sittin there the cuffs round my wrists are pinchin my skin and i know not to say nuthin and the more i keep quiet the more angry the cop gets / i was in the lunch line when this kid came up to me and started messin with me you know pinchin my titties and shit just jokin around

MULTIPLE VOICES (*echoing and layering*):

SHIA: sometimes im not sure thats true and i try to/ hold it together but sometimes i just caint let it go/ you know that moment   that thing i hold it/ tightly i just can't get over it (*Carole stands, repeats above underneath the following text, sits*)

MULTIPLE VOICES (*echoing and layering*): sometimes at night   at night/   when im all alone   i turn on the radio turn out my lights   and just listen to the words/ try not   to think about nuthin   bout all the shit   close my door   turn out the lights   listen to the words close my eyes

and i told em to step off and he just won't quit / keeps up his mess so i told him wait till we get outside cuz you know i aint gonna play inside shit i wanna eat right

LISA: mi abuela owns a ranch in eagle pass she got a big ranch no neighbors

VICKI: I

at night you can see all the stars and it aint like here / you know there its different

I

I

I

KRISSY: so after we eat we go outside into the yard and we start messin with each other / you know hes grabbin me and im slappin at him he pushes me

BIANCA: at night you can see all the stars and it aint like here / you know there its different

its like the stars are brighter there for some reason

LISA (*cont.*):	KRISSY (*cont.*):	BIANCA (*cont.*):
its like	and i push him back	at night
the stars	right and then well	
are brighter	im done playin but	
there	he just wont quit	
for some reason	the little boy is	
	necio i swear so i	
at night	grab him from	
	behind / *i* put my	
	hands round his	
	chest and shoulders	
	and threw him to	
	the floor you know	
	to make him stop	
	and he did	

VICKI (*Stands, words float out slowly*): sometimes at night
at night / when im all alone

i turn on the radio   turn out my lights   and just listen to the words /
try not to think
about nuthin   bout all the shit   close my door   turn out the lights
    turn on the radio   listen to the words   close my eyes
go to sleep / you know   its like when you
high   and you just sit
       listen
to the radio   eyes closed   and its like nuthin can touch
you / you know

you don't have to think bout nuthin
    its like you here   and not here
       at the same time
                   and you can just let go
      no worries /   just float

KRISSY (*cont.*): you see that what happened / thats what they arrested me for and they call it assault put a pair of handcuffs on me in front of everyone / i cant move i cant talk im just sittin there the cuffs round my wrists are pinchin my skin and i know not to say nuthin and the more i keep quiet the more angry the cop gets / i cant say shit but im thinkin fuck you fuck you fuck you motherfucker and i want to kick the back of his seat but i cant even move

LISA: You! You!
You! You!

ERIKA: that man / he walks around the school like hes the shit
  short fuck carries a gun he hits the lockers with the night stick and hes always behind us telling us shit like get to class / hope you not as messed up as your brother / i know your family / i know what you're like but he don't know shit cuz i aint even got a fuckin
brother i done told him that twice already

VICKI (*stands*):
you don't have to
think bout nuthin
its like you here
    and not here
    at the same time
    and you can just
         let go
no worries /   just
float

ERIKA (*cont.*):
so i don't know if hes got me confused
with someone else or what but i do know
he be ridin me from day one and just don't
understand why when he caught me taggin he
signed some papers and now hes got me down
as a gang member cuz i wuz taggin my name in
the bathroom so now im written up as a gang
member cuz i got a tag name /

KRISSY:
but i do know he be ridin
me from day one and just
dont understand why
    when he caught my taggin he
signed some papers and now
hes got me down as a gang
member cuz i wuz taggin my
name in the bathroom

KRISTEN: ill lie
down
on the
zacate
and
just
stare
at the
stars

and sometimes / you know
ill
fall asleep
right
there
and
its
safe

OMI: ill lie
down
on the
zacate
and
just
stare
at the
stars

and sometimes / you know

ill
fall asleep
right
there
and
its
safe

ERIKA: im not even
scared
cuz there ain't no neighbors

ERIKA (*cont.*):
    and you kinda feel like /
        you know
      you kinda feel like you high
     cuz you not really thinkin
           nuthin
and its like you high
     but you aint   you just
chillin

                CAROLE: when he caught me taggin he
                signed some papers and now hes got me
                down as a gang member cuz i wuz taggin
                my name in the bathroom so now im
                written up as a gang member cuz i got a
                tag name / shit we all got tag names!

COURTNEY (*stands, calls out tag names, others repeat and echo*):
baby joker,
    sinner,
bj,
          kid one   CAROLE:
frutitas,   baby joker,
  koner,   sinner, bj,
head,   kid one,
    peanut,   koner, head,
güero,   peanut, güero,
         casper,   casper, cuca, 1800s / we've had em
cuca,   since we were in sixth grade and my
    1800s   mommas been callin me gordo since i
(*Sits*)   wuz a baby / that dont mean shit
                     but now my name is on some paper
                     somewhere (*Stands*) next to the word
                     gang member and im in the backseat
                     of a cop car bein arrested for
                     assault?   what the fuck?

FLORINDA: one day im gonna live there on the rancho

with the stars

ive spent my whole life trying   to prove there was a reason

to my being born

sometimes im not sure   thats true and i try to / hold it together

but sometimes

i just caint let it go / you know

FLORINDA: that   ERIKA (*stands*): my greatest fear
moment   is having life swallow me whole—
         that thing   that one day i will make a giant
   i hold it / tightly   leap and have nothing to soften my
   i just caint get over it   landing. what if i cant stop
sometimes at night   falling lower and lower into the
   at night / when im   dark?   la oscuridad
      all alone   peanut / ive spent my whole life
                                       trying   to prove there was a reason
                                       to my being born (*Sits*)

OMI (*Others echo*):
we did everything
together   my dad
he would pick me up   and take me anywhere i wanted to go
one christmas he bought me a go-cart   we would go out to the
country on
the southside   and ride together   in the country

                                                        the stars
are almost as bright   as in eagle pass   on my buelas
rancho /

                          almost

you know my friend   he has a brother fifteen   in juvie   and
sometimes
well be out   and he will just start cryin
      cuz he misses his brother   and i tell him
at least hes   comin back
        my fathers   never comin back
                    he aint never comin back

Working the Work

FLORINDA: he would pick me up   and take me anywhere i
wanted to go

ERIKA (*singing*):
Quiero verte allá en el cielo donde yo te conocí
Podemos platicar el mundo será igual, como en el mundo allá en el cielo
Quiero verte allá en el cielo, caminando junto a mí.
Podemos platicar, el mundo será igual
Como cuando yo te conocí
(*ERIKA sings this verse three more times as the following text is spoken.*)

FLORINDA:
Shhh . . . it's Abuelita's funeral. Mima. She's dead.

MULTIPLE VOICES (*in conversation*):
 That's my favorite color.
 Tia Sylvia picked it out.

BIANCA: And that man standing over there, with the long chongo,
that's my dad, my Papi. He doesn't let me see him cry, only one time,
when Mami and him almost broke up and she didn't let him back in the
house, but this time, Papi's wearing black sunglasses. All his brothers
are too.

MULTIPLE VOICES: And that song, (*Singing*) Quiero verte allá en el
cielo . . .

MULTIPLE VOICES (*in conversation, sometimes* echoing, *sometimes in*
unison): that's Papi's song. It really is him singing it. I swear. I've seen
Papi on stage singing it and it sounds just like him. Girls go crazy when
Papi sings that song . . . especially those older ladies that wear too much
makeup and look at me and call me mija . . . Mija, your papi sings sooo
beautiful . . . I hate that.

FLORINDA: Except, right now, I rather be at Papi's concert than here.

VICKI: The mortuary man, Don Diego put a tape on this little stereo
and put the microphone yes real close to the speakers so all the familia
could hear it on the ceiling loudspeaker.

(In the following section, performers pass the lines around as if in conversation.)

ALL *(singing)*: Quiero verte allá en el cielo . . . . Quiero verte allá en el cielo . . .

CAROLE: That means, I want to see you over there in the heavens.

VICKI: Yeah. How romantic, huh?
BIANCA: Seeing Abuelita up there in the heavens with Papi, singing to her? Wow . . . I'm gonna sing Papi that song one day when he dies.

FLORINDA & BIANCA: I'm gonna cut his long ponytail off before he dies and place it in a frame.

VICKI: No, I'll place it on an altar by the side of the TV where Mami keeps it, that way whenever we watch novelas together,
ERIKA: Papi will always be there . . . with his long ponytail . . .

VICKI: But I don't want to think about Papi dying right now. Not with Mima dead . . .
COURTNEY: I don't know what I'm gonna do now. I want to sing to her too . . . my own song,

(MULTIPLE VOICES can be heard in conversation.)

FLORINDA: I scream over all the noise . . . ERIKA & VICKI: Mima!
ERIKA & BIANCA: Can you hear me?
COURTNEY: I want to sing you a song . . . I
VICKI: hope you can hear it . . .

SHIA: *(Singing)* ummm . . . ummm . . .
ERIKA: Abuelita, Abuelita . . .
ALL: Yo te quiero tanto . . . tanto . . . Yo te adoro, tanto tanto . . . Adiós mi Mima . . . Mima del Eagle Pass . . . Adiós . . .

(SHIA continues to hum the melody under the following text. ALL echo and loop the following text while alternately standing and sitting on impulse in a random order. The speaking builds in intensity and rhythm.)

ALL: you turned my sky
into a dream

Working the Work

i looked at you
when it rained tears,
you looked for me
with watering eyes
        as i grew into a woman

your reflection gave me hope
i didn't understand
you and i were one
a piece of flesh separated by time

i searched for you

in women of my world
in communities
in the earth
in my-self

you are everywhere
you are nowhere

i find you
in Papi's song
        the needle
playing Tejano records
forever revolving
repeating
circular
movimientos of history

you are a butterfly of songs
coming to me like i was your flower
in between cracks on sidewalks
ready to wilt away

you were no warrior princess
or sun goddess of any tribe.

you are my vague memory of
chickens in the yard, fridge full of brown and blue spotted eggs, kitchen
smelling like frijoles con comino, a wave of black hair on my cheek, a
muñeca with a black and red lace dress you sewed for me

i taste you in my water
because water is what caused your death
a gallon of Agua Milagrosa sold to you by a stranger
promising relief for your aching bones and arthritis.
Miracle Water said to have been blessed pure
from the Río Bravo

you told no one.

drank a cup each day
like a ceremony
faithfully reciting
with rosary
prayers of santos, la virgen, and of the Agua Milagrosa

(*The cacophony peaks,* ERIKA *stands. Humming continues underneath.*)

ERIKA: "Dios perdóname por no estar cerca a mis nietos.
Dios perdóname por no confiar en tu fuerza.
Agua, limpia mi alma—mi espíritu—el artritis en mis huesos.
Amen." (*Sits*)

OMI (*stands*):
i taste you in my water.
wonder how much poison i can take

VICKI (*stands*):
just to remember you existed

OMI & VICKI (*syncopated*):
among the border that birthed you and took your life
like so many other women's lives
lost in between worlds
never found

ERIKA & MULTIPLE VOICES (*echo*):
but it's water that tries to show us how to survive

Working the Work

how to adapt to mother earth
trying to tell us something
> is wrong
> out of balance
> is right
> full of perfections

is it our fault water is part of the cycle of life?
is it your fault you believed in miracles?
is it our fault
> that rivers divide countries
> and that oceans feed and swallow civilizations?

FLORINDA: Abuelita, you tried to tell me something with your death.

ERIKA: Papi, you tried to tell me something with your song.

ALL: Water, you tried to tell me something with your poisons.
VICKI: Sky,
ALL: you tried to tell me.
CAROLE: Earth, you tried to tell me

COURTNEY: All grandmothers become water when they leave this earth
All water becomes us when we enter this life

ALL (*echoing and calling*): Mima, I still see you
I still drink from you
You hear that song, Mima, that's my song for you.

ERIKA and BIANCA: Quiero verte allá en el río
Donde yo te conocí
Podemos platicar, el mundo nunca será igual
Como en el mundo allá en el río
Quiero verte allá en el río
Cuidando a todos para ya no sufrir
Podemos bailar, el mundo siempre será igual
Todos nos tenemos que morir
Todos nos tenemos que morir para vivir

OMI: Mima, I still see you

I still drink from you
You hear that song, Mima, that's my song for you
ALL (*echoing*):
Adiós, Mima. Adiós.

ERIKA: Tlazokamati   Ometeotl

(*ALL move to a different chair in the semicircle, crossing the center.*)

LISA: Dear Mom and Dad,

KRISSY: You were queer bashed?

CAROLE: Dad, there's no way I can tell you how devastated I am.

KRISSY: You were queer bashed?

VICKI: In 1993, when I was queer bashed, I called you from the hospital for help, and you said that maybe I shouldn't be gay. But I still want you to appear here and protect me and let me sleep again. I remember how we'd play catch all spring and summer, and you said that if I kept working hard, I could be the first girl

CAROLE: to be a major
league baseball player.

KRISSY: (*as Carole speaks*) Sometime Wednesday
night, someone broke into my

MULTIPLE VOICES (*overlapping*):
Mom, i can't tell you, because
i feel so selfish. if i had
pawned the stuff myself, i
could have given you the
money. you live in poverty and
won't let me help you, and now
this happened and i'm so
embarrassed.
i don't remember what i did
that made you give up on me,
but i am sorry about it. Mom,
i can't tell you, because i
feel so selfish. if i had
pawned the stuff myself, i
could have given you the
money. you live in poverty and

---

won't let me help you, and now
this happened and i'm so
embarrassed.

KRISSY (*cont.*):
apartment and stole
almost
everything I have (except
my clothes). They robbed
me of all my cameras,
editing equipment, my
laptop computer, even my
violin
and my alarm clock. I'm
so sad. And I've been
thinking of you a lot
since this happened.

CAROLE: Mom, i want to tell you i'm scared and sad. it was my creative
outlet, you'd understand that—you'd come home at night and make
amazing craft things—dresses for Kait and me from chicken-feed bags,
even cut-out pictures from fancy wrapping paper and put them in
frames.

KRISSY (*stands*):
i remember delivering meals
on wheels with you (if you
worked second shift that
week) and how i used to
wonder why we had to deliver
them, when we were one of the
poorest families in town, and
how i knew not to ask that
because you would be
disappointed in me.

CAROLE: i know you'd
understand how lost i feel to
have no tools to express my
hope for something better.

KRISTEN (*stands*): Dad,
when you'd get up so early
and work so hard and tell
us how lucky we were that
we didn't have to grow up
in an orphanage like you
did. but Dad, i did lock
the doors and i worked for

thirteen years to piece
together the skills and the
tools i needed for my studio
and i know that you were
proud of me for you taught me
there's no shame in an honest
day's work. and i worked many
days for those cameras.
(*Sits*)

KRISSY:
i understand now, Mom. My
recording women's stories
was my way of looking
after them. (*Sits*)

SHIA (*some echo*): Mom, i know
that you hear strangers trying
your doorknob at night, seeing
if it's locked. i know your
doorframe has dents and broken
wood around it
OMI: (like mine does now) from
people trying to break in. i
know it would just upset you to
know that happened to me. but i
want you to say
ALL: "ssshhhh, it's going to be
all right," and pat my arm.

CAROLE: Dad, when you'd get up
so early and work so hard and
tell us how lucky we were that
we didn't have to grow up in
an orphanage like you did. but
Dad, i did lock the doors and
i worked for thirteen years to
piece together the skills and
the tools i needed for my
studio.

FLORINDA: Dad, you let me put together electric train sets way too
young, and yeah, i electrocuted myself lots, but i think of you every
time i figure out how to wire something together, or to fix and use the
broken equipment people gave me.

FLORINDA: i doubt the person who stole my stuff will be able to figure out how i rigged it.

OMI & MULTIPLE VOICES: Dad, you let me put together electric train sets way too young, and yeah, i electrocuted myself lots, but i think of you every time i figure out how to wire something together, or to fix and use the broken equipment people gave me.

KRISSY:
Mom and Dad, you taught me to
be a fighter, and those tools
they
stole were what i was
fighting with. i thought if
more people knew one another's
stories, they would treat each
other better. i
wish so much
that i could tell you
and you
could bring them back.

BIANCA: well anyway, i can never send you this letter. but i'm really down about this and i'm in a writing group now so i'm writing. even my writing was on my laptop, and that got stolen, too. weird, isn't it?

KRISSY (*with echoes from MULTIPLE VOICES*): anyway, i love you, Mom and Dad. and i will try to keep fighting and keep working hard and keep trying to be a good daughter.

with more love and understanding every year,
MULTIPLE VOICES (*echoing*):
  krissy
      krissy
            krissy
krissy

(*Song break*)
    ALL: I paid my dues
(*This phrase is repeated in rising melody and rhythm. As intensity builds, ALL stand and cross to sit in different chairs. As song continues under text, FLORINDA speaks.*)

FLORINDA: Shaking, trembling, unable to type
Grounds for dismissal to an accounting clerk
A title I don't wear proudly

But it's what I do
Cause baby needs

ERIKA: I sit

Meanwhile he across town claims to be a father
But ain't raised shit

MULTIPLE VOICES: I freeze

OMI: This is me praying
Not to take a life today

VOICE: Freeze

OMI: This is me praying I can survive one mo' day

VOICE (*whispers*): Freeze

SHIA (*stands*): This is me praying
SHIA & MULTIPLE VOICES (*echoing*): That my son is OK in court
SHIA: delivered to a man who pawns baby's toys for rocks
I light a joint (*Sits*)

VOICE: Freeze

VICKI (*with echoes*): Shaking, trembling, unable to type

SHIA: grounds for dismissal to an accounting clerk
A title I don't wear proudly

ERIKA: But it's what I do
Cause baby needs
I sit

OMI: Meanwhile she across town
FLORINDA: She is twenty-three, a b-girl holds down two jobs
KRISTEN: Has two kids and much more of life to see

(*Singing of "I paid my dues" stops.*)

VICKI: OK Ann, slow down baby, what you mean you gonna die?

MULTIPLE VOICES: Breathe, Ann, slow
say again
VICKI: They told you what

MULTIPLE VOICES (*echoing*): Gestational trophoblastic disease
COURTNEY: Cancer spreads at twenty times its normal rate
There never was a baby

VICKI: What?

OMI: I freeze
This is me praying
For him
Not to take a life today

SHIA: Freeze
FLORINDA: This is me praying
SHIA: I can survive one mo' day

MULTIPLE VOICES: Freeze
This is me praying

LISA (*with echoes*): My homegirl Ann is OK
that cancer won't take another smile
from me
as I light another cigarette

KRISSY (*with echoes*): Shaking, trembling, unable to type
FLORINDA (*with echoes*): Grounds for dismissal to an accounting clerk

---

Spoken-Word Orchestra

A title I don't wear proudly
But it's what I do
Cause baby needs

ERIKA (*with echoes*): I sit
In the bathroom at work
My only chance at solace
For a 3 a.m. studio session

FLORINDA: I freeze

OMI: This is me praying
VICKI: My representation of what a b-girl should be
Is enough

ERIKA: I freeze

MULTIPLE VOICE (*with echoes*): This is me praying
The creator bless me
With one mo' flow

I freeze
(*Song returns under text.*)
    OMI: This is me praying
    MULTIPLE VOICES (*with echoes*): I can do more with these lips
Than suck dicks and kiss chicks
    OMI: I freeze

(*Song rises in strength and sound, harmonizing and improvising, filling the space.*)

VICKI: I paid my dues.

(*Song cuts off.*)

VICKI: Shit that scares me:

MULTIPLE VOICES (*echoing and repeating*):
KRISTEN: Inexplicable noises in the middle of the night
OMI: Losing my mind
SHIA: Dying young

         Working the Work

Death
KRISTEN: Disappointing my father
VICKI: Drunk men downtown who get handsy after a few drinks
FLORINDA: That I'm really not as smart as people say I am
COURTNEY: That I'm really not as strong as I think I am
OMI: Maybe all this shit really can't be changed . . .

(*Echoes of this list continue under the following text.*)

VICKI: I am not always afraid.
Sometimes I am brave.
But more often than not I am angry and seething with a rage that
threatens to burst through like a flooding dam.

COURTNEY: Female rage is an ugly thing. Unfeminine, unforgiving
and unacceptable. Make no mistake, in voicing your anger you will be
simultaneously freed and punished. Such is the nature of the world in
which we live.

OMI: This is the lesson my father
tries to plant inside of me, written
on the flesh. Perhaps more from
knowing the place in the world
carved out for little black girls,
my father attempts to save me by
teaching me to never place myself in
harm's way by being too loud. Which
presupposes the notion that there is
any safe place in the world for any
black woman, any black girl child,
anywhere.

KRISTEN: Inexplicable
noises in the middle
of the night
Losing my mind
Dying young
Death
Disappointing my
father
Drunk men downtown
who get handsy after
a few drinks
That I'm really not
as smart as people
say I am
That I'm really not
as strong as I think
I am
Maybe all this shit
really can't be
changed . . .

COURTNEY: I am not always afraid.
Sometimes I am brave.
But more often than not I am angry and
seething with a rage
that threatens to burst through
like a flooding dam.

KRISSY: Unfeminine, unforgiving, and unacceptable. Make no mistake, in voicing your anger you will be simultaneously freed and punished.

VICKI (*with echoes and layers*): Drunk men downtown who get handsy after a few drinks
That I'm really not as smart as people say I am
That I'm really not as strong as I think I am
Maybe all this shit really can't be changed . . .

KRISTEN (*with echoes and layers*): I am not always afraid
And I fight to be courageous each day of my life.
As a child my favorite color was nine
And my Creolemaroon alter ego refers
to more than my family's
diasporic heritage.
I am a daughter of the Baptist tradition
There are no women models of how I might
release my fear
And dream myself a warrior.
These visions of myself:
Rebel writer
Passionate organizer
Fierce in love and struggle
No, these visions, I believe, belong to Oya
I fancy myself neither religious nor spiritual in
any meaningful way
But perhaps the ancestors, wherever they are,
saw fit to link my dreams to Oya.

COURTNEY: Shit that scares me
Inexplicable noises in the middle of the night
Losing my mind
Dying young
Death
Disappointing my father
Drunk men downtown who get handsy after a few drinks
That I'm really not as smart as people say I am
That I'm really not as strong as I think I am
Shit that scares me
Shit that scares me.

VICKI: This is the lesson my father tries to plant inside of me, written on the flesh. Perhaps more from knowing the place in the world carved out for little black girls, my father attempts to save me by teaching me to never place myself in harm's way by being too loud. Which presupposes the notion that there is any safe place in the world for any black woman, any black girl child, anywhere.

FLORINDA: (*stands, echoes of previous text underneath this text*) When I am nineteen, I date.

I see a man who is ten years my senior, a graduate student in the Department of Economics. One night in the middle of conversation he leans in quickly, crushing my lips and pinning me to the sofa.
　　Startled, I feel my body react in fight or flight mode. I tense, shoulders tighten, breath quickens, and my eyes flutter in alarm as he squeezes tighter until he notices the fear lurking in my eyes and pulls away. (*Sits*)
SHIA: Startled, I feel my body react in fight or flight mode. I tense, shoulders tighten, breath quickens and my eyes flutter in alarm as he squeezes tighter until he notices the fear lurking in my eyes and pulls away.

Repulsed by my fear.

COURTNEY: Inexplicable noises in the middle of the night
Losing my mind
Dying young
Death
Disappointing my father
Drunk men downtown who get handsy after a few drinks

Shit that scares me

Inexplicable noises in the middle of the night
Losing my mind
Dying young
Death
Disappointing my father
Drunk men downtown who get handsy after a few drinks

That I'm really not as smart as people say I am
That I'm really not as strong as I think I am

Shit that scares me
Shit that scares me
Shit that scares me

LISA: I can still see him, confused, wondering what it was I saw in him that he simply can't acknowledge.

VICKI: I hate who I become when I am afraid.
OMI: I am afraid and disgusted by what I transform men into with my fear.

VICKI: I hate who I become when I am afraid.

COURTNEY: I can still see him, confused, wondering what it was I saw in him that he simply can't acknowledge. I hate who I become when I am afraid. I am afraid and disgusted by what I transform men into with my fear.
There is no room for trust.

(*KRISTEN echoes as COURTNEY continues.*)
All lovers are potential thieves wooing me into an illusory state of security
 So they can break into my home and ravage my belongings . . .

LISA: My fear turns both of us into monsters.

COURTNEY & KRISTEN: I do not see him again.

(*A pause and energetic shift. ALL return to their seats in a new configuration.*)

VICKI: I rarely feel safe anywhere.

KRISSY: I move about the world not because I am brave
But because I know that I have to learn to move beyond that fear.

VICKI: I rarely feel safe anywhere.

SHIA & OMI (*with echoes*): As Audre Lorde reminds us,

OMI: we are afraid of so many things:

KRISSY (*stands, echoes from KRISTEN*): When we are loved we are afraid / love will vanish / when we are alone we are afraid / love will never return / and when we speak we are afraid / our words will neither be

heard / nor welcomed / but when we are silent / we are still afraid.[1]
(*Sits*)

SHIA: To which I would add

KRISTEN (*With echoes*): When we are safe we are afraid
We will be violated
And when we are violated we are afraid
We will never be safe again

COURTNEY: And when we are violated we are afraid
We will never be safe again

(*A pause and energetic shift*)

LISA: The deceit, the lies, the poisonous flattery, and most of all the
lethal betrayals all moved through the basement like jealous lovers
looking to get even.

BIANCA: And I sat on the basement steps, peering around the corner
as best I could. Hoping to learn these rites of passage that I would
someday cross, wanting to feel the force these adults generated with
such knowing.

(*Canon or round vocal effect—first performer begins text and continues to
the end. At a delayed time, indicated by a slash (/) and bold* **cue word***, second
performer repeats same text from this point and continues through to the end.*)

CAROL: Light-skinned round-
bodied Melba in her white hot
pants; Eddy with her yellow
eyes—if she wasn't already too
drunk to make it; red-headed
Trina—the skinny temptress
in capri pants and midriff
blouse, and her bumpkin
husband Dino; Percy who looked
like **Santa Claus** / and beat
his howling wife on Sundays
while we ate fried chicken and
corn on the cob; the brothers

Herb and Billy—raw and rowdy.
All of them were in the dark.
Grown and disoriented in their
new suburban lives. No bars to
receive their passions like in
The City, no street corners
where loud talking freely
lived and dissolved into the
sky. The suburbs were neat and
contained, so their most
unclean urges had to find the
right locale. And my parents'
basement on Saturday nights
was it. They gathered at our
house full of a tonic that
looked like desire and
sometimes even love, but was
laced with a sinister
manipulation and a ferocious
competition for conquest.

FLORINDA:
/ **Percy** who looked like
Santa Claus and beat his
howling wife on Sundays
while we ate fried chicken
and corn on the cob; the
brothers Herb and Billy—raw
and rowdy. All of them
were in the dark.
Grown and disoriented in
their new suburban lives.
No bars to receive their
passions like in The City,
no street corners where
loud talking freely lived
and dissolved into the
sky. The suburbs were neat
and contained, so their
most unclean urges had to
find the right locale. And
my parents' basement on
Saturday nights was it. They
gathered at our house full of a
tonic that looked like desire and
sometimes even love, but was
laced with a sinister
manipulation and a ferocious
competition for conquest.

CAROLE: (*The last line is overtaken by the next speaker's first line.*) And
Momma was sitting or talking or doing her bop—that sweet country
two-step swing she did. Her eyes torn between rage and regret, trying
not to see the bold betrayals, trying not to linger in the jealousy. Every
Saturday this competition, and my mother always on the losing team.
FLORINDA: The women came to the basement to be lusted after, and
the men came to lust. The room was like a ravenous dick hunting pussy
all night. The stereo pulsed with "Wang Dang Doodle." The full breasts

that dared anyone to touch them. The red eyes that licked their lips as they looked. The hands placed casually, strategically on the crotch or a thigh. This combat had no rules. Loyalty, respect, and passion, free from the need to control, were checked at the basement door.

BIANCA: And everybody danced with Melba—just grind on that booty, just reach for those titties, play the game recklessly, watch her hot pants rise up higher, wet in the seams from sweat and juice

OMI & FLORINDA: and laugh at the nastiness of it all.

BIANCA: I think it's the little things in childhood that cut us the deepest.

CAROLE (*with* echoes *from MULTIPLE VOICES*): And as time moves forward and back, circling to hold a piece of a birthday party, a bit of a Platters' song,

LISA (*layered in*): It's the little things in childhood that cut us the deepest.

CAROLE: the best line from a well-worn story—the original wound is mostly forgotten, appearing only as ghosts at inopportune times— butterflies in the shoe store, nausea at a lover's touch, sadness at the smell of baking biscuits.

FLORINDA: My heart bent when I saw Momma trying not to see Daddy, pretending everything was just fine.

SHIA: I think it's the little things in childhood that cut us the deepest.

COURTNEY (*with echoes*): Real women were vain killers; weak women were pathetic victims complicit in their own abuse; men, even the best ones

ERIKA: (Mommy always said "*Your* Daddy is a good man") were rendered unaccountable in a room full of perfume, push-up bras, and Johnny Walker Red.

(*Multiple voices in repetition and call-outs build to a sassy cacophony, listening and responding.*)

BIANCA: My heart craved these truths. I fed on them, worked them into my child self, and made them the necessary ingredients for my own satisfaction. Secretly in my bed I would come in my own hands, those images of twisted lust pushing me to a trembling climax and creating a perverse formula for release.

(*ROUND/CANON OF WORDS: each round begins with the words in brackets*)

CAROLE (*with echoes*):
And now as I try
to undo these
[lessons], (*VICKI
begins again*)
to unhook my
desire from
distrust and
conquest, I try
to stop the home
movies in my mind
and feel each
sensation anew.

VICKI (*with echoes*):
[And] now as I try
to undo these
lessons, to unhook
my desire from
distrust and
conquest, I try to
stop the home movies
in my mind and feel
each sensation anew.

KRISSY (*with
echoes*): [And]
now as I try to
undo these
lessons, to
unhook my
desire from
distrust and
conquest, I try
to stop the
home movies in
my mind and
feel each
sensation anew.

LISA (*with
echoes*): [And]
now as I try to
undo these
lessons, to
unhook my
desire from
distrust and
conquest, I try
to stop the
home movies in
my mind and
feel each
sensation anew.

OMI: My heart
craved these
truths. I fed
on them,
worked them
into my child
self, and made
them the
necessary
ingredients
for my own
satisfaction.

LISA: And feel each sensation anew.
OMI: Secretly

(Performers listen and respond to each other, as if in conversation.)

CAROLE (*with echoes from ERIKA*): Daughter
You are part of me
Daughter
I am part of you
Together our worlds
Together our lives
Together we've grown

I tried my best
Didn't always know the answers
I tried my best
Didn't always understand you

I am proud of you, mija
I want you to be proud of me, too

SHIA: You should be sorry for being you
No matter who you are
No matter what you do
You should be sorry for being you

You should be sorry for being you
No matter who you are
No matter what you do
You should be sorry for being you

VICKI: I never liked walls
I never liked barriers
Never liked black and white
Wrong or right
The world is not that simple

I never liked walls
I never liked barriers
Never liked black and white

Wrong or right
The world is not that simple

OMI (*with echoes and above verses repeated*): Ama
1915
South Texas
Your mother died giving birth to you
Eighteen years later you gave birth to your first of twelve
You knew what hard work was
Fields of cotton
Pecan shelling
Sugar beet farming
Childrearing

ERIKA: I never liked walls
I never liked barriers
Never liked black and
white
Wrong or right
The world is not that
simple

COURTNEY: Ama
1915
South Texas
Your mother died
giving birth to you
Eighteen years
later you gave
birth to your first
of twelve
You knew what hard
work was
Fields of cotton
Pecan shelling
Sugar beet farming
Childrearing

ERIKA: I never liked walls
I never liked barriers
Never liked black and white
Wrong or right
The world is not that simple
I never liked walls
I never liked barriers
Never liked black and white
Wrong or right
The world is not that simple

COURTNEY: Mom
1953
San Antonio
Number ten of twelve
Twenty-eight years later
you gave birth to me
To your first of two
And only two
Because
Your tubes were tied
And nine years later
your uterus removed

SHIA: Me
1981
San Antonio
The child you wanted with or
without my dad
Seventeen years later me pregnant
A senior in high school
Off to the clinic
No baby nine months later
(*The voices build in layers and
intensity.*)
    SHIA: I am proud of you, mija
    I want you to be proud of me, too

CAROLE: Ama
1915
South Texas
Your mother died giving birth to
you

OMI: I told her I didn't want to
do my confirmation
Don't you know you may not have
a mother if it wasn't for the
church?
I didn't want to live anymore

MULTIPLE VOICES: I tried my
best
Didn't always know the answers
I tried my best

SHIA: Daughter
You are part of me
Daughter
I am part of you
Together our worlds
Together our lives
Together we've grown

I tried my best
Didn't always know the answers
I tried my best
Didn't always understand you
I tried my best
Didn't always know the answers
I tried my best
Didn't always understand you

VICKI: I never brought it up again
And I was confirmed as Rose
After St. Rose of Lima
And after my mother
Rosemary Lopez Flores
On Christmas and Mother's Day I go to mass with
her
I pray and respond in unison with the rest of
the church
I walk in and put holy water on my forehead,
chest, and each shoulder
Always an expectation or disappointment
Never enough

KRISTEN: Didn't always
understand you
I am proud of you, mija
I want you to be proud of
me,
too

I am proud of
you, mija
I want you to be proud of
me,
too

COURTNEY: Daughter
You are part of me

Daughter
I am part of you
Together our worlds
Together our lives
Together we've grown

VICKI: Always straight A's
But still always suspecting me   COURTNEY: I tried
Was the last one of my friends to start   my best
having sex   Didn't always know
But still couldn't tell you   the answers
Couldn't take my own self to the clinic   I tried my best
And did it without a condom   Didn't always
Because it felt so good   understand you
As long as he didn't cum inside
Even when I knew that was the way Kristina got pregnant

ERIKA: Keep my secret
Still want them to be proud of me
I tell her how I feel about the church
She listens and agrees
But as her brother is recovering from a liver transplant
The family is together one week at my eighty-nine-year-old
grandmother's house
In prayer

OMI (*with building echoes*): Prayer
This prayer is for you
And your mother and your mother's mother
This prayer is for me and my daughter and my daughter's daughter
This prayer is for the women
The women who live and die
Who create and procreate
Who love and cry and feel and pray for their daughters
Daughter
You are part of me   MULTIPLE VOICES (*overlapping*):
Daughter   Daughter
I am part of you   You are part of me
Together our worlds   Daughter
Together our lives   I am part of you
Together we've grown   Together our worlds
                                          Together our lives
COURTNEY: I tried my best   Together we've grown
Didn't always know the answers
I tried my best   I tried my best
Didn't always understand you   Didn't always know the answers
I am proud of you, mija   I tried my best
I want you to be proud of me, too

Spoken-Word Orchestra

Didn't always understand you

KRISTEN: I am proud of you, mija
I want you to be proud of me, too
SHIA: I am expelling my fear.

I am becoming the woman
The warrior
That I was born to be.

I am

Becoming Oya.
KRISSY: I am expelling my fear.

I am becoming the woman
The warrior
That I was born to be.

I am

Becoming Oya.
BIANCA: I am expelling my fear.

I am becoming the woman
The warrior
That I was born to be.

I am

Becoming Oya.

LISA (*with echoes from MULTIPLE VOICES*):
this girl
eight the first time
she evaded her skin
retreated from her bed
to camouflage herself
in midnight corners
that harbor her fugitive
from her own innocence

Working the Work

OMI (*with echoes from MULTIPLE VOICES*):
this girl
unaware of what pieces of herself are lost
which limbs will grow back
what syndrome will thwart her growth
what it means anymore to not know

it is this girl

not the failing economy
not the fatigued and fatherless households
not the flailing red, white, and blue
ribbons on car antennas
or affixed to beds of pick-ups
and minivans
ERIKA: but her
this girl
she reminds me
that we are at war.

war looks different these days
SHIA (*with echoes from MULTIPLE VOICES*):
some trenches resemble tract homes
tree-lined drives
cul-de-sacs
½-acre lots with three treelings on each

others
SHIA (*echoed by LISA*): single/multi/extended families
sectioned eight ways
between liquor stores and Baptist churches
LISA: shrapnel lining streets
where shoeless vagrants pine for pennies
will work for anything edible

ERIKA (*with echoes from MULTIPLE VOICES*):
this girl
this girl
it is this girl
this girl

KRISTEN:
but her
this girl
she reminds me
that we are at war.

MULTIPLE VOICES (*speaking in layers and repetition*):
soldiers are

ERIKA:

preschoolers

this girl

prepubescent

this girl

premenstrual

it is this girl

preteen

this girl

pre anything adult
latchkeys
casualties
who learn to live with a lack of

these soldiers
bury themselves nightly
craft foxholes of flannel and linens
prisoners of war
praying from morning to morning
KRISTEN (*repeated by SHIA*): submission   silence
    amnesia
tactics for suburban warfare where
survival means more than memory
KRISTEN: they plead for stays from sexual execution
for just one more day
to trust
before wounded and dying wolves
in sheep's clothing
SHIA (*with echoes*): feed on their need
brothers uncles fathers steps and grands
VICKI: cousins once removed
sisters aunties mothers grands and steps
friends of the family
wolves, for whom real love is
as distant a memory
as a mother's womb
as distant as living
OMI: living names plaster newspapers and war memorials
VICKI: this girl
this Eve, this Elizabeth, this nine-year-old girl in El Cajon, this Jessica,
this fifteen-year-old boy in the school closet, this Ida, this Kimberly,
this Adam, this eight-month-old baby in Africa, this Edward, this
Ryan, this ten-year-old boy in Tampa, this Jane Doe, this six-year-old
girl on a school bus in New Mexico, this JonBenet, this ten-year-old

girl in Arizona, this Polly, this Samantha, this John Doe, this Jane Doe, this Jimmy, this Bonita,
OMI: this Shia
BIANCA (*echoed by ERIKA*):
this girl and
this girl and
this boy and
this eight-year-old girl
CAROLE (*with echoes*): my daughter is eight
she is consumed with Bratz dolls
finally fashion
SHIA: she covers her eyes when bodies go bare
CAROLE: still finds shock in four-letter words
giggles at what grown-ups do
asks too many questions

she knows what private parts are
what boundaries mean
i pray her wits are about her
or a letter opener near   OMI:
the day some dreamy-eyed creeper   joseph,
with a safe-sounding biblical name   michael,
tries to persuade her into submission silence amnesia   john,
cajole her from being   david,
"Saliah," the pious, virtuous, upright one   abel,
she came into the world   samuel,
eyes open, engaged   or frank

OMI (*echoed by CAROLE*): i knew
she had been here before
she would never walk alone
her roots are far stronger than the world
above this earth she belongs to
she will not wilt
BIANCA (*echoed by ERIKA*): this girl
my girl
ERIKA: i will teach her to fight

Spoken-Word Orchestra

(Pause and energetic shift. Song sung by MULTIPLE VOICES, building and responding to each other.)

MULTIPLE VOICES: I am no one again
Again I am no one
No one again am I
I am no one again

I am not free again
Again I am not free
Free I am not
I am not free again

MULTIPLE VOICES (*in soft echoes*): Confession

COURTNEY (*with echoes*):
Sometimes i punch myself.
Take swings at generations
of pain in my belly.   OMI: curdle
Red, bloody clots of undigested truths,

OMI: curdle in ovaries and harden uterus.
Fingers grope for my tiny penis.
Lust and ego, always tugging.
THREE VOICES: Unforgiving time and place.

COURTNEY: Back of truck, stench of beer,
backyard, backseat,
railroad track, toilet seat,
at the beach, in the water, on the bed,
always at war.
Pushing and pulling like a swarm of lovebugs.
Mate and die
Mate and die
VICKI:
Pushing and pulling like a swarm of lovebugs.
Mate and die
Mate and die
(overlaps with the following verse)
FLORINDA: Who do you love more, mom?

Working the Work

Me or dad?
He's gone again.
We chase out the fear with coat hangers,
wet towels like whips, and kitchen knives.
Around and around the house.
Anger that rips up the stairs
(*Overlaps with the following verse*)
KRISTEN: and falls from the ceiling fan.
There by the skylight,
a view of the clear, blue unfaithfulness.
My loyalty is like my thumb.
My wound is my womb.
MULTIPLE VOICES (*in soft echoes*): Resurrection
COURTNEY: I am the new lover of my body's pain.
I hold her.
(*Overlaps with the following verse*)
KRISTEN: I caress her.
I dance with her.
She is my mother, grandmother, great-grandmother.
OMI (*with KRISTEN & FLORINDA*): We fall together.
There is no space in between
my body and gravity.
(*Pause and energetic shift. Laughing and playing, performers return to the "na na" song with hand gestures. They sing a few verses, building in rhythm and playfulness. Performers exit by crossing downstage and out through the house. Blackout.*)

PART III

The Work of Transformation

Chapter Seven

TRANSFORMING PRACTICE

Artists, Activists, and Academics Working across Boundaries

A key strategy of the Austin Project is to empower women through ensemble writing and performance in the jazz aesthetic, giving them methods and insights they can take back to their own creative, intellectual, political, and spiritual work. In this chapter, an artist, an activist, and two academics talk about the impact of such work on their practices. The contributors are theater artist Florinda Bryant, international development officer Rajasvini Bhansali, English professor Lisa L. Moore, and sociologist Gloria González-López.

Florinda Bryant

How do you break down the science of the cipher?

I HAVE PARTICIPATED IN THE AUSTIN PROJECT SINCE 2002. HOWEVER, my relationship with the jazz aesthetic goes beyond tAP. In 1998, I was cast in Sharon Bridgforth's *blood pudding*, a piece directed by Laurie Carlos. Through that experience, I, at eighteen, would learn jazz and I would learn about the cipher.

At the time, I was not rhyming publicly. I was supporting a large number of male-centered hip-hop groups, singing background, carrying gear, and watching from the sidelines. The cipher then was the sidewalk outside the club where I would rhyme alone to whatever my homeboys were rhyming to onstage. There was definitely a time and place for the sisters to get on stage, but not without a fight. I called myself an actress, or a singer, or a dancer, singularly, depending on what I was auditioning for.

The cipher as I knew it was a straight hip-hop thing. Not a theatre term. The idea of an ensemble in a traditional theatre sense was nothing more than the group of people lucky enough to secure whatever gig was in question. What I would begin to learn in 1998 at frontera@hyde park theatre would change me. What I would learn about my art and myself as a member of the Austin Project has changed everything.

The Austin Project taught me to listen. Being able to work with international artists has been amazing. Having the opportunity to work so extensively with Sharon Bridgforth and her Finding Voice method has been instrumental to my own work and my development of my own techniques, which I use with my youth theatre companies and the students I teach through the Theatre Action Project. Sharon Bridgforth made me examine not just my writing but myself as a writer. It has been like conservatory training that never would have been available to someone like myself who did not graduate from college. Seeing myself beyond labels, beyond lack of privilege, and beyond résumés and talent is one of the best blessings. It is the best teaching method, one I hope I have adopted. The added bonus is how Sharon presents her methods: she takes it to the next level, saying, "I ain't just going to tell you, I'ma show you the method." That is what Sharon does through her teaching and her living. She is in the same hot seat with her own work. She leads the group to be solid because, if you are not standing solid, structure will fall.

For any writer, having the opportunity to work your work with a group of people who have no other interest than making sure you write your ass off is unheard of. The truth sometimes is ugly. On the journey to finding the truth of my work, I have often times found myself in some ugly territory. It has been painful at times, and hard. I have had to fight myself and everything I have allowed myself to believe about myself. The cipher created in the Austin Project has supported me through these discoveries. There is no room to fall off, to be too broken down, to not get back up. You ain't got to win every time but you got to fight and commit to the dance. That is the process, and it is not complete until you get back up.

The Austin Project has created space for me to get clear about a lot of things, particularly around the subject of identity. In year one, Carl Hancock Rux did a workshop where he asked why we give one singular answer when asked, "What do you want to be when you grow up?" It is as if, in the many, many years you are hopefully granted, there is room for only one focus, one thing we can be when we grow up. The idea of duality was enforced when, within the Austin Project space, the call was issued for the scholar to embrace being an artist, and for the artist to embrace being a scholar, and for an activist to do the same. It was a revolution, y'all. For me, a high school graduate, to be in the space with university professors and for them to hear me say, "yes, I am a scholar," and to hear, "yes, you are," the response. Babyyyy. The idea of rejecting the singular was huge. It changed the way

I walked, the way I saw things. It shaped my relationship to myself with regard to race and being biracial. There is space to be all things. Eventually it gave birth to me seeing myself as more than a single mother and helped me open my heart enough to be someone's wife.

I began work on what would later be titled *Half-Breed Southern Fried Check One* while in the Austin Project. I never would have written or had this piece produced were it not for the Austin Project. First off, in the beginning, I was still not claiming space as a writer—at best I was a poet and even then, depending on who was in the room, I wasn't even that. I kept alive the idea that because I was not educated I could not be a writer, and even if they were calling Tupac Shakur a poet that was only because he was male. Second, I had become a new mom in 2001, a single mom at that, and when would I find time to write? It is amazing what we won't do for ourselves. I needed help. Dr. Jones gave me that help. I would never have committed to myself to take four hours a week to work on my art. Shit, I didn't think I had any art to speak of at that time. She had me committing to myself and I didn't even know it. Third, the Austin Project gave me an opportunity to see myself—not as I was but as I could be. I was surrounded by mirrors of possibility. I was able to connect with women so different, yet we found places of sameness. We were given the gift of community and support. As a woman, I have found many moments where I felt alone, but since I have been in the Austin Project, I may be many things but alone is never one of them. That true support and gift of vision help me realize my own position in a sea of stars—as we all shine so brightly.

The Austin Project has elevated me: my writing has become craft, my tools are no longer just my hands or my voice or my face but my entire body, and my work is not just what I do on stage but how I live my life.

So how do you break down the science of the cipher?

Quite simply it is the Austin Project.

Rajasvini Bhansali

From Kathak to Kenya: Creating Political Family in the Jazz Aesthetic

IN 2004, I MOVED FROM AUSTIN, TEXAS, TO KENYA TO WORK WITH THE Wakamba people in the rural Kitui district. This move felt momentous even as it was well-planned and deliberate, not because I questioned my commitment to international development or to the necessary task of returning to the "third world" as a queer, immigrant woman dedicated to forging new collaborations in the Global South, but because leaving the Austin community meant leaving a political family that had, in fact, brought me into adulthood as a poet and activist. So, with equal measures of trepidation and courage, I *became* ready.

My task in Kenya was to support capacity building of leaders who ran local vocational-training institutions to create more robust, inclusive, and youth-focused structures. My work with the Austin Project in the previous year and with Poetry for the People in the mid-1990s had prepared me well to value the process of trust building, so essential for any successful collaboration. I utilized the skills I had fine-tuned in the Austin Project to listen deeply to the stories of the youth, adult staff, and community leaders with whom I was blessed to work in Kenya. Together, we mobilized community support for youth training and employment; strategized new ways to work for economic justice, including upgrading our workshops and supporting our youth in learning twenty-first-century skills; and we influenced national youth development policy. Even more than my public policy and institutional development skills, I had to utilize my learning attitude, commitment to building a team, and most of all, listening and witnessing people's telling and sharing of their stories to engage with them in the context of their communities.

I relearned that instead of allowing political differences to cast a cloud of distrust and self-righteousness, we as activists must embody the joy and possibility in collective reflection, analysis, and argumentation that are essential for us to remain clear in our goals for a more just society. I worked with a core team of managers and community leaders in Kenya. One of the managers was found to be engaging in some unethical practices, those little acts of inequity that ultimately result in bigger corruption, and had to be "dealt with." In my capacity as advisor, I simply helped shine the light on the outcomes of this problem and presented it to his peers to handle the situation. I remember the moment of awe and humility in which I witnessed the most nuanced and yet effective method of "corrections." The seniors on the team sat with him in silence as he reflected on his part in creating the problem. They posed key questions in the spirit of community and appealed to his sense of shared responsibility to address the core issues. Initially, the person under reprimand was defensive, even angry. But in a few hours, his anger turned into reflection and his reflection turned into action that has resulted not only in his own transformation but has also made an impact on youth training in the polytechnic he led. This instance reminded me that as I mature as a political being, I must remember the traditions I encounter in my birth family and my chosen families. Our African and Asian, historic and democratic traditions of listening, debating, and learning from each other are necessary in the production of strategy, community, and art.

I witnessed in my colleagues in Kenya, much as I learned from working in community development in India, that one's seniority as a community leader is not a god-given right. Leadership requires moral rectitude, impeccable ethics, and humility to win the love and trust of the people, whether in rural Kenya or in San Francisco, California, where I currently lead an innovative youth development program. I have been deeply changed by working with extraordinary people who believe that their personal and political power comes from their roots; their power comes from creating the right spaces for young and old, men and women, to share their concerns, voice disillusionments and fears, debate the finer points of social change, and value relationships with each other as a foundation for any growth. It is therefore no surprise that so many leaders are in fact artists and scholars and vice versa.

In our work as ethical leaders and organizers that is oriented in building other people's power, we sometimes forget to find our own voice, seek our own power, and transform our own lives as the foundation from which other good things may come. I know that I became a poet because in my own family, and in my chosen family of activists and friends, I could not always tell my most meaningful and complex truths—ballads which spoke of love and of flaws; stories that equally had room for reverence and irreverence; poems where I could cry, laugh, and be still all at the same time. There was and is always this weight of expectation, of perfection, of being one step ahead and beyond to prove my worth, to make my existence worth the while. With distance from India, when I moved to the United States at seventeen to go to school, and the blur of nostalgia that followed, I had begun to forget experiences that uniquely propel me. The process of remembering, retelling, and reliving these complicated, sometimes pretty, sometimes ugly stories, required a supportive sphere—a sphere of articulated expectations, yet gentleness; a sphere of rigor and love; and a sphere that would never stop reflecting brilliance even when I could no longer recall my own qualities.

The Austin Project, led by Sharon Bridgforth and Dr. Joni Jones in 2003–2004, provided me with such a sphere to rediscover my own power as a human being, a woman, an activist, and a poet, writer, and artist. Through the masterful work of Sharon Bridgforth in the jazz aesthetic and through Dr. Jones's deliberate creation of a magical community of scholars, artists, and activists with shared vision for art as a vehicle for change, the most ordinary of experiences were transformed into extraordinary works of art and self-mobilization for those of us who participated in the Austin Project. Here, we built a community of engagement by witnessing each other's growth; by writing; and by speaking and listening deeply and actively and reciprocating that rare gift of presence and witnessing. In the Austin Project, I once again practiced my forgotten tradition of invoking teachers, spiritual and ancestral linkages, and contemporary influences within my poems. The process of the Austin Project birthed my tribute to my first language: Kathak—a North Indian classical dance and theatre art form. I learned that my story of a being trained from age three to become a Kathik—storyteller and holder of community experiences—is undeniably not part of the mainstream.

During the Austin Project, I learned to be open to writing in a language that lives in my body as much as in my intellect or tongue. The intensity of this work sometimes made me want to give it all up and come to a screeching halt amidst the heartache and the very physical manifestation of this difficulty that became this nagging left-shoulder ache. Sharon encouraged us to use these spaces of discomfort, even pain, to try a new skill, a new tune, a new movement that could be transformative. In discovering language lodged as visceral memory, in finding poems in hidden nooks within me, in developing work in a community of brilliant artists, scholars, and activists, I believe I found my truest voice. As the Austin Project family practiced each time we came together in our circle, and as my Kenyan family taught me each time we took an hour to drink tea and sit with each other, to celebrate this power that is each one of us with a poem, story, song, or dance *is* to fully live.

Lisa L. Moore

Epiphanies Lost and Found

Last night I watched the movie *Akeelah and the Bee*, about the eleven-year-old African American girl from a failing junior high school in South Central Los Angeles who ends up winning the Scripps National Spelling Bee. Laurence Fishburne, who produced the movie, plays her crusty mentor, the former head of the English department at UCLA who left teaching because he couldn't cope with his grief over the death of his little daughter. He has a quotation attributed to Nelson Mandela on his wall that he makes Akeelah read, and that gets repeated in a flashback later in the movie:

> Our deepest fear is not that we are inadequate. Our deepest fear is that we are powerful beyond measure. We ask ourselves, Who am I to be brilliant, gorgeous, talented, fabulous? Actually, who are you not to be? We were born to make manifest the glory of God that is within us. And as we let our own light shine, we unconsciously give other people permission to do the same.

It's so much harder for me to write something that offers simply my own thoughts and perceptions than it is to write an academic piece. Don't get me wrong, I'm proud of my academic writing and I've spent years practicing a style that is, I hope, clear, witty, and authoritative. But the truth is that, like so many English professors, I went to grad school in literature because I deep-down wanted to be a writer and was afraid I wasn't good enough or brave enough to survive as an artist. So instead I studied other people's writing and wrote about it. I have been blessed with a successful and rewarding career as an academic, and I don't regret that choice. But there's no denying it was at least partly based on fear. Only recently has it occurred to me that it might not only have been fear of failure; it might have been fear of success. And that's the fear that's haunting these words now.

Well, maybe if I'm honest, I would have to say that I have a little regret. I have heard myself tell people, "If I had had real support for my dreams, I would be as good a novelist and poet right now as I am an academic. If I had spent all the years I spent in graduate school and as an assistant professor working as a creative writer, I'd be at the same place in that field that I am in this." I'm a little surprised when I find myself saying this because as a rule I don't do regret. I don't like to acknowledge my own mistakes, let alone talk about them. I like to see my life choices as all tending in a positive direction. But one thing the Austin Project has done for me is rip off that particular veil of illusion.

I now know that if I can't connect with and express my regrets, mistakes, vulnerabilities, doubts, and fears, I also can't touch my deepest dreams. I think I have been most afraid of those dreams. What if following my dreams led me away from the hard-won security—career, family, home—that I've struggled to create for myself? I'm a Canadian lesbian living with my partner and our two children in a state with not one but two laws against gay marriage. In the next state over, Oklahoma, my partner Madge's legal adoption of our children, as a second-parent same-sex adoption, has no legal standing. I'm a sexual abuse survivor and the veteran of childhood suicidal thoughts. Aren't I entitled to a little peace and security? What if letting my inner artist out—or any of my other dreams, my desires for overwhelming passionate love that lasts forever, for a big-ass spiritual quest, for toe-turning sex until the day I die—lets the floodwaters in and I just float out to sea with them?

I've already strayed alarmingly from the putative topic of this essay, which is supposed to be how the Austin Project has influenced my work as an academic. And there's certainly plenty to say about that.

I'm pretty sure Omi asked me to participate in the Austin Project that first fall of 2002 by accident. I was teaching a feminist research methods class for the master's students in women's and gender studies. Several of the students had taken Omi's performance ethnography class the previous semester and talked a lot about how inspiring they found it. (Omi went by the name Joni Jones then and I still remember one student's routine whenever her name was mentioned: she would thump her chest hard, twice, then look skyward and murmur adoringly, "Joni.") I decided to invite Omi as one of the guest speakers. She e-mailed me back to accept, and then added, "Can I ask you a favor in return?" She asked me to be a consultant scholar on a new project of hers, a collaboration of artists, academics, and activists. She assured me it wouldn't take much of my time, but that if I could, I might want to attend the first session led by Sharon Bridgforth, who Omi called the "Anchor Artist" for the project. Omi and I didn't know each other at all well then—our departments are in different colleges on different parts of the campus—and I often think that if I hadn't happened to contact Omi that week, the Austin Project might have started without me.

I also owe that initial invitation to Sharon, I suspect. I had met Sharon when I invited her to talk about her then-new book, *the bull-jean stories*, to my gay and lesbian literature and culture class. (I do have to give myself credit for using invitations to my class as a way of creating connections with people I admire!) Sharon read from the book and it was a religious experience—and not just for me. Her deep powerful voice, those unforgettable characters, and her huge presence in the room left me dizzy and my students inspired. That may have been the only time Sharon and I met before the first day of the Austin Project, but at least I was one academic at UT that she knew was interested in her work.

So it took a lot of serendipity to get me into that room that day. The meeting was supposed to be four hours long, which meant I had to ask Madge for four hours of that precious commodity, weekend childcare with our eighteen-month-old Max. Looking back on it now, I can see that I had a whole team of angels (this must be what angels are) getting me to that place. And by the end of four hours, I knew I was going to stay.

The room was full of powerful and powerfully interesting women, African American, Asian American, and Latina. I think that first year there was only one other white woman, Shannon Baley. That in itself was such an unusual experience that I knew I had to come back, just to live in a world more like the real world, in which white people are actually a minority, and less like the academic world, in which people of color are a scarce resource. Every subsequent year there were one or two other white women in the group, but for me the fact that the group's agenda is set by and for women of color has remained powerful. I don't want to say too much here—I'm aware that white people tend to be a little more fascinated with our experiences

The Work of Transformation

among people of color than is strictly necessary—but I do want to mark the importance of that aspect of the Austin Project for me. I remember at the end of the first year there was some discussion about whether or not consultant scholars should participate in the final showing of our work. The actor and playwright Florinda Bryant remarked, "One of our consultant scholars has made herself part of this group. She's been here every week and should definitely be up on stage with us." That's when the penny dropped for me. I wasn't one of the few white women in the room because I had been specially selected by a top-secret panel of people of color based on my impeccable anti-racist credentials. I was here because I kept showing up.

That's been deep—the realization that solidarity is not the same thing as approval or even friendship. I had long cited the Bernice Johnson Reagon insight that "Coalition work is not work done in your home. It is work done in the streets. And it is some of the most dangerous work you can do. And you shouldn't look for comfort . . . It's very important not to confuse them—home and coalition."[1] Inside the Austin Project, I have experienced a new layer of truth in those words. At times I have been very uncomfortable. I have been called out on my assumptions that people might need my "help" with their research (ouch), on my assumptions about parenting, on my sense of time. I have learned that it's important to feed the people, that good snacks help keep us in the room. I have learned that giving priority to process means that I may not emerge from the group, any given year, with a finished piece of writing, and that no one but me can decide when something's finished. In addition to the delicious moments of epiphany, this group has sometimes been difficult, frustrating, and even boring for me. Love, trust, and friendship sometimes blossom out of working together—and sometimes they don't. But I keep coming back, and so does everyone else, for the sake of the work. That's what coalition, what community, feels like right now.

That first day, Sharon immediately plunged us into what she calls The Work. The first thing she asked us to do, in that group of strangers, was to go around and identify ourselves in terms first of gender and then of sexual identity. I'm not kidding. Have you ever tried this exercise? It results in a very revealing combination of terror, shame, and hemming and hawing. Very few people in this all-women group could answer either question in just one word, even "woman." And then Sharon gave us an instruction that would become familiar: "Now, write." About what, people asked? "What was your experience?" Sharon replied. But do we write about our experience of gender and sexual identity, or our experience of the exercise, or, or, or . . . "Just write," Sharon repeated firmly.

I was hooked. A free weekly creative-writing workshop with one of the writers I admire most in the world? Under what possible circumstances would I turn an opportunity like that down?

For that first year in the Austin Project I felt militantly that I was *not* doing my academic work. I had recently gotten tenure and had my first child, and I was engaged in a process I called "refilling the well." Over the previous few years I had tried a lot of things out. I took piano lessons for a while. At one point, I got out of bed every morning and sat down to draw a portrait of the sleepy self I saw in the mirror first thing. I was in a play Madge directed for her theater company, Rude Mechanicals. I was in a dance performance in the burning July heat with one hundred other women dressed in white on the Congress Avenue Bridge. I was in a movie. I taught in England for a few weeks and made a lot of watercolor drawings there. I moved my whole family to Paris for a semester and taught at the Université de Paris–Nanterre. I got Rolfed. I tried to write some personal essays, some short fiction. And now, under Sharon's guidance, I seemed to be writing . . . poetry.

The first poem I wrote in the Austin Project is the one reprinted (with a lot of revision) in Chapter Three of this book. I wrote the poem on a Sunday morning, alone in my university office, trying to replicate the deeply disorienting and exciting experience I'd had the day before when Daniel Alexander Jones had been the Guest Artist in the Austin Project. Daniel had us do some yoga, then talk in pairs, then write. I'm a long-time yogini but it had never occurred to me to use yoga as part of a writing exercise—to connect body, spirit, and breath to the act of writing, an act that I had previously assumed took place mainly in my head. That morning, I took a mat into the faculty lounge, devoutly hoping no one else would show up and discover me acting silly, and did a few sun salutations. Then I went back to my office, sat down in front of my computer, and started having a panic attack. The second stanza of the poem ("Sounds gather like bees / around my mouth / and the taste of blood / eases my jaw open") is actually a description of the numb, tingly feeling I get when I hyperventilate, followed by the realization that I had inadvertently bitten my tongue. I don't clearly remember what happened next, but about an hour later, I had a text that was like nothing I'd ever written before. And I was a writer in a way I'd never been before, either. For the first time I was taking an emotional and psychic risk, writing not to convey information or even make an argument, but writing because I had to. Writing to survive.

What's funny is that I thought I already knew all this. As an English professor trained in composition pedagogy, I've been telling students for years, "Writing is a form of invention and discovery." Certainly my best experiences with my academic writing were ones in which I figured out what I thought about a piece of literature in the process of writing about it. As always, "we best teach what we most need to learn."[2] What was different this time? This time there was no bridge of information, argument, research, or reporting between that discovery and the writing itself. I wasn't discovering something about somebody else's writing and experiencing increased self-knowledge as a by-product, however welcome and sought-after. I was discovering my own voice and story and putting that on the page for the first time. It was terrifying. And I've been trying to recreate that experience ever since.

One of my big disappointments has been that, although I've written lots of poems since that day in 2002, I've never quite recaptured that moment of sheer in-my-body, out-of-control, something-is-writing-me inspiration. And I haven't produced a poem I like as well since then either. The second year of the Austin Project I actually remember saying firmly on the first day that I was done writing poems about my sad childhood, that I wanted to write happy poems for a change. Wasn't there plenty to be happy about? I had a wonderful family, and by fall 2003 was pregnant with our second child. I had a job I loved, a great community, and this new, treasured creative outlet in the Austin Project. I started a series called the Belly Sonnets that fall. After I read the first one, I remember Florinda saying to me, "Why are you trying to write about how great it is to be pregnant? All I hear you do every week is come in here and complain about how sick you feel." Hmmm.

This seems to be the lesson I have to keep learning—that no matter who I think I should be, I'm never anyone but who I am. The best work I can do, as a writer and otherwise, is to try to know who that is and be faithful to her. And that effort has transformed my academic work in any number of ways.

The most obvious difference has been in my teaching. I've begun asking my undergraduates to do different kinds of assignments, not just the analytical argumentative essays I wrote as an English major and that I was expected to teach in my turn. It's great to be a critical thinker and to be able to make a persuasive argument, but not everybody learns best that way, and there are some things that writing an argument will never teach you. So now, although I still assign traditional essays, my students also sometimes write poems. Sometimes they make drawings and write about that. Sometimes they write personal essays. And I hope what I'm offering them is an array of tools for using writing as a form of self-discovery and engagement with the world. In my graduate teaching, I've devised a new course that is markedly different from anything I've ever taught. The course is called Theory in Action, but it's really the Austin Project for graduate course credit. We meet once a week, and the students each devise for themselves a "community engagement project." But the real goal of the class is for each student to take a breath, amid the demands of graduate school, and ask himself or herself, "Who am I and what is my work in the world? What do I most need to learn?" My sense is that people go to graduate school in almost any discipline—but perhaps this is especially true in the arts and humanities—to try to carve out a little niche of creativity and self-direction for themselves in the edifice of capitalism. But then the demands of professionalization and the worry about finding that rare bird, an academic job, start to take up more and more brain space and soon they've forgotten the creative spark, the desire, that got them here in the first place. In this class we use some of Sharon's exercises from the Finding Voice method, along with other things I've picked up over the years: exercises from performance and writing workshops by Maiana Minahal, Deb Margolin, Peggy Shaw, Lois Weaver, Marga Gomez, and Rude Mechanicals; principles of yoga and Quakerism, my two spiritual practices; exercises from Re-Evaluation Co-Counseling, a peer-counseling method I've learned; and principles of feminist pedagogy I've been working with for many years. Typically, in a three-hour class period, we spend some time doing exercises that involve talking and some time doing exercises that involve writing. Some days we do meditation and movement work. The relationship between these exercises and the development of each student's project is pretty loose, intentionally so. It is up to each student to figure out what is required (by his or her own deepest dreams) in order to create work that feels authentic, connected, and driven by the best each is capable of.

In 2007, Omi and Sharon asked me to envision the class as an explicit "graduation project" marking the beginning of a new stage in my affiliation with tAP, a stage during which I would no longer be participating in the weekly circle but rather "doing" tAP in the other parts of my life. For this version of the class, then, I decided to end the semester with a public event I called a "colloquium/performance." The students and I invited friends, family, and community members to witness and talk to us about our semester's work. The students created poster presentations, which they set up around the Center's beautiful gallery space, each poster describing a particular project. Two students had collaborated on a feminist rewriting and staging of Shakespeare's *The Tempest*; someone else had done a capacity assessment of queer-friendly health resources in Austin; a third project was a proposal for a cooperative scene shop to serve local theatres. There were projects on helping African American women make healthy choices in taking care of their hair, a series of interviews about actor-centered theater practice, a performance project to give voice to the experiences of women students of color, and a Muslim feminist book group. We greeted our guests at the door by offering them a small glass of either champagne or sparkling water. This ritual of welcome was a direct steal from a beautiful "performance dinner"

I had attended a few months earlier, hosted by tAP member Ana-Maurine Lara and her partner Wura Ogunji. Ana and Wura had greeted everyone with a thimbleful of palm wine, and it had been a powerful gesture of both welcome and sacredness. After this offering, my students and I gave our guests some time to wander around the space, look at the posters, talk to friends, and meet new people. Ultimately we asked everyone to sit in the circle of chairs we had set up, and then the students gave a performance: a tAP-style "spoken-word orchestra" in which I had channeled Laurie Carlos as best I could to create a piece that would allow the group to share their words and work with each other and the audience. The script was composed of excerpts I had chosen from student writing; for the performance, I asked people other than the author to read those sections, working with repetition, layering, and other choral effects to create a satisfying whole. After the performance, one of the students formally asked the audience to "break bread with us." During one of our "community as classroom" projects that semester, we had helped move supplies and equipment from one storage room to another in the back of a local theater. The project leader, Thomas, had introduced us to the "bucket brigade" method of passing each object along a line of people to move things efficiently from one place to another. We adapted this experience for our performance, forming a long line from the back room where the food was stored out to the table in the performance space where we intended to serve it. As we passed along each food item or beverage, we named it: "Fadi's unleavened bread! Claire's Brie! Lisa's hot tea!" Our final act was to arrange the food and offer it to our guests. The evening ended with this sharing of breads, dips or spreads, and beverages from the culture (or sometimes just the taste!) of each student. I had been anxious earlier in the week about this performance, wondering why I had decided to make this the final project in a class in which I had not taught performance skills per se. But taking this risk with my students added another layer to my understanding of the work of the Austin Project: I realized that the performance was not about the "skills" of the students, even less about my teacherly or directorial virtuosity. Rather, it was about the students getting to speak one another's words, to really internalize one another's stories, and to present them boldly and with respect. It was a deep and intimate experience of community.

In many ways, then, my work in the Austin Project has taken me far afield from my academic training. Yet ultimately this work has caused me to rededicate myself to my scholarly research and writing. As I write these words, I'm working on three books (including the one you're reading right now), and all of them are about communities of women working across differences in a variety of genres. On a deeper level, though, my creativity has been freed up. My academic writing feels integrated with my poetry, my drawing and painting, my love of dance, performance, and yoga, and with my teaching, too. I'm doing the same work, whichever genre or venue I find myself in: the work of clearing out the vessel to let the divine pour through.

I've recently come to realize that one of these projects, a book I'm writing entitled *Sister Arts: Lesbian Genres and the Erotic Landscape*, is my version of what I've heard other Austin Project women call "listening to the ancestors." The book is about four women in eighteenth-century Britain and America who used the landscape arts—garden design, botanical illustration, landscape sketch, and landscape poetry—to express their love for other women. These women were born into fortunate circumstances with only moderate worries about money and safety to contend with. The rewards of a conventional life seemed to be theirs for the taking. But each one of them turned away from that life, following instead fierce and disruptive intellectual and artistic ambitions and finding community, friendship, and sometimes erotic and romantic love with other women.

I have been haunted and possessed by these women. In the summer of 2006 I was in Wales doing research for the book and took a morning off to climb a small but precipitous mountain to look at the ruins of a medieval castle. It took about an hour of steady uphill work, with frequent breaks to catch my breath, to reach the top. Eighteenth-century garden designers often incorporated just such steep and rocky trails into their landscape designs so that visitors could experience the effort required to stay on "the path of virtue." At the top of the mountain, I was rewarded just as those designers would have wanted, with a spectacular view of the town of Llangollen. Far in the distance I could see the trees surrounding the home of the famous Ladies of Llangollen, Sarah Ponsonby and Eleanor Butler, who eloped (twice—the first time they were caught and brought back) from their Irish families and made a home together in rural Wales in the 1770s. I dropped, breathless, to a ruined wall and pulled out my sketchbook. With my watercolor pencils, I made a drawing of the gray-blue sky framed by a glassless Gothic window. After half an hour or so, I put my pencils away. I clambered around the ruined castle site, taking photographs, then found another place to settle. Here, I pulled out my notebook and wrote a sonnet. (I had made a promise to myself that on this trip, freed from the daily domestic routine, I would write a sonnet a day, no matter how rushed or uninspired.) Then I climbed some more, trying to find a surface smooth enough to take a rubbing with my gold and silver wax crayons. A few minutes later, putting my unused crayons back in my bag—they were to be perfect for recording carved epitaphs in the Llangollen churchyard

The Work of Transformation

later—I caught myself laughing. I've turned into a Sister Artist, I thought. I don't mean to compare my output to, say, Mary Delany's production of nearly a thousand botanical illustrations, all completed after she was seventy years old, or the Duchess of Portland's creation of the largest natural history museum in Europe in her home in the 1770s, but the idea that what you should do in the face of overwhelming natural beauty is make something to record the moment is very much in their tradition. As I learn more about these women through their work, I feel them gather around me, asking to be recognized, asking to be read with sympathy and understanding, for their love of women's art forms like embroidery and letters, and for the desires they felt that we would now call lesbian. They all got to tell their stories in some way—they were not voiceless—but these stories have been forgotten or misread. When I sit down to write this book I am not so much trying to explain as to listen and transcribe. My academic writing no longer needs a qualifier—it has become, finally, just writing.

My life as a writer, of course, is not all lived on the mountaintop. As I mentioned, after four years, I was "graduated" out of the Austin Project. Like others who had been in the group from the beginning, I was given the charge of taking what I learned in the group, making it my own, and spreading the word. Putting this book together is one way of doing that. But what will substitute for those weekly meetings? It was such a luxury to have a creative life already organized for me—I used to joke that all I had to do was press play, show up to the meetings, and I knew I would work my work. As much as I love Theory in Action, I am really there to facilitate the work of others, not to do my own. Thanks to tAP, I have great people to read my writing, but without a structure to bring us together, we all tend to drift off into our lives, our other projects, our immediate obligations. Many of us have new commitments to our work as artists that ironically seem to leave us even less time to figure out how to be together outside the Austin Project. The effort of thinking that through is just one more unfinished piece of work.

Gloria González-López

Feminist Epistemologies, Spiritual Activism, and Healing: Women of Color and Performance of Stories of Survival and Pain

I BECAME A MEMBER OF THE AUSTIN PROJECT (tAP) IN FALL 2002, shortly after joining the Department of Sociology as an assistant professor. I received an invitation from Joni Jones, a kind-spirited African American professor at UT Austin, someone I had just met who asked me to play the role of a consultant scholar in a community-based project involving young adult women from different cultural and ethnic backgrounds. Joni introduced me to Sharon Bridgforth, an independent intellectual, group facilitator, and another gentle soul orchestrating this project. I felt deeply honored to get to know both of them as I accepted their invitation to become a member of tAP. These three women along with the rest of tAP gathered on Saturdays at a school located in East Austin, and I joined them on different occasions in the fall of 2002.

What was the purpose of this gathering of women of color from contrasting ethnic and cultural backgrounds? United by common stories of life and struggle, these women participated in meetings designed to explore their inner voices. Among other artistic activities, creative writing became a personal and professional avenue leading to self-exploration. I engaged in and closely observed different group exercises in which participants opened up and shared intimate secrets of their life histories and narratives. As an academic, I saw new expressions of intellectual activism come alive through the fearless self-disclosure of women's stories. Their individual voices were unique yet shared as part of unpredictable spiritual and emotional journeys of discovery and growth. In these meetings, I witnessed endless weavings of words, the unpacking of untold family stories, the ghetto, el barrio, abuse, pain, laughs and joy, cultures in clash and reconciliation, unforgettable and too-painful-to-forget childhoods, the intricacies of intimacy, the labyrinths and fears of sexuality, gender, and relationships—all of them coming alive through women's voices, all woven through creative essays and poetry. Through tAP, I was beginning to discover, to some extent, other ways to unleash the journeys of women on their path to inner exploration. I witnessed the spirit ripening through collective moments of rupture and self-discovery, and the aesthetics leading to the healing of individual yet interconnected souls.

The intellectual journeys that were unfolding in front of my eyes at tAP coincided with a personal encounter I had with Gloria Anzaldúa. Though I had been familiar with her work since I was a graduate student, I had never met her in person. I finally had the privilege to attend a workshop she gave in San Antonio during the fall of 2002, the same semester I joined tAP. I was one of many waiting in line to talk to her immediately after she offered her final remarks that evening. One among my countless questions to her was designed to explore her views on the future of women's and gender studies. During our conversation, I became aware of the urgent need for me (as a feminist sociologist) to look at the multiple dimensions of women's subjective and collective experiences of everyday life, and one in particular: spirituality. While I was (and I am still) exploring a feminist sociological

The Work of Transformation

conceptualization of spirituality, the collection of readings contained in a volume she co-edited with AnaLouise Keating, *This Bridge We Call Home*, reminded me of something I was noticing in these tAP meetings: women unpacked their life stories while crossing borders and languages many times in alternating opposition and juxtaposition. Their voices were so contrastingly different, but they crossed fine lines to encounter one another in these collective conjugations of humanity. Each woman's unique history of womanhood and life united her with the other tAP members through the strikingly diverse yet fluid and common faces of womanhood. As each woman talked to the rest of the group, I became aware of the ways in which women are always united through difference, and as each woman took a turn to talk, I was reminded of Chela Sandoval's emblematic expression: "I am another yourself."[3]

During the fall of 2002, the tAP members got together many times, and I often had to miss the opportunity to join them. I was struggling with my own busy agenda as a deeply intimidated and shy new scholar, a new assistant professor trying figuring out the rigor of academic life in a still foreign but welcoming city. But it was hard to let go of tAP. I decided to remain connected with my sisters in their collective unfolding of fears, dreams, and hopes. Deep in my heart I knew that the exercise of humanity that many times I witnessed with teary eyes was a clear illustration of some of the basic concepts I had learned from leading feminist intellectuals. Anzaldúan theorizing on spiritual activism, for instance, became the only way to explain what women were doing with one another in this collective effort of self-discovery and growth. In her examinations of Gloria E. Anzaldúa's contributions to feminist theorizing, AnaLouise Keating explains, "Spiritual activism begins with the personal yet moves outward, acknowledging our radical interconnectedness. This is spirituality for social change, spirituality that recognizes the many differences among us yet insists on our commonalities as catalysts for transformation."[4]

Though these insightful reflections informed my experience within tAP and my undergraduate and graduate teaching at UT Austin, my sociological research did not engage much with these groundbreaking forms of intellectual work at that moment. However, these reflections helped me reorganize my own professional experience as a Mexican immigrant who had traditionally felt on the margins of academia, especially as a graduate student. In my first year in Austin, the concept of spiritual activism became a foundation to develop a self-critical and more comprehensive view of my professional development as both a researcher and a teacher. I gradually felt more and more deeply connected with my profession, and with my new role as a sociologist working at a major research institution. And as I think of this experience in retrospect, the emblematic phrase I see every time I visit the UT Austin home page ("What Starts Here Changes the World") now reminds me of that sense of interconnectedness I experience as I engage in my teaching and research on sexuality, gender, and qualitative methods; I hope my humble work in the world may unfold avenues inviting both undergraduate and graduate students to engage in larger intellectual movements for social justice and change, locally and on a global scale.

More recently, Anzaldúa's insightful epistemologies began to organize the methodological questions I asked myself as I began to conduct my fieldwork leading to my second major sociological research project: a study of incest in Mexico. In this project, I am exploring the ways in which sexual activity within the context of the family (voluntary and involuntary) is connected to micro and macro social forces, and I am aiming at exploring larger social processes and structures of social inequality affecting both children and women. I recently completed the first phase of this project: I conducted in-depth individual interviews with a total of sixty adult women and men with histories of incestuous experiences who currently live in four urban centers (i.e., Ciudad Juárez, Guadalajara, Mexico City, and Monterrey). Though not all of the adults I interviewed reported their incestuous experiences as negative, damaging, or painful (and that was especially the case for those who voluntarily experienced sex with a relative), in this study, I introduce the concept of "epistemologies of the wound" to identify "the multidimensional state of consciousness I have discovered and explored at the core of the mutually interconnected intellectual, emotional, and spiritual processes I have experienced" and immersed myself in these individual interviews. The human interconnection I have experienced with each of my informants has allowed me, for instance, to metaphorically place myself inside the wound as an epistemological site to generate sociological knowledge on sexual violence against children and women. This process has also helped me to develop a sense of emotional and social interconnectedness with other adults, who may not have their voices included in my study but who have also been involved in similar experiences, especially those who had sex against their will, by force. And as I think of those unknown human beings in Mexico, Latin America, U.S. Latino communities and beyond, some of the women in tAP who had similar childhood histories come to my mind. In the end, spiritual activism unites all of us as we decipher our own marginalities and colonizations, either within the social cracks of so-called "developed countries" or the wounded spaces within "developing" and "underdeveloped" cultures and nations.

SPIRITUAL ACTIVISM: *Todas somos nos/otras*

Spiritual activism was also expressed through what was still unknown to me; at that point, the best was yet to come. I was invited close to the end of the fall semester to observe on-stage presentations of poetry and performance of healing: the women of tAP began to unpack their lives and pain articulated through voices mutually interconnected in deep processes of inner transformation. The women I had met months earlier had been able to completely open up and give life on stage, at times in the dark or under a humble dimmed light, to their stories of pain, stories of childhood and poverty, racism, homophobia, cultural shock, sexual curiosity and fear, love and deception, wounded bodies in struggle, despair and resistance, abuse—the quintessential *lucha*. I enjoyed being lost in my own state of sublime admiration and respect for them. I listened attentively in an act of emotional intimacy that will forever unite me to each one of them. What I experienced at that moment cannot be explained with words, because the spirit has no language or borders, because the soul of tAP was a state of collective consciousness inviting me in my own solitude to explore more than what I was able to explain to myself. Quietly, that night I became invisible in the comfort of that seat in the back, in the last row, but in my silent presence I was deeply connected with them through the tears that caressed my cheeks many times during an event that kept my notion of time in suspense. My own tears became the mirror reflecting back to me to remind me of my very own scars of life and struggle, pain and growth. The performance of humanity I was witnessing reminded me that through creative and aesthetic avenues, women that embrace contrasting cultural, ethnic, linguistic, class, religious, and sexual desires and experiences (among other layers of the human condition) can be united with one another by allowing themselves to be vulnerable and to confess their most intimate stories. I allowed myself to be caressed by their use of language, their body movements, their voices in pain, at times in desperate hope, at times in transition, and always so alive, resembling a powerful way in which women can expose to themselves the complex layers of the human condition: becoming completely vulnerable while placing themselves inside their deep wounds with a fearless and fragile open soul. Their unique yet collective vulnerabilities reflected back to me through the decolonizing feminist ideas that kept coming to my mind. *Todas somos nos/otras*—Anzaldúa's quintessential idea—was one of the refreshing feminist conceptualizations that explained the process I was witnessing, and was the intellectual organizer of that performance of humanity, of spiritual interconnectedness and individual yet collective healing.

January 2003. I never went back to any of the meetings or gatherings of

Transforming Practice

341

tAP, and though I periodically received messages from my sisters in struggle, I had my own battles to survive and kept my physical distance, but all of them were together in my heart. I had a deep desire to remain connected to all of them: with Sharon, who in my mind had became a shining Sol; with Joni, who through her own spiritual journey became Omi, and who reminded me of a peaceful Luna; and, finally, with the incoming groups of women I never met but I knew were rising stars aligned by el Sol and la Luna in interdependent forms of spiritual intimacy. In my silent and distant presence, each semester I visualized a group of women of color with similar stories but contrasting backgrounds getting together to learn the ways to open up and look inside their wounds through the aesthetics of healing. I knew that the women of tAP would continue exploring other avenues, always emblematic of spiritual activism. They were women going beyond the routine of daily life, getting together more than once to explore the quintessential *facultad*—another Anzaldúan concept which identifies the capacity to become "excruciatingly alive" to one's self and to those who are part of our life—to the rest of our world.[5]

Four years have already passed, and when I think of tAP, clear images comes to mind: a woman with open arms and expressive eyes looking up to the limitless sky, a woman in process of rupture and spiritual healing, a woman in communion with sisters sharing a common path, a woman becoming the change we want to see in our wounded societies, a woman for justice and without borders, a woman of universal struggles beyond fictitious differences, a woman who is the clear light and precious expression of the humankind.

Mi solidaridad y amor.

WORK OF THE SPIRIT

A Conversation with an Austin Project Elder

This chapter emphasizes the spiritual aspect of the work of the Austin Project. A partial transcript of a group conversation with a spiritual elder, the chapter offers an opportunity, through raúlrsalinas's insights, to consider the interactions of art, activism, and spiritual practice.

raúlrsalinas

(March 17, 1934–February 13, 2008)

XICANINDIO ELDER, POET, AND HUMAN RIGHTS ACTIVIST RAÚLRSALINAS was the executive director of Red Salmon Arts and founder of Resistencia Bookstore—a literary venue and community center for aspiring writers in Austin, Texas. raúl conducted intensive creative writing clinics locally and throughout the country with disenfranchised youth. These clinics were held in conjunction with a variety of arts organizations, correctional facilities and social service agencies. raúl's work with various political movements earned him an international reputation as an eloquent spokesperson for justice and advocate for the challenges and struggles of youth. Through SOY (Save Our Youth), raúl reached countless marginalized young people and trained other members of the Red Salmon Arts collective to continue this invaluable work nationally. He worked extensively with the American Indian Movement and the International Indian Treaty Council. raúl was the author of four books of poetry (*Viaje/Trip, East of the Freeway, Un Trip Through the Mind Jail,* and *Indio Trails*), as well as three spoken-word CDs (*Los Many Mundos of raúlrsalinas, Beyond the BEATen Path,* and *Red Arc*). Most recently the University of Texas Press published *raúlrsalinas and the Jail Machine: My Weapon Is My Pen,* a collection of his essays, newspaper articles, and letters. Beginning in 2001 he was an adjunct professor at St. Edward's University teaching classes on incarceration and media studies. raúlrsalinas is also the recipient of numerous awards: the Louis Reyes Rivera Lifetime Achievement Award presented by La Causa and the Dark Souls Collective at Amherst College in 2003; the Martin Luther King Jr./Cesar Chavez/Rosa Parks Visiting Professorship Award given by the University of Michigan at Ann Arbor in 2003; the Lifetime Achievement Award from the National Association of Latino Arts and Culture in 2004; Con Tinta, a coalition of Chicana/o and Latina/o cultural activists and writers honored raúl with the Veterano Writer Award in 2006, and finally the Alfredo Cisneros Del Moral Foundation Award in 2007. raúlrsalinas served as a beloved mentor to many artists, writers, and scholar-activists who sought to make a difference beyond the academy.

What follows is an edited transcript of a conversation between raúlrsalinas and the Austin Project, facilitated by René Valdez and Omi Osun Joni L. Jones. Speakers are identified in italics.

Omi Osun Joni L. Jones: This year it is clearer to me that the Austin Project has a spiritual base. It doesn't have to be a particular spiritual base at all, but my own spiritual practice is Yoruba. There is a lot of Yoruba flavor in the things that we do. Yoruba is my life, but what is important about the Austin Project is that is that there is a spiritual reality that undergirds it. I didn't acknowledge that, wasn't clear about that, when I started this in 2002.

So it's exciting that today we kind of sit right up in the middle of that awareness, the spiritual nature of the work that we do. Activism, art, fully being ourselves—those are phenomenal acts of love that spirituality, for me, rests on. So it's great that all these things have come together.

René Valdez: I want to thank everyone for coming together. I want to thank Sharon Bridgforth and Omi for organizing this important conversation. I also want to thank those of the Austin Project that came early this morning to help, and those who brought the treats and the food and the nourishment, thank you for your hard work. Just a brief introduction of our elder, mentor, and teacher, raúlrsalinas. I know many of you know of him, or know of his work, specifically his art, poetry, and activism. Today we are going to have him speak a little about how spirituality ties into his work and informs his art and activism. So a lot of us haven't had the privilege to lay out how spirituality works with activism and art, so we look forward to hearing what my elder has to say about such things.

So I would like to present raúlrsalinas.

raúlrsalinas: I am just going to try to invoke the energies of our ancestors before we turn it over to our sister Omi. I just want to thank all of you for coming here today, for bringing your hearts, your good energy—we sorely need them. I want to ask our grandmothers to just watch over us as we stumble through this time period here together, because we are trying to use some ways that belong to us, but we are ignorant about how to use them, so we misuse them. And so we ask the grandmothers to forgive us for that.

Omi Osun Joni L. Jones: I am wondering if we can start the conversation with you telling us about the early activism.

raúlrsalinas: Well, I think that it's important to understand how spirituality plays a part in our lives and how some people happen to come by it. My early activism had to do with fighting the jail machine from inside. With no sense of anything but fighting, and having been raised in the Catholic tradition, which still haunts me today, I didn't feel like I had any real understanding and, towards the end of my stay in prisons, I began to work through my art, and to connect with people who were combining those elements as one, and I began to look at my art in somewhat of a spiritual sense.

And upon my release from the control center, I went into exile. I wasn't allowed to return to Texas, couldn't return to California. I went into exile in Washington State and became involved with the fishing rights struggle of the American Indian in the Pacific Northwest. They are still fighting, still raging. And it was there that I was introduced to Native ceremonies and traditions, and went to my first ceremonies out West. I began to listen to the elders. They were telling us, for example, that we were following each other as leaders when the real leader was the sacred pipe. We didn't understand those things.

And when the jailing and all that began, we had nothing left but the ceremonies, and when we turned to the ceremonies, they began to attack the ceremonies. Then we realized the importance . . . It was very strengthening to learn that sitting in a circle, praying, receiving the sacred elements, could make one stronger.

And then how to begin to describe that as an artist, as a writer, how to begin to convey those things. And the making the mistakes and it all. And then finally how to utilize the arts. And now we work with youth, incarcerated youth, in schools, in detention centers, and it's about love and a lot of care and genuine honest feeling of wanting to just embrace them. Our poetry transforms people, young people. Not just young people, it transforms me as well. And so I use that and I try to be very conscious that it's not just me that is moving that [transformation], but the fact that I have been placed there to use those energies, and it works. It works. I am very careful about how I use these things, because, as I said, we are very ignorant. We are humans, we sometimes want to take it in another direction.

We are humans. I always make a point to let people, especially young people, know that I am in no way a medicine man or representative of anything. I am just a pitiful human being that got introduced to these things. And people don't know how to take it. People ridicule, some people try to control, people feel awkward, and so they disrespect. So one has to be careful even in how one carries these things. As soon as I wake up I am going to stumble and fall. I have to ask for strength, for guidance, for someone to stop by or call and say, "Hey," for that day that keeps us going.

What is spirituality? *Licencia*, kind of like *las energías*, you know. It happens and you feel it; it changes people and it's obvious. The unspoken. I think it's about turning each other on to whatever it is that makes us feel, and share, and contribute without all the other trappings—what's in it for me or whatever. It's a very good feeling to share, to give, to sacrifice. To give up something we cling to, material things. And I learned that from the elders, the giveaways, these things.

That's how the elders do it, when they set up a ceremony, the spirits tell you what elements you should use and there's a story for every element you use. And there are prayers. Whoever gave you this gift prayed before they gave that to you, and you've had that somewhere, and there were prayers there. This pipe is from South Dakota, or someone in Geneva, Switzerland, or Paris. So when you pass something on to someone, it's got all those prayers. It's not any hocus pocus, I mean, these are things that are all around. Tobacco, cigarettes, I just received some knickaknick tobacco. Somebody brought some back. These are the things our people use—water, corn, sage, tobacco, cedar, plants—these are the things that were meaningful at one time, but they've reduced them to nothing. They make us think that these things aren't valuable to us. And they are valuable to us, because they are left to us. I've seen federal agents kick our altars because they know how much strength there is there. So in all the tribal people throughout the continent, all continents, we all have the same elements: the Europeans before whatever happened; Africa, Asia, the sacred fire, the sacred drum. So those are things that are also protectors for us. And whenever people say yes, we put it on, our colors—this is what we are about—these are our ancestors. The sacred deer, the sacred eagle. All these things.

Omi Osun Joni L. Jones: You have been active in a number of kinds of communities. I wonder if you could share some of that journey with us, what it's been like for . . . you to build a community.

raúlrsalinas: I guess the first experience in community building that I was involved in was the prison community. After having spent, like, nine years in three different prisons, I was sent to a control unit in Marion, Illinois. We began to organize as Native Americans and Chicanos within the prison

The Work of Transformation

around educational issues, around the identity questions of the period about the things that were happening on the outside.

And the more we organized, the more we got to know our strengths and our weaknesses. One of our weaknesses was that we were isolated within the prison for any type of action that we wanted to take to articulate our grievances to the administration. As a result of study groups we began to form alliances. We forged alliances first with the Puerto Rican political prisoners, where we were social prisoners.

Through them we began to make inroads into the Black liberation issues of the times. They had quite of few Nation of Islam prisoners with us. We formed a very strong alliance. We saw how strong we could be against the prison systems. All we were fighting for was better medical attention, more attention paid to the indiscriminate sentencing and antiquated parole law. We were challenging our confined situation and becoming educated in the process, which Joy James calls "imprisoned intellectuals." We got so strong we were able to close the prison down. We were sent to a control unit—because we had formed that strong of a community, of jailhouse lawyers, of artists, of communicators. It took us days to research these tired behavior modification programs that the Feds had initiated—which was the later version of the lobotomy . . . And it was a laboratory to break prisoners, especially the political prisoners.

And, my God, I wound up being right in the middle of it, man. How rewarding and how educational, and how enlightening and how strengthening that social prisoners and significant druggies, or whatever they were in there for, could make the system listen and make changes. So that's what I left prison with, that transformation, which is the subject of this coming book, which combines my art and my spirituality with my politics.

I was released from prison and went to Washington State and my mentor immediately took me to the scene of an abandoned school in Seattle that was being occupied by the Chicano community, with the help of the African American and Asian community, that became the Centro de la Raza, which today still exists in many different changed forms. That was the parent organization, that was the first community I came to. They allowed me to try my politics, to try my art. They allowed me the space to see if something had really happened to me to make a difference, or was I just jiving. From there, we learned of the plight of the Native Peoples, being arrested, beaten up for exercising their treaty rights to fish. We joined them. I got taken in by a beautiful tribal chairwoman on the reservation, and so I became part of that community. From there we took on many of the major American Indian movement issues—self-determination. The Washington–

Work of the Spirit

347

Oregon Walk, the standoff on the river, trips to Geneva, and twelve years as the founder of the Leonard Peltier [Defense Committee] staff, different communities in Europe who've been so supportive of indigenous struggles, the young people in Holland. The real religious community that finally, through the Native ways, we were able to sit with, who were able to send representatives of their religious groups without fighting or arguing. The Buddhist community, who are very supportive wherever Leonard Peltier is taken to trial.

We had a bookstore in Seattle. They said "Let a poet name it: Resistencia." This [store we're in today] is the heir. So we came here twenty-four years ago to the east side, back to where I had grown up and left and got in trouble and everybody knew me. I rented a little storefront on the east side, and opened a little bookstore with a book that I had just published, and three other books. Somebody made the shelves, like we still do. We started out doing poetry readings. We'd have maybe two people. We had the first Chicano Kwanzaa. We didn't have any heat, but it was a very beautiful gathering. We began to bring a Native consciousness—because we were involved with the Peltier movement. We then organized a cultural exchange. We took twenty-one youth from here to Pine Ridge Reservation. We spent twenty-one days there, meeting people and relatives, learning all about the ways. So then we came to the south side, every time something happens we have to move. Last time the sisters painted the outside turquoise, and the landlady kicked us out. So then we began to work here and the people came.

This bookstore, everybody has put money into it. My mom, my family, everybody, students, teachers, and that's what has kept this space going. We don't own the space. We've always worked with the student community at all levels. Writing clinics—we do a writing workshop. We [work with] incarcerated youth, and middle school youth. We have interns that come here.

The gay and lesbian community was also growing here in Austin. We had friends [from that community] here as artists, couple of friends there in academia, but we began to be more a part of that with our sisters and brothers. Again, it was an education. I mean, we're relatives and we don't know who the hell we are. People say "those others" and that kind of stereotyping—backyard *chisme* that we have. We are part of the gay/lesbian community and they are a part of us, and we began to do events together, and hey, they're all right! What the hell? So it has been a learning experience. It's been an education every step of the way. Because it's opened our eyes more. Like you were saying, the more we open our eyes to culture, to different ways, the richer we are, the better we are for it, the better we can have the inner strength to say, "Here I am. I got nothing. Take me. Why should I act

The Work of Transformation

like I'm anything, I'm nothing, just earth. Just dirt. And I am ready to help you. And I don't want anything in return." That's what I keep learning.

Struggle. What a beautiful word. That is all we have. Struggle. Every day. Continuous. Struggle. Education. It comes no other way. That's education of the heart, education of the mind and spirit. When folks can feel each other. We talk about that. How to feel. Make them feel that we care. But how do we do that? Don't ask me, man. That's just when people show up, try to get everything that's bothering us and hurting us and say [raúl makes a hugging motion]. And it's not easy. We all have scars. We're all hurting. We all have stuff. But the more we open up, the more we learn, the more we are not afraid. That's what this space has become, not because I am saying it, but I've heard many of you say it. It's a "safe space." A safe space. It's safe because you can say whatever you want to. We are the strength. Here is one of those spaces. That's what we have tried to keep going.

We keep it going because of you. People bring us things every day, from all over the world. Every day—teachers, students, just passing through. Elders. Medicine people. That's what's here. That's what we have when we receive help. What should we say, I don't know what to say. Who puts the words in my mouth? Grandma, grandpa. Mom. We have all that community, all those relatives. And that's who we call on.

Hailing from El Paso, Texas, René Valdez is a working-class Chicano cultural worker, community organizer, and media activist who migrated to Austin in the late 1990s. He began as a volunteer for both Red Salmon Arts (RSA), a literary/cultural arts nonprofit organization (where he is now executive director), and community-based Resistencia Bookstore. Since 2000, he has worked as a student, close political comrade, and caring son of Xicanindio elder poet/human rights activist raúlsalinas. For the past three years, he has co-facilitated the intensive writing workshops of the RSA project, Save Our Youth (SOY), at Johnston High School.

Chapter Nine

NARRATING THE AUSTIN PROJECT

The First Five Years

OMI OSUN JONI L. JONES

In this final chapter, Omi Osun Joni L. Jones maps out the first five years of organizing the Austin Project in a personal narrative. Interweaving autobiography, advice, and documentation, this chapter is designed to be a springboard for organizing in your community.

IN *June Jordan's Poetry for the People,* JORDAN AND MANY OF HER STUDENTS meticulously describe the steps they took toward publishing their work and presenting their work in public. Jordan writes "For anyone interested, this Blueprint will spare you most of the trial and many of the errors of my own gradual discoveries."[1] Likewise, I have laid out the details of tAP's development to provide others with a guide as they work to establish similar projects in their communities. Rather than instruct readers on how to transform their artistic community activism into published texts and community poetry trainings as Jordan did, I chronicle the weekly workshops, exercises, Guest Artists' residencies, Austin-based artists' contributions, the culminating performances, and the managerial and interpersonal challenges and triumphs. It is my hope that the successes and failures of tAP will help other women map out transformative strategies in their neighborhoods.

How We Began

Jazz provides the space for the necessary inner freedom that spurs activism. This is not an unfettered, unbounded freedom, but a mature, responsible freedom that requires the virtuosity of self-introspection and the wisdom of group creativity. It was this freedom—to be one's true self in the company of open fellow travelers—that was terrifying in the preliminary planning meeting with Sharon Bridgforth when I invited her to be Anchor Artist for tAP. In that first meeting, Sharon's passion and persistence suggested that my dreams might come true. The expectation of rejection had left me so accustomed to working in a mindset of lack, of struggle, or stunted growth and deprivation, that her enthusiasm, clarity, and specific strategies for financing the Austin Project were, frankly, off-putting! I had barely stumbled through the embryonic ideas about tAP when Sharon instantly said, "Yes, I would like to work on this with you, and this is what you will need to do." I learned to appreciate her experience and her eagerness, and not be threatened or suspicious when my desires were taken seriously.

Within twenty-four hours, Sharon had e-mailed me a budget for tAP. After realizing that this was not an attempt to usurp my ideas—knee-jerk fear and suspicion are signs of living a dwarfed life—I considered the budget, made modifications based on the reality of what I knew was available, and discussed the idea with Edmund T. Gordon, then the director of the John L. Warfield Center for African and African American Studies (JLW/CAAAS) at the University of Texas.[2] I was surprised by how willing Ted was to commit Center funds to this work. Ted and I assumed the roles of director and associate director, respectively, of the Center in 2001. During our tenure, the Center offered approximately sixteen teaching assistant positions annually, collaborated with more than fifteen departments representing a wide range of disciplines to hire faculty working on African and African diasporic issues, sponsored a host of undergraduate activities, produced a series of guest lectures through Diaspora Talks and African Feminisms seminars, premiered productions of theatrical jazz in a Performing Blackness series, provided travel and research assistance for forty-five faculty affiliates, and worked to push the university to be more responsible in its education and employment of people of African descent. Given this pressing agenda, I was timid about committing the Center's funds to something I could not fully articulate. But Ted's understanding of art, politics, and activism meant that even my nascent vision was recognizable as compatible with his own.

With a budget of ten thousand dollars from JLW/CAAAS, and additional financial support from the Zachary T. Scott Family Chair in Drama at UT, held at that time by Jill Dolan, the Center for Women's and Gender Studies, and the Center for Asian American Studies, the Austin Project began. The money provided an honorarium for Anchor Artist Sharon Bridgforth, and three Guest Artists annually, as well as accommodations, meals, and transportation for the Guest Artists. The Austin-based Artists who performed a brief program on the same bill with the Guest Artists, performed for free. From the initial budget, I also purchased food for workshops, rehearsals, and post-performance receptions. Obviously, many in-kind services made tAP possible. The Anchor Artist and Guest Artists worked well below their customary fees, mostly because they believed in my idea and because we had worked together for many years. I relied on the goodwill of my exceptionally talented friends, and they in turn encouraged their talented friends to support this work without requiring their standard fees. I had been in conversation with Sharon and most of the Guest Artists for more than ten years as we created jazz-inflected work together; tAP became a way for all of us to continue the conversation and more fully explore the particular brand of theatrical jazz we were developing. The Guest Artists' standard fees for a workshop and performance *begins* at five thousand dollars, and I was quite appreciative of their willingness to work hard for much less money than they deserved. The Center bore the cost of photocopying and publicity, and the Center staff folded these new responsibilities (travel arrangements, hotel reservations, reconciliation of receipts, coordination of performance receptions, preparation of the performance space, staffing the box office) into their already packed commitments.

Ideally, each woman in tAP would be paid for her work. Paying the women would add another level of professionalism to the work, and would appropriately acknowledge the commitment and talent they bring. I see tAP as job training for the work the women will take out into the larger world, and for this they should be paid. Unfortunately, I have not yet been able to make this happen.

During the first two years of tAP, I paid for the participants' babysitting needs. I did not want the women with children to feel constraints on their participation. In more recent years, the women have worked out their own babysitting arrangements, often in a situation that allows all the children of tAP mothers to spend the workshop hours together.

Musical jazz relies on multiple voices and possibilities. Simultaneous multiple voices generate something new and unknown. Rather than a repetition of the familiar techniques for changing society (debate and negotiation, confrontation and revolt, coercion and torture), which have still left massive inequities in place, tAP rests on the principle that merely bringing a diverse group to work together would in and of itself generate minimally explored strategies for social change.

For this reason, the working group must be diverse. Cross neighborhoods, race, sexuality, education, class, self-performance—cross everything, and people are pushed to see themselves and others anew. Work together, and people are given an opportunity to learn respect, accountability, and true collaboration in which everyone contributes her absolute and idiosyncratic individuality, and everyone yields to the group process.

While a mix of people is a productive starting point for social change, I wanted the group to be predominantly people of color, and Sharon wanted specifically to work with women. This refining of participants still allowed

The Work of Transformation

for ample differences among us that challenged us to examine our self-constructions and our presumptions about others.

I had thought for some time that my jazz practice as a producer was connected to democracy, but democracy is not the issue at the heart of it all. The heart is personal freedom and group accountability. That's the real deal in the Austin Project. When a woman is hiding behind her own mess (insecurities, fear, isolation, doubt, numbness), we call her out on it. It is hard to hide from a room full of women determined to help you fly.

In an attempt to get as wide a range of women as possible to participate, I initially invited women from the NAACP, the Nation of Islam, SAHELI (an organization for Asian American families dealing with domestic violence), and Arte Sana (a Latina arts and healing organization). None of these leads panned out. In the first year, I developed another list of women Sharon and I knew directly, and after conferring with Sharon, I invited twelve women to become the first group of tAP participants. Eleven women completed the first year. As we considered who might participate, we consciously selected women of varied class backgrounds and sexualities.[3] All of the women lived inside of multiple identities as artists, scholars, and/or activists. In the first year, four identified primarily as artists, two primarily as scholars, and at least two felt activism was as much a part of their lives as scholarship or art. In that first year, four were in straight or gay marriages, two had children, and various sexualities (straight, gay, bi, curious) were represented. Although all of the participants identified as women, there was a range of gender performances within the group. There was one Latina, one Afro Latina, one Asian American woman, two white women, one first-generation Greek American woman, one Caribbean woman, and the rest were African American women. Most of the women had undergraduate degrees, some were in graduate school, and some were university professors. Many women identified as middle class, or struggling middle class, and some acknowledged present or past lives of poverty and economic deprivation.

FALL 2002

Members: Adrienne Baker, Shannon Baley, Detine Bowers, Florinda Bryant, Angela Kariotis, Jacqueline Lawton, Gloria González-López, Carole Metellus, Lisa Moore, Jane Park, Tracey Swan

Guest Artists: Laurie Carlos, Daniel Alexander Jones, Carl Hancock Rux

Austin-based Performers: Zell Miller III, Martha Pérez (Eric Dannenbaum and Danse Adje), Darla Johnson

---

During this first year, the group met for eleven weeks, each Saturday in the lobby of King-Seabrook Chapel at Huston-Tillotson University, a historically Black university in Austin. I brought an array of snacks to sustain us through the four hours of self-exploration and writing, and as the weeks progressed many woman also contributed to our bounty of fruit, chocolate, hummus, nuts, and tortilla chips. We generally began each session with a "check in" in which each woman briefly shared what energy she was bringing to the circle that day. We sat around large circular tables and looked out over the campus onto Seventh Street in East Austin, a predominantly Black and Latino/a part of town. We had signed Letters of Agreement that gave me permission to use their words and images for educational purposes, and gave them the assurance that I would fulfill my producing responsibilities as thoroughly as possible. Shannon videotaped our meetings as she participated, Sharon led our sessions, and we each hunkered down to do some of the toughest personal work we have faced. The women often remarked about how these sessions became like "church" for them, a spiritual commitment. We looked forward to our meetings all week and were revitalized after each gathering.

I had wanted to attract to tAP women from even more varied professions and organizations. In order to increase the diversity of representation in the first year, I held a small workshop outside of the regularly scheduled weekly tAP meetings. This smaller group included Mamata Misra, then the director of SAHELI, Ane Ebie, a performance studies graduate student in the Department of Communication Studies, and Theresa Burke (later Theresa Burke Garcia, who officially joined tAP in 2003), an elementary school teacher and actress. I used Theatre of the Oppressed techniques as writing prompts, and I included their writing in the lobby display that was part of the public sharing of the Austin Project work that year.

This first year cracked open many doors that I had unconsciously sealed shut. I had spent years walking in loneliness and isolation created, in part, from my unwillingness to release old—albeit crippling—ways of walking. Then, on the very first day of our gathering in 2002, Sharon had us sit in a circle on the floor where we could all easily see one another. "I am the producer, not a participant," I told myself, but was seduced by the sheer joy of being in a room full of women—mostly women of color—who were committed to being stronger better selves. So I, too, sat on the floor—a supreme release for me at that time, to sit with rather than sit apart from. To sit *with* risks being seen. But I sat there, full of delight and anticipation. Then Sharon firmly told us to respond succinctly to each of her questions about identity. "What is your race/ethnicity?" And, one by one, we thought through the right words. It was exhilarating! Such a simple question took us

The Work of Transformation

to the core of history, lineage, spirit, geography, politics, storytelling. "What is your gender?" Hmmm. It was heating up. "What is your sexuality?" And I was either paralyzed into wide-eyed silence, or I whooped my big old laugh—my two responses when I am scared. For the first time publicly I said, "Well, I've been historically heterosexual but I am sometimes attracted to women, though I've never had a relationship with a woman. But I think I could." And with that, everything changed. This is what tAP was for—prying open the truths that will help us to walk as ourselves. This is what is needed for abiding social change—for each of us to utterly name our desire—sexual, political, sartorial, gastronomical—all of it. And I cried inside because I knew I had waited years to finally say that, to not be who I imagined others to think I was, or who I thought they thought I should be, but instead to just be me.

Daniel Alexander Jones, Laurie Carlos, and Carl Hancock Rux were the Guest Artists in 2002. It was important for tAP women to see established artists working within unconventional forms as models for their own choices, and I also wanted to feature the less well known Austin-based artists who were likewise challenging form with the work they created. When Anna Deavere Smith produced the Institute for Art and Civic Dialogue, she brought internationally renowned artists to Harvard for performances and conversations with the people of Cambridge. This is an important model, but it seems to slight the local artists who may be engaged in equally powerful work. I wanted to be sure that the local and national could come together. It was another way to extend the cross-fertilization that is central to my jazz understanding of how to generate social change.

As Guest Artist, Daniel gave us movement-based exercises. There was yoga, and an extended session in which each woman sat across from a partner and looked into her eyes for at least fifteen minutes. No fidgeting, no turning away, or staring instead at noses. I worked with Jane and felt such love for her as both our eyes pooled with tears. I moved between many feelings—self-consciousness, generosity, humility, humor, appreciation. I realized how much I don't see of others, and consequently, how much I don't see of myself. Looking at Jane gave me a profound sense of shared humanity. Daniel instructed us to write a poem about our partner. Jane's poem about me—a beautiful tribute that made me stand taller—lived on my refrigerator door for a year. Daniel used the body work to open us up to others, and to open our creative passages. It seemed that for Daniel, the body and the written expression were intimately linked.

It was during his public performance that Daniel first tested his now nine-part autobiographical series with *The Book of Daniel*. With slides of his grandparents projected on a sheet and a flip-chart lesson on the nature of jazz, Daniel created a heavily improvised ride through identity, lineage, and the creative impulse. Martha Perez, Eric Dannenbaum, and Danse Adje were the Austin-based performers that evening, sharing the Haitian drum, dance, and song that characterize their work.

In Laurie's workshop session with the group, she pushed us to say what we were afraid to say. In a particularly difficult exercise, Laurie asked each woman to choose another woman in the room, then say "I love . . . ," then, "I hate. . . . " The sentence had to be completed with a comment about the woman being addressed. Laurie did not allow us to simply say, "I love your curly hair." She asked us to speak a deeper truth. It was startling how difficult it was to hear people say they loved something about me. I rejected the appreciation I was given. At that time, as I struggled with so many fears and hidden personal corners, I didn't have a place to put such comments. Then one woman turned to me and delivered an "I hate" statement, and I was enraged! Not because she hated something about me, but because she introduced into the circle an issue that I thought we had resolved. I rarely speak publicly from a place of fire, but it was easy for me to access that place as I turned to this woman and returned an "I hate" statement. I spit the words at her with a certainty I had not known before. This was not my usual carefully measured comment; this was the site of passion born of truth, and the beginning of a new way to know who I am.

For her public performance, Laurie presented *If the Butter Burns, It Ain't Biscuits*, an improvised piece about loneliness and community. tAP women could see Laurie embody the essential principles of risk-taking and truth-telling as she made discoveries on the spot. With her distinctive blend of breath and modern dance–inflected movement, Laurie presented new ways of telling stories and walking erect as an artist of a little-known theatrical form. Zell Miller III—who lovingly calls Laurie "Mama Carlos"—offered an opening performance that demonstrated his debt to Laurie's brand of direct address to the audience, and created an environment of warmth and professionalism that replaced formal introductions of Laurie.

Carl gave the women a workshop about the professional side of the performance world, and guided us through group performances that we wrote and presented within the four hours we were together. His attention on group performance foreshadowed the work we would do with Laurie in 2005 and 2006. For his public performance, he read casually and authoritatively from his *Pagan Operetta*, sitting on a stool. Before Carl's performance, Darla Johnson danced an homage to her mother titled "Waiting," a duet with a tree limb that trembled and bent under her guidance.

The workshops were designed to get us to be present, to truly feel what we are feeling, to be honest about what we know of ourselves and the world. This is the key in a jazz aesthetic that unlocks the idiosyncrasy and community, the vitality and fragility of the most profound art and activism and scholarship. The guest performances were an opportunity to see how the jazz of the workshops could be shaped into professional public work.

At the end of the eleven weeks, the women performed the work they had created in the style of a poetry reading with each woman sharing no more than five minutes of her work. The performances were held in room 2.180 of the Winship Drama Building at the University of Texas, and in the music classroom at Huston-Tillotson University. These different locations were chosen to attract different audiences.

During the spring of 2003, I asked the women to participate in local events sponsored by groups that were as committed to social change as tAP is. Florinda and Jane performed pieces about physical abuse and sexual identity for SAHELI, a support group for Asian American families coping with domestic violence. Lisa and Carole shared their work at the annual Peace and Justice Day sponsored by the John L. Warfield Center for African and African American Studies. Florinda and Carole performed their work at UT's "Take Back the Night" celebration, designed to increase awareness about domestic violence. In a moment of foreshadowing, D'Lo was in town and performed alongside Florinda and Carole. D'Lo later became a member of tAP in 2006.

Fall 2003

Members: Rajasvini Bhansali, Florinda Bryant, Theresa Burke Garcia, Monique Cortez, Geeta Cowlagi, Amber Feldman, Virginia Grise, Rosalee Martin, Carole Metellus, Lisa Moore, Deisi Pérez Pérez, Shia Shabazz
Guest Artists: Sharon Bridgforth, Laurie Carlos, Robbie McCauley
Austin-based Performers: Daniel Davis Clayton, Jeffrey "Da'Shade" Johnson

In the second year of tAP, I followed my initial governing principle that once you are in tAP, you are always in tAP. With that in mind, I invited all of the women from the previous year to return for another eleven-week session. Some women were already over-committed, and some had moved out of the state. This left only three members returning. Using the same principles of diversity that guided my original list of participants, I once again looked for women from divergent class, race, geographic, and sexual backgrounds. By the second year, word about tAP had spread, and many women sought Sharon and me out to inquire about participating with us. Sharon has been conducting writing workshops since 1995, and women who knew of her strength in that context were eager to work with her in a deeper way. Through my work at the University of Texas, and through my work in the local theatre scene, I, too, knew several women who wanted to work with me in a rigorous, systematic way. In order to curb the forces of hegemony and ensure that the space was dominated by women of color, white women needed to be a clear minority. It would have been easy to only select women in the academy because that is a world I could easily tap for participants. It would also have been easy to draw from the deep pool of exceptional Austin writers. But choosing solely from either of these groups would have blunted the necessary edginess and unpredictability that comes from diverse groupings, and would have diminished the potential for exacting transformation.

After the first year of the Austin Project, I was reminded that producing is exhausting. The logistics of coordinating space for workshops and rehearsals, keeping the women informed about the progress of the work, shopping for and transporting the workshop food, hosting the Guest Artists who need meals, transportation, and company in a new city, publicizing performances, creating lobby displays for the public performances, photocopying work, fliers, and handouts, and toting video equipment for documentation, along with maintaining my responsibilities as a faculty member and associate director of JLW/CAAAS was almost debilitating. The thing that kept me going was the absolute thrill of the work itself. I could see what was happening to each of us, how important this work had become to us, how it was changing our lives—and this kept me shopping for specific sugar-free snacks at 1:00 a.m. or schlepping equipment in the rain or changing the hotel in the middle of the night for a guest who found the original hotel too noisy or facing down the daunting red tape that UT creates in order to pay anyone for anything. I asked one of the tAP women to be my assistant in order to stave off delirium, but ultimately she was not able to do so.

While it was important for us to meet at Huston-Tillotson College, an often-overlooked HBCU (historically Black college or university), the logistical difficulties of using the chapel had intensified by the end of the first year. Monique, a physician, had access to an Austin Regional Clinic facility that was not being used, and this became our new weekly home in the second year of tAP.

After seeing the power of the first year, I decided to fully immerse myself as a participant during the second year. Sharon once again used some of the introductory exercises from her facilitation method, Finding Voice, to get us familiar with each other and with ourselves in a new group, and in 2003 she had entirely new Finding Voice techniques to get us to see who we are. It felt good to write creatively after the years of demanding

     The Work of Transformation

career-dependent academic writing. The creative writing gave me a new way to actually see myself as a writer and to eventually claim that title. My academic writing put the emphasis on theorizing or critiquing rather than writing per se. My subsequent scholarly essays following my work with tAP had a clearer voice because of the authority I was finding as a short story writer. I became passionate about the possibilities of blending the content with an appropriate and distinctive writing presence.

In the second year, we once again videotaped all of our sessions to document how we did the work and how the work was evolving.

Robbie McCauley conducted a workshop for tAP in which she spread newspapers on the floor and asked us to find—almost randomly—a piece of text to write about. She also conducted body work in which we had to put our backs to the group and move with the passion of whatever we were feeling right then. Robbie honored the creativity in each of us, and spoke intimately about her own journey as an artist. It was particularly important that Robbie—an acclaimed artist and activist who teaches in the academy— could speak from personal understanding about art, activism, and scholarship. On October 31, 2003, Robbie performed "How I Make Pieces, *Sugar*, and Other Excerpts," an improvised conversation with the audience about sugar production, the transatlantic slave market, the conflation of Black bodies with stimulation and pleasure through coffee, tobacco, and sugar, and her private relationship to diabetes. As she ate fruit and injected insulin into her arm, she became the embodiment of the racist history that continues to grip the world. Jeffrey "Da'Shade" Johnson performed in the local artist slot prior to Robbie, and through spoken word and capoeira, Da'Shade wove a rhythmic history of alienation and exile.

On November 7, 2003, Sharon read excerpts from her award-winning book *the bull-jean stories*, and from her performance piece, *con flama*. Her respect and familiarity among a wide range of people and institutions brought new audiences to the Austin Project experience. Daniel Davis Clayton performed his jazz-inspired poetry to set the stage for Sharon's performance.

Laurie was now familiar with many of the women in tAP, and she understood the potential in the process. She did not feel the medical clinic where we had been holding our weekly meetings was conducive to the work she wanted to do with the women, so her workshop was held at The Off Center, a popular theatre space operated by the avant-garde Rude Mechanicals theatre collective in Austin, Texas. As with all the spaces that tAP has used thus far, The Off Center was donated as an in-kind contribution. We sat in a circle and Laurie preached about what it means to make art. No matter how each woman identified, in that moment we were all artists being pushed out of our timidity. Some of us cried at the painful recognition that Laurie exposed. She taught us jazz principles of deep listening and courage as we sang "Row, Row, Row Your Boat," in a layered musical round, and once again marveled at what we could create together. The common children's song became a scatting, bluesy, spirited, improvised collaboration of surprise and union. On December 5, 2003, Laurie was scheduled to perform excerpts from her newly written *Marion's Terrible Time of Joy*, but moments before the audience entered the space, she turned to me and Sharon, handed us scripts and said "I want you to do this with me!" Sharon and I moved through the shock and the terror, performed on stage with Laurie, and relied on everything we knew about how jazz is made—fierce individuality, communal responsiveness, and play, play, play.

A significant development in 2003 was the transformation in the relationship between Sharon and me. We fell in love, and my life became a lush green field of possibilities.

At the end of the eleven weeks, each woman presented her work as a series of individual readings in the Winship Drama Building, room 2.180, at the University of Texas. Geeta had to leave for India to be with her ailing father-in-law, so she videotaped the reading of her poetic essay, and it was shown during the performance. There was a second, more informal reading at the clubhouse of Vini's apartment complex. Families and friends joined us as we each shared the work we had created.

SPRING 2005

Members: Florinda Bryant, Bianca Flores, Kristen Gerhard, Erika González, Virginia Grise, Krissy Mahan, Rosalee Martin, Carole Metellus, Lisa Moore, Courtney Morris, Shia Shabazz
Guest Artist: Laurie Carlos

In the third year, I moved tAP from a fall to a spring activity. As associate director of the JLW/CAAAS, I received a course reduction in the spring. I decided to fill the "extra" time not only with my expanding JLW/CAAAS duties, but also with the increasing responsibilities associated with producing tAP. In this year, Sharon and I co-facilitated rather than Sharon assuming the primary responsibility for facilitation and me taking the less interactive role of producer. I introduced a series of physical strategies for exposing those psychic spaces that keep us stuck in our daily interactions. My increased role as a facilitator shifted our relationships with the women and with the work itself. Our weekend workshops were held at the Center, which solidified tAP's alignment with the radical politics of JLW/CAAAS.

The Work of Transformation

This year, Sharon and I thought it would be good to vary the structure. By this time, some women would be in their third year with tAP and we wanted to keep them stimulated and challenged with new forms. I was also aware that the scholarship component of our work had been given short shrift. In the first year, Lisa Moore prepared some materials on feminism and distributed those to the women, and Gloria González-López created a lobby display on Latin jazz. For the most part, this was how scholarship was addressed during that first year. In the second year, scholarship was mentioned but not woven into the weekly workshops. So in the third year, I worked to bring scholarship to the fore. With this in mind, Sharon and I introduced a research element into the women's work. Sharon asked the women to consider the writing they were working on, and identify how that writing might benefit from further study that could be acquired at a comprehensive library. Lisa gave the women a brief orientation to the Perry-Castañeda Library (PCL) at UT and allowed the women to check out books on her card. Some of the women seemed intimidated by participating in such a formal institutional structure, but others were excited to make use of these resources. Many of the women came to understand their subjects—such as child molestation, the wars of the United States, the history of colonization—through the statistics, ethnographic documentation, and empirical data available at the PCL.

I also began a series of movement workshops with the women, borrowing techniques from Theatre of the Oppressed, yoga, and my own performance exercises, to encourage them to find places of tension in their bodies where trauma, stress, and fear might be lodged. In solo, paired, and group "dances" the women explored the connection between their physical, psychic, and spiritual selves. At the conclusion of each session, they wrote what they felt and what they discovered. Some of this material made its way into the pieces they were working on, and much of this material was solely designed to help free them into deeper creativity.

The greatest structural change in 2005 was in the shape of the final public performance. Rather than invite Guest Artists to tAP, in the third year I invited Laurie to do an extended residency with tAP wherein she worked with the women five days each week for two weeks. Laurie came near the end of the eleven-week session, took the writing the women had generated so far, and melded it into a jazz concert. In the workshops leading up to the performance, Laurie helped us to pay attention—a key feature in a jazz aesthetic. One evening she played Sting's "Fill Her Up." The music started out in a traditional country-western style, evolved into a driving urban rhythm, then returned to the country style. Laurie helped us listen to the details in the lyrics that anticipated the musical shifts. We took apart the words and the sounds, noted which instruments were used when and to what effect, recognized the moment when Sting's voice moved from white Southern pathos to lilting jazz longings. This was the kind of listening and appreciation Laurie demanded of us in performance. A jazz aesthetic chorus does not unconsciously speak simultaneously, but finds the moments when amplification, allegro, whisper, juba, retard, staccato, or glide are the best choices to make; and "best" is determined by studious listening.

Everyone's work was included in some form in the final performance, though few of us had our entire pieces performed in the public showing. This new text required that everyone be willing to allow her work to be reimagined through Laurie's sensibility. The public would not experience us as individual writers, as was the case in previous years. Instead, the audience would receive a blended text of our writings. This also meant that we had to trust other voices to express our work. Rarely did Laurie assign the writer as the primary voice in her own piece. She applied the techniques of choral work, listening, repetition, layered music, and polyphony to the performance so that a single page of text might transform into three pages of shared voices and varied understandings. It was quite moving to hear my own story through the spirits of the other women. I heard things and felt things that I didn't know were there. I was struck by how respectfully and empathically the women handled my words. They seemed to understand at a depth that I thought could only belong to me. I think such collaboration would have been awkward in earlier years because the trust in the process and in the "elders" would not have been as strong. Laurie had returned to tAP for the third consecutive year, and even the new members had seen her previous performances and heard the legends surrounding her past workshops.

The public performances were held in the Lab Theatre at the University of Texas and at allgo, a statewide queer people of color organization. There were several teenage girls in the audience and their presence gave a heightened energy to the performance. Unfortunately, Rosalee was not able to perform with us; her ex-husband died near this time and she traveled to support her children through the family's grief.

In the spring of 2005, Sharon learned that she had cervical cancer. Her surgery was in May, after the tAP session had ended, but the fact of her cancer and impending surgery colored all of our relationships that year. After her surgery—which was successful and did not require radiation or chemotherapy—tAP women were excellent caregivers as they organized food deliveries, cleaned her apartment, ran errands, told jokes, moved her from a second-floor apartment to an accessible one on the first floor, and demonstrated their respect and gratitude for their much-loved elder.

Members: Florinda Bryant, D'Lo, Dulani, Bianca Flores, Kristen Gerhard, Erika González, Virginia Grise, Alyssa Harad, Amanda Johnston, Ana-Maurine Lara, Krissy Mahan, Rosalee Martin, Lisa Moore, Courtney Morris, Jaclyn Pryor, Shia Shabazz
   Guest Artists: Laurie Carlos, Daniel Alexander Jones
   Special Guest: Maiana Minahal

The fourth year of the Austin Project was markedly different. In this year, the exuberance that Sharon and I felt for the process of tAP led us to work with a significantly larger number of women than in previous years. Ten women were returning, and we invited six more to join us. While this larger number may have created some unique challenges in 2006, the tensions also stemmed from the new emotional and physical terrain that Sharon and I inhabited as she recovered from cancer and I was her primary caregiver. I do not think either of us realized what a toll this had taken on our ability to be fully present and generous as facilitators.

In addition to the size of the group and the sheer exhaustion of the facilitators, a host of other factors may have contributed to the strains of the fourth year. There were more absences and tardies than in previous years. Sharon insisted that women miss no more than one workshop during the eleven-week session, but several women went beyond this number. There seemed to be less enthusiasm and willing vulnerability than in the past. The work is always difficult, but it had been the kind of challenge that we welcomed as part of our growth. In the fourth year, the challenge seemed to be around being rigorously self-reflexive and committed to the jazz structures that were presented. I felt that some of the subgroups that developed created collective identities that hampered the process of individual self-exploration. Groups of women sometimes spoke as a unit, which made me feel as though I was not really knowing them or working with them as specific distinctive women. There also developed a "group within the group" of women who periodically gathered for parties and conversation. These gatherings did a lot to create solidarity and group identity, but might have left those who did not participate feeling somewhat alienated.

It is also important for me to note that many women did not feel that this year was as difficult as I did. Some of those who had just joined tAP experienced similar revelations and reached places of growth as did women from previous years; indeed, some were surprised that many of us felt various levels of discomfort and dissatisfaction with the fourth year.

In spite of any weaknesses that year, the year also had significant high points, including specifically locating spirituality within the work of tAP. Over the years, it had become clear that spirituality was central to the work we were doing together. The ability to face the truth of one's self seems at the core of many spiritual practices including Buddhism's quest to help human beings discover and nurture the Buddha nature within, the consciousness of Christ that Christians must embody, and Ifá's principles of obedience and self-development. Several spiritual traditions were represented in the group over the years including the Religious Society of Friends, Judaism, the Ifá and Orisa traditions of Yoruba-based practices, Danza Azteca/ Chichimeca, Catholicism, Jainism, Islam, Buddhism, and various Protestant denominations.

To underscore the spiritual foundation of our activist, scholarly, and artistic journeys, I invited spiritual leaders from different traditions to speak with the group about the intersections of their activism and their spiritual practice. One Sunday at the Resistencia Bookstore, raúlrsalinas talked to tAP members about how each of our choices are acts of social change that are fueled by spirit.

Another powerful addition to the work in the fourth year was the presence of Maiana Minahal, who was mentored by June Jordan and became one of Jordan's teaching artists for Poetry for the People. After Jordan's death, Maiana was at the helm of this transformative poetry-based activism that Jordan had begun. Poetry for the People was undergoing a metamorphosis that was threatening to break the spirit of the program, and Maiana sought relief from those challenges by coming to Austin to replenish with the Austin Project. I was moved that Maiana accepted Sharon's invitation to come to tAP. Having Maiana present was a kind of validation that the work we were doing was important and was carrying on a distinguished tradition. Near the end of the eleven-week session, Sharon offered to train the women in her Finding Voice method of facilitation. Maiana attended tAP specifically for this training, and she welcomed her role as student as a respite from the rigors of her years as group facilitator.

Daniel and Laurie returned as Guest Artists. The continuity that results from working with the same artists helps solidify tAP's identity, and provides the Guest Artists with an ongoing space for examining their own work. During the workshop with Daniel, the women engaged in a passionate discussion about whether or not they could call themselves artists. Uncharacteristically, neither Sharon nor I were present for this workshop. The women reported sharply different accounts of what transpired, but it seems that issues around class and the utility of art dominated the discussion.

Laurie once again came for a two-week residency. As in 2005, she took our writing and shaped a group text of our work that we performed in room 2.180 of the Winship Drama Building at UT, and at The Off Center. At the final performance, Laurie, Sharon, and I made several exciting announcements to tAP and to the audience. Virginia had been one of only two persons chosen that year for participation in the prestigious CalArts writer's program. Florinda had been selected to have her own full-length work produced in the Performing Blackness series of the John L. Warfield Center for African and African American Studies. And Shia had been chosen to shadow me in my work as producer for tAP. In making these announcements, it was clear that most of the members who had been with tAP the longest were now "graduating" to the next levels of their development.

SPRING 2007

Much of 2007 was devoted to rest and reorganization—and to developing this book. No new members were invited to join as we all continued to catch our breath from the rigors of 2006. It became clear that it was time to reexamine tAP's structure and create new plans for moving forward. Several of us met twice to discuss tAP's shape and future possibilities. I sent a simple questionnaire to all of the women who had participated from 2002 to 2007, and asked them to e-mail responses if they could not make the meetings. Those questions provided the organization for our planning sessions.

That spring some of the women also worked with Sekou Sundiata as part of his America Project. Sekou is very much a part of the jazz tradition that shapes tAP, having worked with Laurie and Carl and other members of the tAP extended family, including composer and singer Helga Davis. Several years earlier, I had interviewed Sekou and his long-time collaborator, trombonist Craig Harris, as part of a theatre conference sponsored by New World Theatre of the University of Massachusetts. I had been moved by his work, and was thrilled that tAP would have the privilege of working with this visionary. A handful of women worked with Sekou on their writing, and several of us attended his *51st (dream) state* that was produced by the Performing Arts Center of UT. During the fall of 2005, some of the women worked with Sekou when he was in Austin for a conference on art and policy. Sekou enjoyed working with tAP so much that he specifically requested to work with us when he returned in 2007. It was unfortunate that more women did not work with this nationally recognized poet and activist, and I believe that their lack of availability had as much to do with the lingering disappointment from 2006 as it did with their busy schedules. On July 18, 2007, Sekou died of a heart attack. I have not been able to fully feel this loss; the enormity of it is so great. On September 11, a day of particular significance to Sekou and his work, tAP joined other Austin organizations to celebrate his life. Helga also came at my request to sing "The Sea," a song from his production, *Elijah*. Sekou's passing is a shocking reminder of how important it is that we do this work, that we be courageous and joyful, and that we pass the light on.

As part of a new selection process, some of the more senior tAP members conducted a workshop designed to allow potential members an opportunity to get an idea of the work and to allow tAP members to participate directly in deciding who might comprise the next tAP ensemble. As a result of the organizational meetings, I determined that we should not work with more than nine women (well, maybe ten if we found someone we *must* work with!), and that the women should make a two-year commitment to tAP. After two years, another group of women will be asked to work with us. The two-year cycle will help to keep all of us fresh and open, and will create a culminating experience for each woman.

tAP has now expanded to include the Austin Project Performance Company (tAPPCo) which is headed by Florinda as the artistic director. Florinda had suggested this addition as a way to expand tAP's reach, to keep previous participants actively engaged, and to provide tAP artists with a knowledgeable ensemble that could perform their jazz-inflected works. I retain the philosophy that once you are in tAP, you are always in tAP, but after two years of work, the women would no longer attend the weekly circles. They could participate in guest workshops and mentor new members, and they would be expected to "give back" to tAP in specific ways. And, indeed, the women are finding their own ways of helping to sustain tAP; one woman has been documenting our work and creating DVDs that Sharon and I show at conferences, another is creating graphics for tAP, another is working on developing a website for tAP, others have invited Sharon to offer Finding Voice workshops for their jobs and readings in their cities, and others have developed university courses specifically around the Finding Voice method. I have asked all the women to put tAP on their résumés and vitae, and to acknowledge publicly each time they use exercises and structures they acquired from tAP. I believe it will add another layer of commitment if the women understand they have a responsibility to tAP that will continue beyond their time in the weekly circles. I have to be clear with the women about my expectations in this regard when I extend the invitation.

It is important to continue expanding the diversity of the women who are invited to participate. Most of the women have been connected to Sharon or me in some way prior to their work in tAP. This is a good way of knowing the personalities that will be participating, but I fear it doesn't spread the work as far as it could. The circle will benefit from more women who do not already identify as artists and who are not already in our spheres of influence. It is critical that this work pervade society; the more diverse selection of women that carry tAP practices to their homes, the wider the dissemination of these strategies for social change will be.

The addition of the spiritual leaders in the fourth year was very important in solidifying a base for tAP. The intent is to stretch the ways the women think of the work so that all aspects of their lives can be housed together rather than compartmentalized—in the same way that a poem is activism and academic scholarship is a political campaign. I intend to identify leaders from many other spiritual traditions and invite them to share the truths of their lives with the tAP women.

I would also like to include Guest Artists from many disciplines. Composers, singers, musicians, installation artists, filmmakers, and painters would extend the way in which the women of tAP imagine art in their lives and as tools for change.

And perhaps I will include Guest Scholars who consciously create research as an act of resistance. I have yet to fully integrate scholarship into the Austin Project, and am anxious to do so.

As tAP continues to grow, it would be good to figure out what to call ourselves. Are we tAP members? tAP participants? Some of the women felt "members" seemed too exclusive, yet "participants" seems too sterile for the intimate transformative work we do. As women added tAP to their résumés, I think most settled on "members." Perhaps if we call ourselves the tAP *ensemble* we get away from the sense of exclusivity and move toward a jazz notion of collaboration and inspiration.

Between 2002 and 2007, the *ensemble* has had five babies, two marriages, two divorces, two books published, one online journal launched, one doctorate completed, two master's degrees, one nursing degree, two admissions into graduate study, one new job as assistant professor, several productions of original works around the country, the creation of new organizations and companies, "coming-outs," countless readings of their work, and even more individual epiphanies about how to live life. These milestones are what keep the jazz flowing, making change everywhere it goes.

And I excitedly embrace my own reincarnation as tAP evolves. When I look around the circle, I know that I must honor myself as a writer, that I must dance and garden and leave the office before 10:00 at night. I realize once again that my daily minute choices are indeed the ones that make grand changes possible.

NOTES

CHAPTER ONE

1. The website for the Institute on the Arts and Civic Dialogue includes this quotation by Smith along with extensive profiles and Institute production histories for each of those who collaborated on projects. Although the summer intensives ended in 2000, the Institute continues to support work that fosters the kind of contestation, critique, communion, and conversation that characterizes much of Smith's work

2. *Animating Democracy: Strengthening the Role of the Arts in Civic Dialogue* (Austin: Animating Democracy Institute, 2003).

3. Lauren Muller, *June Jordan's Poetry for the People: A Revolutionary Blueprint* (New York: Routledge, 1995), 3.

4. In 2003, Rajasvini Bhansali joined the Austin Project after having been a student-teacher poet with Poetry for the People from 1994 through 1996. In 2006, Maiana Minahal was a Special Guest with tAP. Maiana was mentored by Jordan and became a teaching artist with Poetry for the People. Maiana also took leadership of Poetry for the People when Jordan died in 2002. Samiya Bashir, who was a member of Poetry for the People and was named Poet Laureate of the nine campuses of the University of California in 1994, became an ensemble member with tAP in 2008.

5. I have chosen to refer to the work of the Austin Project as the jazz aesthetic though I am aware of the many critiques surrounding the use of the term "jazz." Most notably, Robert G. O'Meally examined the complexities of using jazz to understand non-musical forms in the preface to *The Jazz Cadence of American Culture*, and at one point in his career, activist/artist/scholar Fred Wei-han Ho simply refused to use the term, as he explained in *Sounding Off!: Music as Subversion/Resistance/Revolution*. But because jazz continues to evoke ideas of opposition, spontaneity, and Blackness, the term suits the politically conscious, Black, feminist, anti-racist work of the Austin Project well.

6. The Combahee River Collective of Black lesbian feminists wrote:

> We might use our position at the bottom, however, to make a clear leap into revolutionary action. If black women were free, it would mean that everyone else would have to be free since our freedom would necessitate the destruction of all the systems of oppression.

7. Katherine McKittrick describes the enterprise of her book *Demonic Grounds* in this way: "I explore the interplay between geographies of domination (such as transatlantic slavery and racial-sexual displacement) and black women's geographies (such as their knowledges, negotiations, and experiences)." While McKittrick sees the slave ship as "materially and ideologically enclosing black subjects" and contributing to "the formation of an oppositional geography . . . of black subjectivity and human terror, black resistance, and in some cases, black possession," I see academic institutions also existing as "vessels of human violence" in the way they seek to eradicate Black femaleness through structures

that negate our existence. Katherine McKittrick, *Demonic Grounds: Black Women and the Cartographies of Struggle* (Minneapolis: University of Minnesota Press, 2006), xi.

8. In *Utopia in Performance: Finding Hope at the Theatre* (Ann Arbor: University of Michigan Press, 2005), Jill Dolan concludes, "[perhaps we should] focus our activism on getting more and different kinds of people into the theater in the first place, so that they, too, might experience their affective power." It is also my feeling that gathering the widest range of audience members lays the foundation for social change, and this is the world of non-hierarchical differences that I would like to inhabit. It is the world I seek to create through the Austin Project.

9. I have used Augusto Boal's Theatre of the Oppressed techniques in the Austin Project, sometimes as writing prompts, sometimes as a tool for encouraging the women to explore their histories more deeply through physicalization. Mady Schutzman and Jan Cohen-Cruz's persuasive critiques of these techniques require that I use the techniques mindfully, with particular attention to the way in which my role as facilitator (or Joker) may unconsciously introduce a dominating force into the space. This impulse on the one hand and the role of elder on the other hand must be gingerly negotiated.

10. During the spring of 2005, Sekou Sundiata came to Austin through the Humanities Institute at the University of Texas to conduct workshops and present his *51st (dream) state*, a production that explores national identity in the United States. As part of his residency, he worked with some of the women of the Austin Project. Almost all of the white tAP women participated while few of the women of color were available for this work. This created the unusual circumstance of having white women as the primary participants and representatives of tAP.

11. White feminists have written about the safety and sanctity of the circle as the site for self-exploration and group solidarity. As they write of such circles, it seems they were considering predominantly white circles, not circles with women of color who bring their own histories to their relationships with white women. In the Austin Project, the circle becomes the place to "go toe to toe"—and it is safe only to the extent that the women offer each other trust and respect. It is not always the gentle space associated with other feminist healing circles. For further discussion and critique of "feminist circles" see Nel Noddings, *The Challenge to Care in Schools: An Alternative Approach to Education* (New York: Teacher's College Press, 1992), and Mimi Orner's "Interrupting the Calls for Student Voice in 'Liberatory' Education: A Feminist Poststructrualist Perspective" in *Feminisms and Critical Pedagogy*, eds. Carmen Luke and Jennifer Gore (New York: Routledge, 1992), 74–89.

12. Ntozake Shange references "combat breath" in her foundational essay "unrecovered losses" in *Three Pieces* (New York: Penguin, 1982). Shange notes that such breathing is required for Black women writers who dare to speak the truths of their lives. Frantz Fanon spoke of this breathing as a way to be ever on guard for the collapse of individuality into essentialism.

13. Deborah G. Marin, Susan Hanson, and Danielle Fontaine, "What Counts as Activism?: The Role of Individuals in Creating Change," *Women's Studies Quarterly* 35 (Fall–Winter 2007): 78–94.

14. Joanna Brooks, "Renovations and Revolutions," (lecture presented at Transatlantic Feminisms in the Age of Revolution conference, University of Texas, Austin, Texas, May 9, 2008), 20.

15. Theresa Jenoure, *Navigators: African American Musicians, Dancers, and Visual Artists in Academe* (Albany: State University of New York, 2000), 203.

16. M. Jacqui Alexander, "Remembering *This Bridge*, Remembering Ourselves," in *Sing, Whisper, Shout, Pray: Feminist Visions for a Just World*, eds. Lisa Albrecht, M. Jacqui Alexander, Sharon Day, and Mab Segrest (EdgeWork Books, 2003), 627.

17. Before an audience expecting her to give a lecture on women and fiction, Virginia Woolf famously declared, "a woman must have money and a room of her own if she is to write fiction." In order to fully experience how Woolf's courageous words suit so well the dilemma of women of color in the academy and the need for the Austin Project for women from diverse experiences, I think it useful to include an extended passage from her work *A Room of One's Own*.

> Alas, laid on the grass how small, how insignificant this thought of mine looked; the sort of fish that a good fisherman puts back into the water so that it may grow fatter and be one day worth cooking and eating. I will not trouble you with that thought now, though if you look carefully you may find it for yourselves in the course of what I am going to say.
>
> But however small it was, it had, nevertheless, the mysterious property of its kind—put back into the mind, it became at once very exciting, and important; and as it darted and sank, and flashed hither and thither, set up such a wash and tumult of ideas that it was impossible to sit still. It was thus that I found myself walking with extreme rapidity across a grass plot. Instantly a man's figure rose to intercept me. Nor did I at first understand that the gesticulations of a curious-looking object, in a cut-away coat and evening shirt, were aimed at me. His face expressed horror and indignation. Instinct rather than reason came to my help, he was a Beadle; I was a woman. This was the turf; there was the path. Only the Fellows and Scholars are allowed here; the gravel is the place for me. Such thoughts were the work of a moment. As I regained the path the arms of the Beadle sank, his face assumed its usual repose, and though turf is better walking than gravel, no very great harm was done. The only charge I could bring against the Fellows and Scholars of whatever the college might happen to be was that in protection of their turf, which has been rolled for 300 years in succession they had sent my little fish into hiding.

Woolf elaborately continues, noting the many times she was barred from entering spaces on the university campus because she was a woman. The Austin Project is committed to open doors, open spaces where women know they belong, where women are in control, where their lives are unfettered by white supremacist patriarchies—multiple sites of domination and terror.

CHAPTER THREE

1. Audre Lorde, "A Litany for Survival," in *The Black Unicorn* (New York: W. W. Norton and Co., 1978).

CHAPTER FOUR

1. Ntozake Shange, *for colored girls who have considered suicide/when the rainbow is enuf* (New York: Macmillan, 1977).

2. Malcolm X, "Letter from Mecca, April 1964," Malcolm-x.org, http://www.malcolm-x.org/docs/let_mecca.htm.

3. Waldo Selden Pratt, "Primitive or Savage Music," in *The History of Music* (New York: Shirmer, 1907).

CHAPTER FIVE

1. Houngan Max Beauvoir, "Haitian Internet," http://www.haitianinternet.com/resources.php/10.

2. The meaning of the chants is cryptic. I have attempted to render the image, rather than translate: *Creole people, search in the depth of the mirror; Legba and Ayizan turn, turn.*

3. The imagery conjured in the chant is that in the sacred mirror Ayizan carries Vodoun on her back.

CHAPTER SIX

1. Audre Lourde, "A Litany for Survival," in *The Black Unicorn* (New York: W. W. Norton and Co., 1978).

CHAPTER SEVEN

1. Bernice Johnson Reagon, "Coalition Politics: Turning the Century," *Home Girls: A Black Feminist Anthology* (Latham, New York: Kitchen Table Women of Color Press, 1983), 359.

2. This oft-repeated aphorism is attributed to the movement educator Moshe Feldenkrais.

3. Chela Sandoval. "Foreword: AfterBridge: Technologies of Crossing," in *This Bridge We Call Home*, eds. Gloria E. Anzaldúa, and AnaLouise Keating (New York: Routledge, 2002), 21–26.

4. AnaLouise Keating, "Charting Pathways, Marking Thresholds . . . A Warning, an Introduction," in *This Bridge We Call Home*, eds. Gloria E. Anzaldúa and AnaLouise Keating (New York: Routledge, 2002), 6–20.

5. Gloria E. Anzaldúa, *Borderlands/La Frontera: The New Mestiza* (San Francisco: Aunt Lute, 1987).

CHAPTER NINE

1. Muller, *June Jordan's Poetry for the People: A Revolutionary Blueprint* (New York: Routledge, 1995), 4.

2. In 2008, the Center for African and African American Studies at the University of Texas was officially named the John L. Warfield Center for African and African American Studies in honor of "Doc" Warfield, a former Center director who set the standard for activist scholarship, community engagement, and politically grounded artistic work. I refer to the Center by the name it now bears though it did not acquire that name during the time span covered by this book.

3. As we have considered participants over the years, Sharon and I have yet to address mobility as thoroughly as we have other identity markers. Including women who identify as physically impaired would be an important way to confront the body-centeredness of tAP from different perspectives.

INDEX